ANARCHY AND SOCIETY

Studies in Critical Social Sciences Book Series

Haymarket Books is proud to be working with Brill Academic Publishers (www.brill.nl) to republish the *Studies in Critical Social Sciences* book series in paperback editions. This peer-reviewed book series offers insights into our current reality by exploring the content and consequences of power relationships under capitalism, and by considering the spaces of opposition and resistance to these changes that have been defining our new age. Our full catalog of *SCSS* volumes can be viewed at www.haymarketbooks.org/category/scss-series.

Anarchy and Society

Reflections on Anarchist Sociology

Jeff Shantz
Dana M. Williams

Haymarket
Books
Chicago, IL

First published in 2013 by Brill Academic Publishers, The Netherlands.
© 2013 Koninklijke Brill NV, Leiden, The Netherlands

Published in paperback in 2014 by
Haymarket Books
P.O. Box 180165
Chicago, IL 60618
773-583-7884
www.haymarketbooks.org

ISBN: 978-1-60846-384-8

Trade distribution:
In the U.S. through Consortium Book Sales, www.cbsd.com
In the UK, Turnaround Publisher Services, www.turnaround-psl.com
In all other countries by Publishers Group Worldwide, www.pgw.com

Cover design by Ragina Johnson.

This book was published with the generous support of Lannan Foundation
and the Wallace Action Fund.

Printed in the United States.

10 9 8 7 6 5 4 3 2 1

Library of Congress Cataloging-in-Publication Data is available.

CONTENTS

ACKNOWLEDGMENTS

We would like to extend our earnest gratitude to the following people who offered helpful thoughts and critiques: Brian Martin, Mark George, Jamie Heckert, Nathan Jun, Matthew Lee, and Jonathan Purkis. We also would like to express our appreciation to the editors and anonymous reviewers of *Contemporary Justice Review*, *Theory in Action*, and *Race, Gender & Class*, in which earlier drafts of some of these chapters appeared.

Jeff: Thanks also to Dr. Heidi Rimke for many lively conversations on the nature of sociology and of anarchism. Special thanks must go to my youngest comrades Saoirse Shantz and Molly Shantz as well as P.J. Lilley (who also indexed this work). My work on this project was supported by a Minor Research Grant from the Office of Research and Scholarship at Kwantlen Polytechnic University.

Dana: An unfathomable debt is owed to my closest and dearest friend and partner, Suzanne Slusser.

PREFACE

PLAIN WORDS: AN INTRODUCTION TO ANARCHY
AND A CHALLENGE TO SOCIETY

We, the authors, have endured long, circular meetings with professional activists, obnoxious riot police, and the presentation of boring academic papers at conferences. We have also enjoyed and relished the occasional political victory, or moment when our students "get it" and a metaphorical light-bulb flashes on. Such monotony and excitement compose the essence of social existence. The challenge is to determine how best to understand these experiences. Do such experiences better explain the worlds we straddle or do they just confuse us?

This book aims to address a few key questions: Can we create social structures—which provide regularity, pattern—that decrease the frequency of debilitation and depression, and increase the chances of inspiration and empowerment? In other words, can we—perhaps as, if the label fits, anarchist-sociologists—critique the social order around us, noting what we like and dislike, what lives up to our values, and then develop strategies for moving towards a better future? It is in this respect that anarchism and sociology have both been "progressive" and part of the Enlightenment tradition, seeking to improve upon past victories and move society towards greater equality, justice, and liberty. The main difference we see between the two traditions is that sociologists have tended to have a more reformist orientation towards the question of progress and the anarchists a more radical orientation.

To Whom it May Concern...

Writing a book like this has been fraught with challenge. First, the audience is nebulous. Will sociologists read this book? Will anarchists want to? Will both find it too distant from their core interests? We hope not. Second, what book can possibly accomplish all that different readers may want it to? Some will want this book to be more theoretical, or historical, or methodological, or empirically-based, or more introductory, of higher-order, or simpler, or deeper. Alas. In an inclusive effort to accommodate the potential trajectories of an anarchist-sociology, we offer the first chapter as a tentative declaration of what anarchist-sociology might already be and what it *could be*.

We wonder if many anarchists who read sociology books, and more do than imagined, might see themselves and their perspectives in this book. They might even express some bemusement: "Yeah, okay, what's the big deal? Sounds like Emma Goldman to me..." Certainly such a sense would mark them as distinct from most sociologists who have overlooked anarchism (even while reading authors inspired by or engaged with anarchy). Curiously, there are also some sociologists—honestly, a surprising number of them—who do not immediately discount anarchism when it is mentioned. There seems to be a genuine tolerance for the perspective, at least amongst sociologists who have bothered to explore anarchist ideas. Thus, it could be that the boundaries between anarchism and sociology overlap for many people, or perhaps that *there may be no boundaries*.

This book is for these very people, and the familiarity, the intuition, the resemblances between anarchism and sociology that they perceive are not accidental or random. There's a reason why some anarchism and some sociology resonates so well together. The following pages draw stronger lines of connection between the two traditions and fill-in more detail than has been previously attempted. But, this book is also for people who either like sociology or who identify with anarchism, but cannot imagine how the other perspective would be relevant. While not all is relevant to the other, some is, and a sampling of these areas of intersection are included herein. Finally, still others might not know anything about anarchism or about sociology, and might not even care about them. But, taken together, as an "anarchist-sociology," these two separate, but intertwined traditions might make more sense and might even be attractive ideas to pursue.

Seize the Moment (and the Imagination)

We have felt the deficit of a book like this for a long time and have found ourselves doing the next best thing for interested persons: recommending Colin Ward's *Anarchy in Action* as a premiere example of a sociological take on anarchism, written by Britain's most famous 20th century anarchist. In a sense, our book is an extension to Ward's excellent book. Then again, Ward admitted that his book was simply a "footnote" of Peter Kropotkin's work (Ward 1996). And Kropotkin, perhaps more than most classic age anarchists, mined history's wide ocean for evidence of anarchistic tendencies, traditions, and ideas. Everything, it seems, is connected, recycled, and updated in the grand narratives on anarchism.

There are various reasons why it is crucial to have an updated and reflexive book on this subject. First, both anarchism and sociology have matured, have survived many generations worth of intellectual and physical strife, and are decidedly better for the experience. For example, anarchism has experienced an analytical and ideological renaissance since the late-1960s, but particularly since the 1990s. During that same time period, sociology has been broadening its horizons and has engaged in rigorous self-criticism, incorporating numerous critical traditions, including Marxism, feminism, post-structuralism, queer theory, and so on. We consider the present moment to be a wonderful opportunity to push sociology's boundaries even more!

Second, even with all the aforementioned advances, an "anarchist-sociology" simply does not exist in any meaningful, real-world sense. We've noted the usage of such a phrase in the writings of various authors in the recent past, but a few references does not a phenomenon make. We suspect it is a precipitous time to make some declarations, plot some schemes, and invite interested people to participate. With a flag planted firmly in the ground (a black flag, of course), people can congregate and we can all exchange ideas with each other.

Third, the medium and the syntax matter. Thus, despite an ever-expanding array of media attracting our attentions, people still read books, especially the very audiences we first aspire to reach: students, scholars, and activists. The presentation of anarchist history in the context of sociological theory (and vice-versa) should not only prove provocative, but we hope is also of *practical use* to readers.

Then there are personal reasons why this book is important to us and why we wish that such a book had existed during our early political years and during our graduate school experiences. We have our feet planted firmly in multiple social worlds and the borders between those worlds (as any permaculturalist would tell you) are the most interesting and fruitful territory. We have spent years as organizers (around various causes) and as anarchists. These experiences have been informative and important, and a close reading of this book will show the impact of such experiences. But, we have also spent much of our lives in the academy—as students, scholars, and educators. While college-life is a strenuous, patience-testing, and constraining experience for many—particularly graduate school (they call them "disciplines" for good reason, as a Foucauldian scholar might say)—it has also been rife with opportunities, not only for enlightenment and empowerment, but the university can also serve as a staging-ground for social transformation efforts.

Many anarchists have an intuitive, sociological mind: we hope to lend additional focus and support for these inclinations. The highly-engaged and analytical anarchist movement only rarely interacts with an equally active, although more stodgy and pro-status quo, intellectual tradition in the academy. Our fellow anarchists may be pleasantly surprised to find that those academic Ivory Towers (which are mostly metaphorical: most university buildings are ugly and utilitarian) contain many critical people willing to challenge (although often only intellectually) corporate capitalism, bureaucratic statecraft, and entrenched patriarchy and white supremacy. We hope such current and future academic workers can find their way into radical movements for change, contributing where possible.

By some estimates, as many as a million college students in the US alone take sociology courses every year: is it possible to introduce even a fraction of those students to an *anarchist* interpretation of society? If so, we hope this book can serve as a helpful primer for those educators interested in taking up such a task. And, more pointedly, for those countless students plowing their way through sometimes boring, pedantic survey courses for general education requirements, we hope this book offers a fresh and provocative intervention, critique, challenge, and supplement to their assigned curriculum.

In summary, we hope this book accomplishes two goals. One: to bridge the gap between self-identified sociologists and anarchists. They ought to meet, socialize, hold hands occasionally (although they likely will do such hand-holding metaphorically), and be more cognizant of the other. Sociologists and anarchists need not become best friends—in fact, it's likely they will not—but rather become colleagues, contemporaries, comrades, and erstwhile companions who sometimes share convergent missions. The first half of this book (Chapters 2 through 5) focuses on teasing-out the sociological characteristics of well-known anarchist thinkers (including Pierre-Joseph Proudhon, Peter Kropotkin, Emma Goldman, Gustav Landauer, Colin Ward, and others). There is a surprising amount to say, so much that we can only scratch the surface in this volume. We also dedicate space to sociologists, such as Ferdinand Tönnies, who have offered sociological ideas that are particularly compelling for anarchists. And two: we aim to inspire, formulate, and engage with an anarchist-sociologist praxis. Sometimes anarchists have talked each other to death about the minutiae of Proudhon and Marx, or responded viscerally to an injustice with little forethought of consequences. And, sometimes sociologists have buried their heads in their journal articles and statistical output tables, feigning impotence, just as often as they have preached and pleaded for reform to other privileged people who hold Power. We seek to identify a tentative, flexible middle-ground, between analytical theorizing and robust direct action. We want to analyze and critique society, but also explore solutions aimed at slowing (and stopping!) destruction and violence, as well as constructing a saner, more liberatory future. Both of these goals are important. We believe *Anarchy and Society* meets these challenges, but also believe that such a broad, formidable task cannot be completed by a single book. True attainment of these goals will undoubtedly require organizing, friendship development, bridge-building, research (of the militant and less-than-militant varieties), and, yes, likely more books. You, the reader, can contribute to these necessary tasks.[1]

We then offer two chapters (6 and 7) as critiques of two of the most entrenched social problems addressed by sociologists—and of intense concern to anarchists: the enduring and proliferating forms of inequality and domination that beset societies, and the stubborn inertia of social order that is reliant upon people's adherence to non-liberatory social norms. We attempt to give these two social juggernauts their due consideration, by focusing our analyses on both their insidious strengths as well as methods of challenge offered by anarchists.

Into the Future (Which Shall Remain Unwritten)

To be clear, we are not of the opinion that there is one explicit road to social revolution. Revolution, by any definition that we believe has meaning, refers to the comprehensive transformation of all social life, from the micro to the macro, from the typical to the rare, through all institutions (including economies, political orders, cultural systems, media), re-ordering a society—preferably from the bottom-up. Such revolution cannot take a single trajectory. Thus, revolutions cannot be made on the backs of a long-successive series of insurrectionary moments, nor can it occur through mere reforms. Political campaigns will play a role and so will all manner of organizations (including, we admit with gritted-teeth, sectors of the non-profit industrial complex). Education and re-socialization efforts are necessary, both within and external to existing learning institutions: conflict resolution training in grade schools, revolutionary-theory

---

[1] We look forward to meeting you in a classroom or conference hall, on the Internet or a library shelf, in the streets, or on a future barricade.

classes in high schools, and pre-figurative strategy courses in colleges can be nurtured, concurrently, alongside a proliferation of free skools, skill-shares, reading clubs, and popular education efforts. Any revolution has and will involve all the above and much more. Revolutions are messy affairs, but they offer multiple points of entry. As such, both anarchists and sociologists can play supportive roles in all these efforts.

This need not be a "long march through the institutions" as recommended by some of our New Left comrades and forbearers of the 1960s and 1970s. There is great value in dialogue between students, organic intellectuals, tenured professors, and activists. Some of this dialogue may focus upon studying the movements we are part of. To this end, our final Chapter 8 discusses some of the risks and pitfalls associated with studying radical movements like anarchism—we do not mean to dissuade this activity (in fact, both of us authors have done this research), but to be honest and reflexive as to its challenges. Anti-authoritarian knowledge and insight can only be generated from multiple vantage points, not privileging any particular group of creators (please see this book's Afterward for a more in-depth rumination upon these issues). As authors with feet planted somewhat precariously in the academic world, we possess some of that privilege, perhaps more than we deserve. We welcome comradely criticisms and debate, hopefully with the intention of advancing not only anarchist-sociology (in whatever form it takes), but also social revolution.

As a starting point of inspiration, we humbly quote the words of an anarchist of a decidedly sociological-inclination, Emma Goldman (2003). She gives us direct inspiration with her encouragement to act on principle and to act *now*: "Today is the parent of tomorrow. The present casts its shadow far into the future. That is the law of life, individual and social. Revolution that divests itself of ethical values thereby lays the foundation of injustice, deceit, and oppression for the future society. The *means* used to *prepare* the future become its *cornerstone*" (262).

In solidarity,

Dana M. Williams
Valdosta, Georgia

Jeff A. Shantz
Surrey, British Columbia

CHAPTER ONE

DEFINING AN ANARCHIST-SOCIOLOGY: A LONG ANTICIPATED MARRIAGE

Introduction

Anarchism is of increasing significance in the world of social movements (Graeber 2002). There are anarchist currents running through many of modern social movements, such as the global justice movement (Epstein 2001). But, this influence is not isolated to movements. The influence of the anarchist movement has also infiltrated the academy and has linked anarchist scholars across discipline into something called "anarchist studies" (Amster et al. 2009). This development is of fortuitous importance to the discipline of Sociology (especially in the United States), which has been going through an identity crisis as of late, as many sociologists seek out activist currents and "public sociology" (Clawson et al. 2007). These factors crucially illustrate the need for a clearly-stated anarchist-sociology.

Numerous authors (Griffin 1991, Ehrlich 1971, Purkis 2004, Welsh 1997) have written of an "anarchist-sociology," but almost always in the abstract, never referencing a specific set of ideas or scholarship. For example, Griffin's (1991) chapter is a mere explication of classical sociological theory, written for an anarchist audience, and he does not introduce any distinct anarchist elements. Purkis (2004) comes closer than most by seeing anarchist-sociology as a potential tradition to grow and build, but does not describe it as a means to analyze society as well as transform it. Welsh (1997) is principally concerned with critiquing sociological social movement theories, particularly the work of Alberto Melucci.

This essay will establish the groundwork for the ontological understanding of anarchist-sociology—what it is or, more importantly, what it could be? The major goal is to answer: What does "anarchist-sociology" mean to the discipline of Sociology? There are lots of potential understandings to the phrase "anarchist-sociology"; it is a rather flexible noun, particularly since it lacks any prior definition. We do not claim that anarchist-sociology is exclusively any of these, but offer the following as descriptions of possible meanings.

This essay explores possible meanings of "anarchist-sociology," compares the two traditions of anarchism and sociology, establishes a basic definition of anarchist-sociology, and re-conceptualizes Sociology along anarchist values.

Against the State: Anarchy is Order

As Hartung (1983) notes, any suggestion that the state and other forms of imposed authority might be replaced by a decentralized network or federation, as contemporary anarchists propose, is likely to be met with a sustained and vocal opposition. This is especially likely given that those who find current systems of imposed authority much to their liking are often those with the resources to mobilize public opinion in support of their preferences. There is certainly no doubt the opposition to the state and other systems of imposed authority "undermines the dominant mode of political organization and the number of vested interests within it" (Hartung 1983: 83). Thus the mighty force of resources, both material and ideological, that have been mobilized to condemn and discredit "the beast of anarchy." As anarchists ranging from Murray Bookchin to Colin Ward suggest, anarchism as a practical approach to social transformation has been neutralized to a certain extent by its designation as "radicalism."

Any social or political theory that suggests possibilities for social transformation is almost certain to be set upon quickly with claims that it is merely an expression of idealism or naïveté. As a social theory, or perhaps more accurately, a cluster of social theories, anarchism has been subjected "to a great deal of pejorative analysis and gross misunderstanding" (Hartung 1983: 87). Partly this charge relates to the extreme difficulty the modern mind, ensconced in statist social structures and ideologies, has in envisioning a society held together without the "cement" of government in the form of the state. The accumulated experiences, histories and mythologies of centuries of nation-state hegemony make it difficult to even imagine anything that suggests alternative means of arranging society. So ingrained is the worldview of nation states that many conflate the notion of society with the notions of state or nation-state. There is a tendency, even within some critical theories, to assume a correspondence between the state and society.

The idea that the state is the means to social order, even to the extent that it can be equated with social order, has made it very difficult for non-statist visions of social order to be heard. Indeed such visions are most likely to be branded utopian and dismissed out of hand. Significantly this is true even from the perspective of many on the political left. This privileging of the state or statist order and the equation of anarchy with disorder has conditioned the reception of anarchism within social sciences.

> Within sociology, critiques of anarchism are more likely to be theoretical, centered specifically on (1) the notion that social order cannot exist without inevitable structural inequities (i.e., hierarchical organization); and generically upon (2) the idea that the "scientific" constructions of modern sociology do not lend themselves to the study of the local and the particular. This second dilemma is at the heart of wedding political practice to social theory. Certainly, the "problem of order" is an important and unresolved one. As concerns anarchism, the popular image still corresponds to a "state" of anarchy as the equivalent of chaos. (Hartung 1983: 84)

For anarchists, society and state are counter-posed or even oppositional notions. For Kropotkin (1972: 132), the state, the formalized rule of dominant minorities over subordinate majorities, is "but one of the forms of social life." For anarchists, the absence of the state does not mean that order will dissolve into chaos. Anarchists emphasize the capacities of people to develop effective forms of order to meet specific needs and desires. Order, thus arrived at, is also preferable for anarchists since it is not ossified and extended, often by force, to situations and contexts different than those from which it emerged, and for which it may not be suited. This order, on the contrary is flexible and evolving, where necessary giving way to other agreements and forms of order depending on peoples' needs and the circumstances confronting them.

Anarchists propose what the philosopher and sociologist Martin Buber calls "the community of communes" in which social order is based, not on imposed authority but upon cooperation. Buber makes the distinction between the social principle and the political principle. For Buber, the social principle is expressed in informal organizations, co-operative groups, unions and, often, families. The political principle finds expression in domination, authority or, in a word, the state.

Anarchist forms of organization, however, do not look anything like state forms or even the types of formal organization that are typically the preferred subjects of sociology. Anarchist projects provide a framework for practicing, learning about and exploring new forms of social relationship. As Graeber (2004) suggests, the examples of viable anarchism are almost endless. These could include almost any form of organization, from a chess club to the postal service, as long as it is not hierarchically imposed by some external authority (Graeber 2004). Anarchism highlights the voluntary cooperation and largely non-violent socio-political activities that widely characterize social life, as opposed to the state which is understood as the major source of violence in the world (Turner 1998).

Situating Anarchist-Sociology

Most simply, "anarchist-sociology" may be a *subject*. As a subject, anarchist-sociology would be something studied, analyzed, and written about. It could be treated like many other subjects in the classroom as a thing to be taught to students. This subject involves understanding the many ways in which people are dominated by hierarchy and authority, as well as exist autonomously, cooperatively, and without domination. In this respect, anarchist-sociology is like any number of topics of interest to sociologists, ranging from theory to social problems, families to the economy.

Anarchist-sociology may also be conceived of as a *subfield* or specific area of inquiry. As part of the Sociology discipline, it might require similar amenities, such as its own journal(s), an American Sociological Association section, reading lists, and a research canon. Sociologists (and non-professionals) could specialize in this subfield and dedicate more of their scholarly efforts to researching, teaching, and nurturing anarchist-sociology. People could cluster around it as an intellectual entity within the broader scholarly profession, in a fashion similar to social psychologists or criminologists.

The people who have an interest in anarchist-sociology could represent a *caucus*. Such folks within the Sociology profession are oriented towards the particular interests of anarchist-sociology and wish to advance, protect, and foster it within and outside of the larger discipline's boundaries. Other caucuses have formed overtime in Sociology, by folks from backgrounds, identities, and constituencies as varied as humanists, women, African Americans, Latinos, queers, and others.

The phrase "anarchist-sociology" could also describe an *ideology*. Adherents of this ideological orientation would possess a unique attitude about sociology and social order. Anarchist-sociology would refer to the political identity and program that drives adherents, in a comparable way that Marxist sociologists are driven by Marxist ideas or feminists are by feminism. An anarchist-sociology ideology would suggest a radical orientation towards society: a critical and cynical analysis of large institutions and social domination, and the belief in a revolutionary society organized around principles of freedom, anti-authoritarianism, direct action, mutual aid, and decentralization.

Anarchist-sociology may be considered a *theoretical perspective*. This useful framework suggests a particular way of looking at society or maybe a specific orientation towards society. Like most theories, anarchist-sociology would be a utility or tool useful for analysis, or a metaphorical "lens" to look through in order to examine some aspect of social life. In this respect, anarchist-sociology could become a perspective of analytical importance as with structural functionalism or symbolic interactionism. For example, an "anarchist imagination" could permit anyone to observe forms of domination in their own life and identify their roots in hierarchical systems in society.

Lastly, we believe that a minimal anarchist-sociology would involve a particularly radical *praxis*. Anarchists must look deeper at society (using sociology!), and interpret it and its social problems, for the purposes of devising strategies to transform society. Both these critiques and the corresponding prefiguration efforts ought to fit within anarchism's ethical framework. Thus, anarchist-sociology would diagnose the many short-comings, inefficiencies, and domination forms found within bureaucracies—followed by prognostic responses and actions aimed to topple such organizations and construct anti-authoritarian, self-determining, and cooperative forms in their place. Consequently, it would be morally indefensible to study and describe a bewildering array of domination forms without articulating solutions—or at least partial strategies—for overcoming such problems.

Clearly, many interpretations of "anarchist-sociology" exist. Most are mutually reinforcing and represent merely contextual differences. Still, it is unfair and premature to say with absolute certainty what anarchist-sociology means without many people consciously, openly, and meaningfully grappling with such questions and distinctions. Since such experiences and percolation has yet to occur, perhaps the next best thing is to consider what "anarchism" and "sociology" have meant separately.

Comparing Anarchism and Sociology

As Purkis (2004) has noted, anarchism and sociology appeared within the same tumultuous social and political milieu in Europe known as the

Enlightenment. This social revolution spurred all sorts of new intellectual traditions, which helped to lay the necessary groundwork for the creation of radical social movements and the scholarly study of societies. Despite these shared origins, anarchism and sociology are very different. Before noting areas of overlap and commonalities between the two, we explore the major ways in which anarchism and sociology can be critically contrasted with each other. In other words, how best can we organize and order these traditions in relation to each other?

The origins of anarchism can be found in the left-intellectual critiques of state, church, and capitalism, such as those of William Godwin and Pierre-Joseph Proudhon, as well as the burgeoning internationalist and radical labor movements of the second half of the Nineteenth Century. Anarchism's golden age produced activist-intellectuals (or revolutionary philosophers?) such as Mikhail Bakunin, Peter Kropotkin, Emma Goldman, and Errico Malatesta. Each faced exile and imprisonment, while writing numerous volumes each and establishing long-lasting traditions for future anarchists. Sociology has somewhat tamer origins and emerged from academic philosophy departments in universities. Sociology began to slowly constitute itself as a separate discipline, apart from economics, history, and political science (see Collins 1994). Early sociologists such as August Comte, Emile Durkheim, Max Weber, Georg Simmel, Jane Addams, Harriet Martineau, and W.E.B. DuBois skirted the intellectual boundaries between academia, professional social work, and public policy creation. The foci of these intellectuals are comparable to the anarchists, although their analytical frameworks differed and their conclusions were far less likely to lead the sociologists to advocate revolutionary transformation.

Anarchist practitioners have included countless varieties of radicals and anarchists, some of whom do not publicly identify or know they "are" anarchists. Given its outsider and oppositional status, anarchism does not have a method of professionalization to institute long-term adoption of anarchism within communities. Consequently, anarchism's permanency is constrained and limited to flexible and short-term organizations and projects; it is regularly under attack from major societal institutions (especially capitalism and the state). The popularity and traction of anarchism is attributable to the salience of ideas to people in the present, in light of contemporary conditions. As such, when consciousness about social disruption peaks, anarchism has tended to thrive and vice-versa. Anarchism resides in the margins, existing in a variety of collective and cooperative organizational spaces, including affinity groups, networks, and federations, all of which have little coercive capacity over their membership. Sociology is very different: its practitioners are mainly professional, university-trained sociologists or students within universities. While many are academics and teachers, some sociologists also act as policy-makers, analysts, or community organizers. Sociologists are professionalized through formal education via course work, exams, and degrees (often advanced ones). Training in research methods, statistics, and sociological theory are often mandatory, culminating in professionals' own research projects which take the form of theses, dissertations, and academic journal articles. Due to these institutionalized structures, sociology endures overtime, particularly to the extent it is funded (through student tuition and state subsidy) and popularly respected (in some periods, Sociology may become controversial and lose support). Most sociology is sequestered away, outside of public view, in educational organizations—principally universities and colleges—but also professional associations, research institutes, and policy agencies.

Anarchism's realm of engagement has traditionally been within the world's working-classes, other variously-dominated populations, oppositional movements, and—in spatial terms—the streets. To casually encounter anarchism, one must usually be in society's "temporary autonomous zones," including social centers and infoshops, or the meeting-places of anarcho-syndicalist unions. Anarchism's position in the periphery is due to its antagonistic relationship with authority, particularly bureaucratic, hierarchical, and dominating institutions. The public tends to fear anarchism, due to relentless, multi-generational anti-anarchist propaganda. At the same time there is tendency to avoid the fact that in each modern case in which people have worked to produce stateless societies on a larger scale, they have been met by extreme military violence from the representatives of states or nation-states.

> Obviously this would never be allowed to happen. In the past, whenever it looked like it might – here, the Paris commune and Spanish civil war are excellent examples – the politicians running pretty much every state in the vicinity have been willing to put their differences on hold until those trying to bring such a situation about had been rounded up and shot. (Graeber 2004: 39)

Marginal interaction between the public and anarchists and their organizations would likely dispel the most absurd myths about the latter. It might also contribute to a recognition that for many their lives are already organized on the basis of anarchy—mutual aid and affinity outside the state.

Sociology, on the other hand, engages within the realm of ideas and scholarship; although anarchism has its theorists, they are outgunned by the overwhelming influence of professional intellectuals, especially academics who are paid to think and write. It has thrived within the spatial domain of "learning sites," ranging from college campuses to think-tank offices. Authority figures have a mixed relationship with sociology; if its research and teaching is supportive of the status quo, then the state, university administrators, foundations and grant-givers, and policy-makers are congratulatory. If sociology is critical, such authority figures tend to reduce their support or initiate campaigns of opposition. The public tends to know little about sociology—in fact, regularly confuses it with similar sounding things, such as psychology, social work, or socialism—with the exception of the many millions of students who take classes annually. Yet, given the simple lecture-exam character of most education, this "instruction" often does little to re-acculturate most students to more favorable views of sociology or social criticism.

Change is viewed by anarchists as something to be deliberately pursued—in so far as it expands the domain of social freedom—but something that should be resisted if of a right-wing, totalitarian, or fascist character. The goal of anarchism is to radically transform society, to aid revolution through the spread of radical ideas and support for cooperative, alternative culture. Anarchism's impact upon society has been rather limited, especially in terms of its most dramatic goals. There are numerous examples of small-scale anarchistic projects and organizations, such as food cooperatives, social movement networks, alternative media outlets, and other such counter-institutions, but none that have (as of yet) created long-lasting revolutionary change. Sociology has also viewed change as a mixed-proposition. Research has indicated that lots of things cause change—everything from war to technology, natural disasters to social movements—but that change is not necessarily "good." Sociologists have also held conflicting views regarding their own participation in change (c.f. Feagin and Vera 2008). Instead, sociology has mainly aimed to study society, conduct research, advance "knowledge," teach students, and sometimes, moderately impact society (usually within the framework of objective rationalism). Consequently, sociology has had a muted impact upon society, especially in comparison to other social sciences. The discipline has had only limited policy reach and influenced other academics.

Even considering the major areas of disagreement and divergent focus, anarchism and sociology could generate a compelling synthesis, one that we attempt to define next.

Defining Anarchist-Sociology

There are many ways to delineate the boundaries of what anarchist-sociology could be. Perhaps the best way to sketch out these boundaries is to describe the most useful and radical aspects of both anarchism and sociology, and to see where they could potentially converge. Over time, these observations could be worked into a consistent framework and research program. The first, and best, starting place is to observe that sociology is organized for the purpose of studying society, while anarchism is organized to radically transform society. As such, anarchist-sociology is the action-oriented study and theoretically-informed transformation of societies. Not all sociology is done in a liberatory fashion, nor is all anarchism concerned with social relations (although the best of each are). There are anarchist sociologists practicing in academia (and society), just as there are sociologically-informed anarchists acting within social movements. The overlap between these two traditions—while not massive—is large enough to be compelling, and perhaps paradigm-altering for each tradition.

This overlap suggests the study of what perpetuates hierarchy and inequality—the organizational forces that structure society, and the socialization and social norms that instill the existing, conservative status quo social order with so much enduring momentum. Then, anarchist-sociology scholarship would include the complimentary study of how liberatory alternatives are and could be developed. Since some of these alternatives have already been explored by scholars (e.g. since the 1970s by activist-scholars like Rosabeth Moss Kanter, Joyce Rothschild, Frank Lindenfeld), it may be wise to expand and build on these studies, then propagate them widely to advocate for broader application of such approaches. An anarchist-sociology would not only be interested in *studying* the "bad" and "good" potentialities of society, but *advocating for and working to* reduce the bad and spread the good.

As such, anarchist-sociology might aim to help people develop an "anarchist imagination" comparable to C. Wright Mills' "sociological imagination" (Mills 1959). Mills—himself a sociologist, and a self-identified "Wobbly" and "goddamn anarchist"—argued for the importance of identifying the social causes behind the personal troubles one experiences in their life. To do so, one much consider the ways in which time and place have impacted one's biography, even in ways that initially seem impossible or unlikely. Anarchists could extend and refine this imaginative power to identifying the linkages and root causes of inequality in one's life that extend from a varied nexus of social hierarchies. To "use" one's anarchist imagination would be to practice anarchist-sociology. For example, when a White working-class woman identifies her disadvantaged position in society as being the result of her social class and gender—but also that she gathers benefits from her privileged race—she would be exercising her anarchist imagination. Her next step as an anarchist-sociologist would be to find individual and collective avenues for resisting these forms of hierarchy and manifesting new egalitarian, horizontal, and cooperative social forms in their place. This is very much the "typical" process of how an individual seems to come to identify as an anarchist: they struggle with certain forms of domination or authoritarianism in their own biographies, but then begin to see those experiences as a broader pattern affecting *many* individuals. This realization can serve as a catalyst to organizing to end such forms of domination—such as the institutions of patriarchy and capitalism, but also White supremacy (see Chapter 6 for more on the intersection of various forms of domination). This "anarchist imagination" could very well serve as a key concept within the burgeoning field of anarchist studies.

An anarchist-sociology would be a more pragmatic/applied anarchism and a less cynical sociology. Most sociology focuses upon a multitude of social problems, with each new research project seeking to identify new forms of inequality and domination. While this work is important, it is equally crucial to explore avenues for radically altering hierarchical systems of domination. Thus, sociology requires an anarchist sensibility that focuses on the practicalities of power and change. Anarchism, has sometimes lacked the rigorous—although not necessarily quantitative and positivist—scholarship and critique that sociology has been built around. Sociology's intense focus upon social relations, which includes economic, political, and cultural elements, has developed finely honed theories for how society perpetuates inequality, why people put up with subordination, the limitations to resistance by the disadvantaged, as well as an intricate analysis of how social movements function. Sociology's skepticism is not a blanket with which to smother anarchism's wild aspirations, but a helpful lens to view the potentially most successful avenues towards change.

Jonathan Purkis (2004) has written more directly of this synthesis than anyone before:

> To develop an anarchist sociology is to offer a different explanation of why particular social problems emerge, based on a different vision of how society is and ought to be. The development of an anarchist sociology is, however,

still in its infancy, and the institutional possibilities for its emergence are probably somewhat limited. However, what is important is that there is enough evidence already to be able to advocate a substantial anarchist research agenda. There are endless research questions to be formulated: how is power formed and perpetuated? why do people desire their own oppression? how should we research these things sensitively? and what should we do with the results when we get them? If anarchists stick to the kind of principles that most have long held in their hearts, then there may well be answers to these questions. The opportunity for an anarchist sociology to emerge in a contemporary context should therefore not be underestimated. (53–54)

We agree with Purkis that an anarchist-sociology could be a powerful tool to understand society, but that its chances as an insurgent academic movement (especially in colleges and universities) is limited—which is not necessarily "bad." Infinitely more questions will come to be addressed under the moniker of "anarchist-sociology," many of which will have to be more practical, transformation-oriented, and liberatory in character.

Re-Conceptualizing the Discipline: Toward a More Anarchistic Sociology

Since anarchism seems more sociological than vice-versa, we now aim to anarchize the sociological tradition. Thus, we seek out things that indicate an anarchist appreciation of society, an interest in anarchistic elements of society, or anarchistic practice in the field of Sociology itself. Since anarchism is rooted in values and practice, we seek to re-center sociology upon key anarchist values and foci, particularly freedom, anti-authoritarianism, direct action, mutual aid, and decentralization. The following discussion describes general characteristics in society, how the discipline of sociology could incorporate these values, and specific examples of such values in action that could serve as research subjects.

The Sociology of Freedom

"Freedom" is an overused word, often meant to refer to things that have little to do with what anarchists would consider to be real freedom, e.g. the "freedom to buy something," "freedom to vote for the candidate of one's choosing," "freedom to use as much gasoline as one can afford," and so on.[1] Instead, *real* freedom is key. A sociology of freedom is not merely concerned with "freedom to choose" which toothpaste brand to purchase,

---

[1] We discuss conflicts derived from un-agreed-upon definitions more in Chapter 7.

to believe in one god or another (or not), choose politicians in a voting booth, choose to watch TV, or to drink beer. Pierre Bourdieu (1990) argued this pointedly: "It is through the illusion of freedom from social determinants... that social determinations win the freedom to exercise their full power... [P]aradoxically, sociology frees us from the illusion of freedom, or, more exactly from the misplaced belief in illusory freedoms" (15).

As such, the typical meaning of "freedom" is highly circumscribed. Freedom is not merely a market-based or state-derived phenomenon. Its meaning is also broader in utility. As Sullivan et al. (1980) write:

> The freedom we are talking about is not simply a freedom *from*. It is also a freedom *to* or freedom *for*... Freedom is a direction, a process of becoming more the person we are, more the person we have been inhibited from becoming because of imposed identities and the interests of external forms of authority, the state, law, custom, religion, bureaucracy, forms of control... (347–348, emphasis in the original)

There is a long list of things that people could gain freedom *from*, including: the state, boredom, fossil-fuel dependence, abusive relationships, apathy, exploitive work, dirty/unhealthy environment, paternalism, prejudice, aggression, and so forth. Instead, the quest *for* freedom as an individual and collective effort could involve people finding freedom for themselves as individuals (e.g. control over immediate decision in one's life: "I want to learn this skill," "I want to move to this location"), or one can work with others to create a broader, communal form of freedom (e.g. a community is able to formulate and execute its own long-term plans... "we can plan this event," "we can build this community center"). Thus, the freedom one has is not merely rooted in one's individual mobility, but the structural mobility of an entire community.

Freedom is also not a zero-sum game, but rather a continuum. As Ehrlich (1971) notes, "I am at once free and unfree, and my lack of freedom precludes me from fully comprehending the state I am in" (204). Universals—especially those focused upon something so crucial as freedom—are dangerous and inaccurate. Therefore, it is important for anarchist-sociologists to be honest and specific about the ways in which people are free and unfree. As a continuum, there is a perpetual quest to enlarge the spheres of freedom, as some say "to expand the floor of the cage." Eventually, the "cage" will be so cavernous that it will, in effect, disappear. According to this view, freedom is a trajectory of society struggled over during all epochs, a social impulse in which people in groups see the potential for expanding these cage floors.

Restraints on freedom *do* exist, but some of these help to enable the freedom of others. Completely unbridled freedom can lead to chaos. Should everyone have the "freedom" to wander around and randomly assault others? Of course not. Anarchists seek an egalitarian social order thru freedom-maximization; but, eventually, individual freedoms cannot be increased any more without harming others and restricting *their* freedoms. Thus, some "restrictions" must stop someone from intruding upon someone else's freedom.

Generally, freedom is acquired through struggle. People must be able to gain their own freedom, since a "freedom" delivered to others can easily be retracted. Self-acquired freedom creates confidence, independence, experience, and interest, while freedom handed-over fosters dependence, ignorance, a lack of self-efficacy, and taken-for-granted-ness. This is why vanguards and welfare states are bad—not because of most of their practitioners' intentions, but due to the detrimental consequences of such approaches. Mills (1959) went further by noting the false dualism between the individualized freedom of a marketplace and the freedom of representative democracy: "Freedom is not merely the chance to do as one pleases, neither is it merely the opportunity to choose between set alternatives. Freedom is, first of all, the chance to formulate the available choices, to argue over them—and then, the opportunity to choose" (174). Thus, freedom is empowering.

A sociology of freedom would be concerned with studying examples of freedom in society, such as those areas that empower people to do what they wish—as long as they do not tread upon others. For example, freedom may be found in many varieties of social movements, particularly those concerned with expanding human freedom. Within such movements, freedom is likely an impulse practiced internally. Also, an anarchist-sociologist ought to seek out the ways in which political rights operate in society, especially as "rights" that are universally-recognized through social norms and mores, and are not dependent upon or derived from state approval or enforcement. Finally, how do people maintain their independence and gain self-determination from hierarchical power? These are important questions that a sociology of freedom could seek to answer.

In practice, the sociology of freedom would have to allow anyone to participate in it—scholarship, research, and theory-building ought to not only be the privilege of the highly-educated. As such, this form of sociology should be used to find ways towards greater freedom in society. The Sociology discipline could eradicate copyright, and the hoarding of valuable data and information within the Ivory Tower. Knowledge should not be sequestered away within the academy, but liberated and accessible to all people, in all societies, regardless of social position, history, or geography. Finally, the elimination of tuition is another clear step towards freedom for students.

The Sociology of Anti-Authoritarianism

Public opinion polls have noted for decades a general lack of confidence in major institutions throughout the West.[2] This vague anti-authoritarianism could easily serve as an organizing principle for a new anarchist-sociology. Many people regularly find various "legitimate" forms of authority to be meaningless, detrimental, corrupt, or simply illegitimate—consequently, they choose to not respect them (while often giving them subtle endorsement through a lack of visible opposition). Symbols of hierarchical authority implicitly invite acts of rebellion, while horizontal authority is embodied with agreements and understandings (e.g. cultural norms and mores) that do not require external enforcement by hierarchical institutions (e.g. laws and the state). Instead, many agreements are regularly based upon respect, trust, handshakes, and the like—or what some scholars might call positive deviance that is anti-authoritarian in character (see Chapter 7 for more on norms and deviance).

Anti-authoritarianism keeps people independent from the control of others through opposition to various forms of domination and hierarchical institutions. To the extent that such anti-authoritarianism accurately represents broad sectors, an anarchist-sociology could seek to understand how these processes function. For example, Max Weber considered three principle forms of legitimate authority that allowed some to wield power over others (Weber 1958). Is there not, logically, some type of anti-authoritarian authority type that Weber overlooked? Perhaps some form of trusted, non-hierarchical power? If so, this type of legitimacy is decentered from any institution, office, or single person. It rejects the legitimacy derived from other varieties of authority. Anarchists would do well to take note of Weber's observations: authority's strength resides in its legitimacy. For those wishing to eliminate hierarchical authority and its corresponding power over others, then it is crucial to destroy the legitimacy that accompanies that authority.

---

[2] Note that this opposition is not just expressed towards specific individuals, but to institutions generally.

Anarchist-sociologists could research the ways in which people self-organize *sans* authority. How do people deliberately avoid discrimination and domination? Is it through heightened tolerance and egalitarianism? Maybe through the creation of new, radically democratic social norms? We suspect we will find that people employ both passive and aggressive strategies that avoid, subvert, confront, and overthrow so-called "legitimate" authority. Evidence will not be hard to come by. Historical and contemporary examples will likely demonstrate many strategies and tactics, whether via cynicism in large bureaucracies or distrust of politicians, or through slave resistance, worker sick-ins and wildcat strikes, or the refusal to participate in mass consumer culture. Ample evidence will also emerge from observing the collective behavior of crowds involved in resisting authority. How do resisters identify authority figures and structures? Can they see past baton-wielding riot police to the sometimes faceless institutions the police protect? How do crowds of people manifest action with or without new authority internal to their groups and organizations? Anti-authoritarianism does not just suggest resistance to long-established, status quo authority figures, but also incipient and informal authority that may evolve within movements and social change networks themselves, regardless of how professedly radical they may be.

A consistent anti-authoritarian sociology would act to remove titles, statuses, and ranks between people interested in studying and transforming society (for example, the varied distinctions between "assistant professor," "full professor," "instructor," "student," "non-academic," and so on). A truly egalitarian learning environment requires breaking down the walls between the "learner" and the already "learned." Also, a reflexive anarchist-sociology needs to encourage a critique—and attack!!—upon privileged, powerful, dominating, and elite persons, organizations, institutions, and practices. It is not enough to profess opposition. One must help to further its ends, through resistance to hierarchy and through the positive creation of alternatives.

The Sociology of Direct Action

People typically do not channel their behavior through intermediaries, especially political elites. People self-organize themselves all the time to immediately address their collective needs and desires. Direct action is often seen as more efficient, nuanced (i.e. it can allow for localized variation), and empowering. For example, many large protests today involve collections of "affinity groups," who are all individually involved in carrying out their own self-determined and self-managed plans. They sometimes coordinate with each other ahead of time through "spokes-council" meetings, where participants directly solve problems. Activists also act directly within the protest context itself, making decisions within affinity groups and addressing short-term tactical problems themselves—filtering-out undercover police officers, debating the efficacy of property destruction, protecting each other from attacks by external forces (like police or fascists), and of course successfully executing protest plans. In no instance do activists turn to authority figures for "help" in solving these problems. Police are not appealed to for security, city governments are not needed to provide logistical coordination for march routes, and the corporate media need not be relied upon to correctly transmit the ideas and message of protesters. These tasks are all accomplished internally, by participants themselves.

Direct action subject matter is readily found in society by anarchist-sociologists. For example, all types of do-it-yourself activities could fall under this research program. The activities of community organizations, mutual aid and self-help groups, neighborhood watch groups or assemblies, or hobby clubs take care of their own business themselves, without appeals to authority. Or, consider the multitude of friendly societies, traditional unions, work guilds, and mutual aid societies from the not-too-distant past: they provided health care, pensions, educational and cultural activities to their members, long before the social-welfare state had launched its own bureaucratic, partial answer to these needs (e.g. Cordery 2003).

A sociology of direct action would seek out answers to questions directly, without going through bureaucracies, foundations, or governments first. While resources are always an important concern, anarchist-sociologists should not rely upon funding and paternalism from such dominant and hierarchical institutions. Instead, anarchist-sociologists should interview people directly and involve these people immediately in research that benefits them (see Martin 1998b). Ordinary people, the disadvantaged, and communities should set the terms of scholarship that affect and involve them. Then, as opposed to filtering empirical findings through traditional channels—the stodgy peer-review process that is more concerned with theory-creation as opposed to problem-solving—a true sociology of direct action would share research with other relevant public(s) first and foremost.

The Sociology of Mutual Aid

People are social beings and they have shared needs. Throughout recorded (and likely non-recorded) history, people have associated with and helped others in a non-exchange and non-coercive fashion. This sociability or mutual aid—as Kropotkin called it—is the basis of both human and animal societies. Sustaining a community is good for everyone, not just certain individuals. Even though this is a "natural" human impulse—helping people out for group benefit, not just individual benefit—certain things (namely hierarchy) can get in the way of the social inclination towards mutual aid. Anarchist-sociologists might generally define all manner of hierarchical institutions as leading to this unfortunate end, and Kropotkin (2006) was specific in assigning blame to governments and bureaucracies (but also changing norms and social expectations):

> In the guild – and in medieval times every man belonged to some guild or fraternity [and] two "brothers" were bound to watch in turns a brother who had fallen ill; it would be sufficient now to give one's neighbour the address of the next paupers' hospital. In barbarian society, to assist at a fight between two men, arisen from a quarrel, and not to prevent it from taking a fatal issue, meant to be oneself treated as a murderer; but under the theory of the all-protecting State the bystander need not intrude: it is the policeman's business to interfere, or not. And while in a savage land, among the Hottentots, it would be scandalous to eat without having loudly called out thrice whether there is not somebody wanting to share the food[...] all that a respectable citizen has to do now is to pay the poor tax and to let the starving starve. (188)

Rational choice theorists (e.g. Olson 1965) have countered the sociology of mutual aid by proposing the so-called "free-rider problem," in which it is contrary to one's individual interests to do something that contributes to the greater good if there is no requirement or immediate incentive to do so. While this purports to demonstrate the reasons for incomplete participation in societal activities and human selfishness, it actually ignores the many instances in which people are selfless. The free-rider problem turns every situation into a calculated, rational-choice scenario, even though most people do not conceive of situations as such. In order to presume that people want to slack-off and take advantage of other people's labor, one must studiously ignore the many instances—in fact the vast majority of time—in which people cooperate and participate in society without hope for reward or status. For example, people regularly join voluntary associations, help strangers by lending their know-how and resources, donate money or time to local charities, and help each other freely in the aftermath of natural and social disasters.

It would not be difficult to promote a sociology of mutual aid within the academy. It is important to allow and encourage researchers to regularly collaborate with each other, especially in respect to problem-solving (the Anarchist Studies Network and the North American Anarchist Studies Network both provide mutual aid to academic and non-academic scholars, providing reading suggestions on interested topics, requesting hard-to-find research articles, soliciting help on projects, and creating a free forum to discuss current events). Beyond the constraints of professional sociologists, anarchist-sociology would compel those within universities and colleges to work with communities outside the academy, in particular the most disadvantaged and dominated within those communities. This collaborative, outside-facing orientation is often called "service" within the academy—reading others' research, doing peer reviews, helping to provide information and data, and so on. Certain types of research are even more important to communities, sometimes called "participant action research" or projects that lend their services to social movements to better understand their own conditions and potentials (like Howard Ehrlich's Research Group One). To anarchize the discipline of sociology, this type of community "service" would need to be evaluated and prioritized, on par with research published in peer-reviewed journals or classes taught.

The Sociology of Decentralization

Even though many things have been centralized in modern societies during recent decades and centuries—tax-collecting, census-taking, customs and border patrolling, policing—other things remain *de*centralized. An anarchist-sociology would note these elements and raise-up their enduring importance. As Mildred Loomis (2005) explains:

> Decentralization is not turning back the clock. Through decentralization, independence would replace dependency; honesty and justice would replace delinquency. Health would prevent disease and degeneracy; creative work and folk art would replace decadent and inhuman activities. For these desired ends, Decentralization would organize production, control, ownership, government, communication, education, and population in smaller, more human units. (23–24)

Thus, decentralization refers to the social relationships and organization lacking a centralized mechanism, structure, or authority, while not precluding coordination, cooperation, or communication. In fact, many people like smaller things, such as being able to talk with individuals, and tend to identify with their local areas, immediate surroundings, and lived situations. The desire for an immediate connection to others—not one mediated by large, impersonal institutions—is a very real one. Decentralization is not simply a means of facilitating a more thoroughly lived life, but also an avenue to being more democratic and participatory. As Robert Michels (1958) argued, centralization and largess causes problems of leadership consolidation and elitism within organizations, thus stunting the potential for rank-and-file democracy.

If humans live in scaled-back, local communities, trust is likely to develop in people living elsewhere. Others are apt act in ways roughly similar to one's own community. If larger structures of coordination seem to be required between locales, they can connect via horizontal federation. Thus, it is possible to create a complex society, based around direct democracy, local control, and larger-scale coordination, all without resorting to authoritarian leadership or bureaucracy.

These sorts of phenomena—decentralized groupings and federation structures—exist throughout society, from computer networks like the Internet to collections of friends and neighborhood groups. All sorts of organizations have chosen to federate with each other, as shown by the massive networking between individuals and organizations that compose modern social movements. The study of social networks has been exploding within sociology, hinting at the extraordinary ways in which most people interact with each other in largely—although not completely—horizontal patterns. Decentralization can be witnessed in the protest strategies regularly employed by anarchists at demonstrations: autonomous affinity groups that work separately within the larger protest event, all pursuing their own independent goals and objectives, but often coordinating actions between affinity groups through horizontally-organized spokesperson councils.

To practice a sociology of decentralization would require the placement of sociologists in all sorts of places in society—not just clustering them within universities and government agencies. Social movement organizations, community groups, and neighborhoods ought to have their own sociologists who help people to understand their social environments. Or, more radically, all could learn to think more sociologically and to exercise their anarchist imaginations. The means by which people share such sociological analysis ought to simulate a network-style approach modeled upon principles of horizontalism and decentralization—no one able to tell others what information they may or may not have. In other words, it is important to put knowledge and the power to use that knowledge in the hands of anyone and everyone, regardless of one's ability to pay for or monopolize it.

Conclusion

Anarchist-sociology does not exist in any true fashion as described in this chapter. It is not an established research subject, nor is it a subfield within the discipline of sociology. No caucus of people within Sociology presently identify with "anarchist-sociology," as a formal ideology or otherwise. There is no theoretical perspective called "anarchist-sociology" that scholars use in their research, nor is there an agreed-upon praxis that would allow others to practice anarchist-sociology. Even considering such deficits, it is clear that all of these things could be created, albeit with intentional care and action.

We do not presume to argue that the vision for anarchist-sociology described herein is the only one available. In fact, we sincerely doubt that. But, we do not think the framework we construct here is in any way unreasonable. Anarchism and sociology both have very reasonable goals, and we do not see cause to suspect that their wedding together is inconceivable, despite some dramatic differences (such as those detailed above).

Opponents of anarchism typically respond to it by claiming that it rests upon a naive view of "human nature" (see Mayer 1993). The best response to such criticisms is simply to point to the diversity of anarchist views on the question of human nature. What commonality is there between Max Stirner's self-interested "egoist" and Kropotkin's altruistic upholder of mutual aid? Indeed, the diversity of anarchist views regarding "the individual" and its relation to "the community" may be upheld as testimony to the creativity and respect for pluralism which have sustained anarchism against enormous odds (Shantz 1997). Anarchists simply stress the capacity of humans to change themselves and the conditions in which they find themselves. "The aim is not therefore to liberate some 'essential self' by throwing of the burden of government and the State, but to develop the self in creative and voluntary relations with others" (Marshall 1993: 642–643). Social relations, freely entered, based upon tolerance, mutual aid, and sympathy are expected to discourage the emergence of disputes and aid resolution where they do occur. There are no guarantees here, the emphasis is always on potential. Such an approach by anarchists has led some commentators to see certain affinities with critiques of essentialism.

In this regard anarchism takes a highly sociological approach. Human capacities and proclivities are profoundly situational, constructed through everyday practices of living and very much related to social contexts. In as much as those contexts are constructed by human collective interaction, they are open to change through collective efforts.

Hopefully this explication of an anarchist-sociology will help inform the thinking and action of both anarchists and sociologists. With time, a truly unique anarchist-sociology could emerge, straddling and blurring the boundaries between each tradition. We believe this task is important and it requires others' participation to develop.

CHAPTER TWO

RETHINKING COMMUNITY, ANARCHY, AND SOCIOLOGY

Sociology as an organized approach to understanding human society emerged in the turmoil and strife of the late 19th and early 20th centuries, as was the case with other academic disciplines of the so-called "social sciences" such as psychology and criminology. This period was marked by rapid development in the Industrial Revolution, mass production and social conflict based around struggles between social classes (the proletariat and bourgeoisie), and new forms of political mobilization in mass movements of labor. In addition, movements demanding increased access to justice and respect for previously oppressed groups, especially women and racialized communities, gathered strength and challenged social elites. This was also a period of substantial cultural change marked most notably by the large scale movement of populations from rural to urban areas, urbanization, and the migration of people internationally. These migrations brought about major cultural transformations, bringing large numbers of people from diverse backgrounds into close proximity in expanding urban and suburban areas. Other important transformations included the introduction and spread of new, mass technologies, from the telegraph to the radio to television, which allowed for the rapid transmission of information across great distances and which shifted communication from local to national and even global levels. Taken together these many economic, political, and social transformations represent conditions of what social theorists came to call modernity—urban, technologically advanced and industry-based, multicultural, mass societies. Early sociologists sought to understand the structures and processes that drove these modernist societies, how they were developing and changing, and what benefits and threats they might pose to human well-being, individually and socially.

Since their origins in the Industrial Revolution, anarchism and sociology have had ongoing intersections and engagements with one another. Yet, anarchists have often been excluded from the history of academic disciplines such as sociology, or, where included, marginalized and muted. This contribution critically examines intersections of anarchism and early sociological works by figures such as Durkheim, Weber, Spencer, and

Tönnies on issues of community and social change to rethink both anarchism and sociology. The largely forgotten work of people like Gustav
Landauer and Emma Goldman, and the overlooked sociology of Peter
Kropotkin, offer interesting touchstones in the current (re)envisioning of
anarchy and sociology.

Community, Society, and Anarchy

Anarchists argue that for most of human history people have organized
themselves collectively to satisfy their own needs. Peter Kropotkin notes
that the state, the formalized rule of dominant minorities over subordinate majorities, is only one of the forms of social organization, and a
minority one in human history at that. Anarchy uncovers and makes visible the presence of the state in people's everyday lives, including the internal socialization of the state's rules, ideas, and practices. For anarchists,
people are quite capable of developing forms of organization to meet specific needs and desires. As sociological anarchist Colin Ward (1973, 28) suggests, "given a common need, a collection of people will...by improvisation
and experiment, evolve order out of the situation – this order being more
durable and more closely related to their needs than any kind of order
external authority could provide." Order arrived at in this fashion is also
preferable for anarchists since it is not rigidified and imposed, often by
force, on situations and contexts different than those from which it
emerged, and for which it may not be suited or welcomed. Self-determined
order is flexible and evolving, where necessary giving way to other agreements and forms of order depending on peoples' needs and the circumstances confronting them at specific intersections in time and place.

Anarchistic social organization is conceived of as a network of local voluntary groupings. Anarchists propose a decentralized society, without a
central political body, in which people manage their own affairs free from
any coercion or external authority. These self-governed communes could
federate freely at regional (or larger) levels to ensure co-ordination or
mutual defense. Their autonomy and specificity must be maintained,
however. Each locality will decide freely which social, cultural, and economic arrangements, to pursue. Rather than a pyramid, anarchist associations would form a web. This order is both desired by anarchists for the
future, but is also actively created in the present (Ward 1973).

Anarchists look to the aspects of people's daily lives that suggest
life without rule by external authorities and which might provide a

foundation for anarchist social relations more broadly. This commitment forms a strong and persistent current within diverse anarchist theories, expressing what might be called an anarchy of everyday life, at once conservative and revolutionary. Colin Ward suggests that anarchism, "far from being a speculative vision of a future society...is a description of a mode of human organization, rooted in the experience of everyday life, which operates side by side with, and in spite of, the dominant authoritarian trends of our society" (Ward 1973, 11). As Graeber (2004) suggests, the examples of viable anarchism are almost endless. These could include almost any form of organization, from a volunteer fire brigade to the postal service, as long as it is not hierarchically imposed by some external authority (Graeber 2004).

The sociologist Herbert Spencer's social Darwinism has been taken up by some as a sociological justification for inequality, and for the dominance of capitalist markets and social rule by economic elites. Anarchist theorists, most notably Peter Kropotkin, challenged this emphasis on competition as the central factor in evolution and human social development alike. Instead, Kropotkin's research (1902) showed the significance of mutual aid and supportive relations in survival of species.

The positive value accorded notions of community by anarchists, and their distrust of and opposition to the state, were not unique or exclusive to the early anarchist theorists. Strikingly similar positions were put forward by the sociologist Ferdinand Tönnies (1855–1936). Tönnies expressed his perspectives and concerns in the foundational sociological work *Gemeinschaft und Gesellschaft* as early as 1887. In *Gemeinschaft und Gesellschaft* Tönnies appears as perhaps the first modern social analyst to detail distinctions between community (*Gemeinschaft*) and society (*Gesellschaft*). His work warns of the danger posed by the undermining of small, personal, face to face, communal associations, and the growing dominance of large scale, impersonal, distinct organizations of modernity and industrial capitalism. Under economic and political pressures, norms and values reinforced in direct kinship relations and communities are replaced by social control procedures through the state (laws, police, prisons) under anonymous *Gesellschaft* conditions. Tönnies argues that the shift toward modern conditions, dominated by *Gesellschaft* arrangements, would threaten social life if aspects of *Gemeinschaft* relations did not survive as an alternative way of organizing social life. Those writings would provide central concepts and analyses that would be taken up by key figures in the founding of sociology, including Emile Durkheim, Karl Mannheim, Georg Simmel, and Max Weber (Haaland 1993, 26).

In addition, recent scholars in the history of ideas have begun to note the influence of Tönnies' ideas on social movement organizers including, perhaps particularly, major figures in anarchist movements (Drinnon 1961; Nisbet 1966; Day 2005). Yet it is probably more accurate to suggest that these ideas were developed simultaneously by the sociologist as well as anarchist theorists (such as Peter Kropotkin). Indeed, hints of this social schema are found in works of the anarchist Pierre-Joseph Proudhon at least a decade earlier.

Richard Drinnon suggests that the works of anarchists like Emma Goldman, Gustav Landauer, and Peter Kropotkin "was directed to keeping such scattered seeds alive and thereby to [in Tönnies' words] 'fostering a new culture amidst the decaying one'" (1961, 111). The visions asserted by the anarchists—concerned with abolishing social regulation by states, capital, and church, and affirming a new social order based on voluntary arrangements and agreement rather than state compulsion or law—is consistent with Tönnies' notion of *Gemeinschaft*. *Gemeinschaft* is based on commonality of values, place, and relations. This is rooted in face to face interactions in specific spatial sites of interaction. This is, in many ways, the prototype of social relations as envisioned within anarchist alternatives to capitalism. As the sociologist Bonnie Haaland suggests: "In addition a 'Gemeinschaft of mind,' or common will, brings about a reciprocal understanding between and among members of community—a norm of reciprocity which governs social and economic relations (1993, 26–27). This understanding of reciprocity is what is described by anarchist notions of mutual aid.

Resonance between anarchism and Tönnies' notions of *Gemeinschaft* can be seen "in terms of the reciprocity and mutuality of social relations, the primacy of primary relationships, and the predominance of group sentiment and concord" (Haaland 1993, 27). For historian Richard Drinnon, anarchists such as Emma Goldman understood that "a distinction needed to be made between relatively inflexible abstract organizations such as the state and the more primary, flexible organizations such as communities" (1961, 111).

The anarchist Gustav Landauer was directly influenced by the works of Ferdinand Tönnies. Perhaps the most significant anarchist theorist in Germany, after the proto-anarchist Max Stirner, Landauer identified himself as an "anarchist socialist" to distinguish himself from popular currents of Stirnerist egoism. Drawing explicitly upon Tönnies distinction between *Gemeinschaft* (organic community) and *Gesellschaft* (atomized society), Landauer desired, and analyzed, the rebirth of community from within the shell of statist and capitalist society. The forms within which the new community would gestate were to be the *bunde*, or local, face-to-face associations. Like Proudhon and Bakunin before him, Landauer advocated the formation of producers' and consumers' cooperatives as alternatives to statist and capitalist institutions.

The anarchist-socialist community, for Landauer, is not something to emerge from a future revolution somewhere in the distant future. Rather it is the growing (re)discovery of something already present. Landauer writes: "This likeness, this equality in inequality, this peculiar quality that binds people together, this common spirit is an actual fact" (cited in Marshall 1993, 411). In as much as anarchism would involve revolution, this "revolution," for Landauer, would consist of elements of refusal and reconstruction in which individuals withdraw co-operation with existing state institutions and create their own positive alternatives. Notably, Landauer offered a relational definition of the state that in some ways prefigures the work of Michel Foucault. Rather than a rigid and reified structure, the state is composed of relationships and processes of interaction and governance. Landauer argued that:

> The state is a condition, a certain relationship among human beings, a mode of behaviour between them; we destroy it by contracting other relationships, by behaving differently toward one another...We are the state, and we shall continue to be the state until we have created the institutions that form a real community and society of men. (cited in Marshall 1993, 411)

Landauer thus advocated the development of self-directed communities that would permit a conceptual and practical break from institutions of authority. Revolution, re-conceptualized by Landauer as a gradual rejection of coercive social relations through the development of alternatives, was not a linear demarcation between social conditions (marking temporalities of "pre-" and "post-") but a continuous principle spanning vast expanses of time (Marshall 1993, 412).

At the same time as they draw upon Tönnies' conceptual tools, anarchists like Goldman are critical of the patriarchal gap or oversight in ideas of *Gemeinschaft*. Tönnies' notion of *Gemeinschaft* took for granted—as did structural functionalists later—a sexual division of labor and sex-specific roles in the family and community. Even more, these are suggested as rooted in biological difference. For Tönnies:

> Although all individuals participate as social members in both forms of social organizations so that, for example, the Gemeinschaft encloses men as much as women in the communal collective experience of life; nevertheless,

there are critical differences for the sexes at the biological and psychological levels of analysis that have consequences for the division of labour. (Sydie 1987, 140)

Tönnies even suggested different expressions of will. Rational will was assigned to the supposedly male-dominated public forms of *Gesellschaft* (Haaland 1993, 27). The domestic realm was said to be a realm of natural will.

There is a fundamental tension between Goldman's anarchist views on community and *Gemeinschaft* based on the assumptions of patriarchy. Goldman did not accept the naturalized duality of the sexes that appears in Tönnies as well as with in the works of some anarchists, such as Kropotkin. Goldman worked to overcome notions of sexual duality or the construction of the world as divided into antagonistic male and female spheres (public/domestic). As Haaland notes: "To suggest the appropriateness of patriarchy as an organizing principle would appear to a feminist to be a gross violation of anarchist tenets. Given that the rejection of man-made laws and restrictive repressive institutions is central to anarchist theory, patriarchy would appear to violate the basic theory of anarchism" (1993, 28).

As discussed in greater detail in a following chapter, Goldman was aware more than most sociologists and male anarchists that women's opportunities were restricted by social custom and tradition. For Goldman, anarchists must be attuned to and "acknowledge the tyrannies of custom and habit" (Woodcock 1962, 202). In her view, desire was not necessarily a threat to order. Anarchism as political and social theory should encourage people to understand their desires to experience them fully.

Against Dualism

Early sociologists from Comte to Spencer to Durkheim sought "laws of society." This approach often led to the construction of dichotomies distinguishing society from nature, body from intellect, country from city, and emotions from knowledge. Nature signified the realm of instinct, desire, and identity. Society was posed as the realm of norms, laws, and politics.

Often, this division was gendered. Nature was viewed as a female realm. This realm, like women themselves, was to be the subject of regulation and control by the realm of society, politics, men. Sociologist Marilyn French has suggested that women are trained for private virtue while men

are prepared for public power (1986, 582). This echoes Goldman's writings
on moralism and women's treatment socially.

In *The Feminization of America*, social scientists Elinor Lenz and Barbara
Myerhoff provide an overview of dominant tendencies in Western social
thought:

> Dualism and polarization have marked much of our history, replacing the
> natural wholeness and unity of life and humankind with separate, discon-
> nected entities, alien to each other and to themselves. The principles of
> rational analysis and cognitive absolutism of opposites that have dominated
> Western culture perceive the world in terms of opposites that exist in a state
> of mutual suspicion and hostility...proletariat versus bourgeoisie, scientist
> versus humanist, masculine versus feminine (or yang versus yin). The sensi-
> bility that divides the world into opposition inevitably ranks them after
> dividing them, then sets itself up a superior—in value judgments, clarity
> and order. (1985, 230)

The dominant social views constructed a dualistic notion of males and
females and placed women on the body end of a mind/body dichotomy.
This also represented a hierarchical relationship with men on the top (in a
position of strength and authority). Haaland argues that in her rejection
of the dichotomy of reproduction and production and given the social and
historical context in which she wrote, Goldman's claims are actually
revolutionary.

For Goldman, the impacts of dualism are harmful not only for theoretical understanding but for human experience as well. In her view:

> But woman's freedom is closely allied with man's freedom, and many of my
> so-called emancipated sisters seem to overlook the fact that a child born in
> freedom needs the love and devotion of each human being about [her or]
> him, man as well as women. Unfortunately, it is this narrow conception of
> human relations [dualism of the sexes] that has brought about a great trag-
> edy in the lives of the modern man and woman. (quoted in Haaland 1993,
> 53–54)

Goldman challenged, in order to destroy, sexual dualism and the patriarchal ideologies of gender that sustain it. She, like many anarchists who
followed, sought to re-conceptualize notions such as individualism that
have been cornerstones of modernist social discourse.

Contemporary anarchists find themselves in general agreement with
post-structuralist feminism and queer theory, which considers gender to
not necessarily correlate with biological sex, but also to be pliable and
flexible. Thus, there is no "instinctive" dualism rooted in genetics between
males and females. Male-bodied individuals may act in "feminine" ways

(through their free will, if they can break free of patriarchal norms). Likewise, female-identified people can perform "masculine" actions, with just as much competence as males. The wider range of gendered expression sought by anarchists indicates an interest in empowering people to experience more and learn new skills. The nurturer/leader dualism for women and men is artificial. Men can take care of children, be good cooks, and competent cleaners, just as women can of course do physically strenuous and taxing labor, and negotiate tense situations. Countless examples and daily evidence demonstrates this, although artificial dualisms still reign ideological supreme. Dualist assumptions unnecessarily divides, segregates, and creates unequal conditions, while an integrative, reflexive, and open relationship towards gender norms is more anarchist and more sensible. A later chapter, focused on inequality and domination, explores these issues in even greater detail.

From Individualism to Individuality

During the period of sociology's emergence and consolidation as an academic discipline, social thought was dominated by political liberalism and *laissez faire* economics. Liberalism is associated with the notion of competitive individualism, particularly of individual competition and "success" through the market.

Goldman drew a sharp distinction between her conception of individuality and liberal notions of individualism. In her view, the individualism of liberalism reflected an economic and social agenda of the capitalist market and liberal democratic states. For Goldman: "Rugged individualism has meant all the 'individualism' for the masters, while the people are regimented into a slave caste to serve a handful of self-seeking 'supermen'" (1972, 89). Individuality is based in diversity, while individualism derives its power through the indistinguishable characteristics of atomized individuals as represented through the liberal state and markets (Haaland 1993, 84). Goldman's analysis echoes concerns raised by Tönnies in his discussion of the instrumental relations between people that mark conditions of *Gesellschaft*. Goldman saw her theory as bringing together the communitarianism of Kropotkin with the individuality of Nietzsche or Ibsen, which strains against limits of social conformity.

Goldman sought to address the lasting sociological tension of the relationship between the individual and society. She recognized and sought to understand the interdependence "of social organization and individual well being" (Haaland 1993, 6). Goldman identified the dangers of mass organization as well as the threat posed by the unfettered, socially irresponsible individual.

Consequently, she did not join the liberals in uncritically celebrating the individual. Neither did she join the Marxists in associating the individual with bourgeois thought and uncritically subsuming concern for the individual into the collective. Indeed, Goldman and her colleague Max Baginsky issued a statement at the 1907 Anarchist Conference in Amsterdam (that was accepted by those in attendance) in which they attempted to rethink relationships between individuality and social structure. They sought to correct "a mistaken notion that organization does not foster individual freedom; that, on the contrary, it means the decay of individuality" (Goldman and Baginsky 1907, 310). The development of individuality is, for Goldman and Baginsky, a "mutual process" that is based in "co-operative effort with other individualities" (1907, 310). Organization requires creative individuality as individuality requires cooperative creativity in production. Thus, anarchism is the never-perfectible balance between collective unity and individual autonomy, the equilibrium between collective power and restraint, and individual responsibility and choice.

Goldman, as with other anarchists, was wary of claims such as those made by the communist theorist Alexandra Kollontai that communist morality "demands all for the collective" (1977, 231). Goldman opposed economic determinism and the materialism that dominated socialist analysis. Reordering society would not occur only on the basis of economic reform, redistribution of wealth, and infrastructural change. The inner life of people required attention—their values, principles, and desires.

Concerning Bureaucracy

Another key historical force in the emergence of modernity that was analyzed and contested by anarchists as well as sociologists was the expansion of bureaucratization. Bureaucracy extended to all aspects of social life and the life of the individual. Bureaucratic values of rationality, functionalism, administration, management, and universality defined public discourse and practice. As early as the 1880s, sociologists like Max Weber discussed the significance of emerging forms of authority in modern capitalist societies and shifts away from forms of organization and authority that characterized rural feudal arrangements, especially traditional authorities such as the monarchy and church.

According to Weber, the new forms of modern authority were legal-rational, based on written rules, and consistent standards and practices. Legal-rational authority was viewed as an advance beyond traditional and charismatic authorities given that it promised to be based on rational decision-making, on the basis of argumentation and evidence, rather than arbitrary and irrational claims as existed within feudal religion based knowledge systems and institutions (with notions of "divine right" or nearness to god on a "chain of being"). The organizational form of legal-rational authority is bureaucracy, a structure of organization becoming dominant within modern societies. Where feudal institutions were based in particularism, bureaucracies are founded in universal practices.

Social engineers like Frederick W. Taylor viewed bureaucracy as beneficial, at least for industry. Bureaucracy promised efficiency, regulation, and social control—specifically with regard to labor and the extraction of surplus value, and exploitation, within the workplace. Scientific management of industrial production offered a model of social life organized around competitive productivity. Haaland observes:

> Premised upon the theory of social Darwinism, Taylor's theory placed the industrial worker in a competitive context struggling to do better than his fellow workers in order to maintain his position of employment. The principle of competition was seen to operate in the relations between workers as well as in those between corporations. (1993, 89)

Anarchists, like Emma Goldman, were vocal critics of these one-sided views. Drawing upon Kropotkin's works on mutual aid, anarchists, like Goldman, stressed cooperative aspects of social production. Against bureaucracy, they emphasized mutual aid and voluntary cooperation which still marked most of the relationships between workers. Anarchists noted that even within capitalist enterprises, the central feature of production was *shared* labor even if under conditions that were certainly not voluntary.

For anarchists, scientific management and bureaucracy were elements in the extension of the exploitation of labor rather than neutral features of progress and efficiency as champions of bureaucratic control claimed. Indeed, efficiency typically meant the efficiency of exploitation and surplus value extraction from workers by capital.

Bureaucracy offered a means for newly emergent elites, including academic professionals in disciplines like sociology, to extend their influence and power. As sociologist Bonnie Haaland notes: "In pursuit of this goal, sectors such as government, education and industry became central targets for bureaucratization, as the "reformers" attempted to exercise political control with the hope of altering the structure of authority and decision-making" (1993, 91). Against the unitary and arbitrary authority of non-modern social life, the professional strata claimed expertise in administration (social, political, and economic) through the regularity and continuity of rules and procedures.

Bureaucratization led to conformity and self-regulation. Individuals became subordinated to organizational ideals. Durkheim expressed what he saw as the need for the internalization of social control and regulatory impulses in his famous statement that "to be free is not to do as one pleases; it is to be the master of oneself" (1956, 90). Durkheim argued:

> The individual submits to society and this submission is the condition of his liberation. For man freedom consists in the deliverance from blind, unthinking physical forces; this he achieves by opposing against them the great and intelligent force which is society, under whose protection he shelters. By putting himself under the wing of society, he makes himself also, to a certain extent, dependent upon it. But this is a liberating dependence. (1964, 72)

Anarchists recognize that society is not only structured by major hierarchical institutions, but also by the unwritten rules that govern the practice of daily life within those institutions. Peoples' unreflective observance of these norms helps to perpetuate inequality and domination in society (see the later chapter in this book for more on this). Thus anarchists have analyzed processes of what are called governmentality in everyday life. This concern is apparent especially in the work of Emma Goldman, as discussed in a subsequent chapter.

By the first decades of the twentieth century, the modern state and professional bureaucracies (including the medical establishment) had replaced the church and religion as the central authority on issues of morality. While some sociologists suggested that bureaucracy would replace morality with legal and rational perspectives and discourses, Goldman recognized that the bureaucracies, rather than replacing or superseding the religious would take up religious discourses in bureaucratic or state form—through moral regulation and practices of governance.

As Haaland notes: "The role of sexual moral education had shifted from the pulpit to the physician's examining table. The medical profession played a key role in mediating the relevance of social values to its citizens (1993, 73). As former president of the American Gynecological Society proclaimed in a 1908 article in the *Long Island Medical Journal*, medical professionals held a "high function as confessors and advisors" (Gordon 1976, 170). Class-based explanations and moral judgments were passed off as "science." The connections between the new bureaucracies and religious moralism was asserted explicitly. As one physician put it, religion must be viewed as "an unrecognized branch of higher physiology" (Gordon 1976, 171).

State repression of sexuality and control over birth control practices was related with eugenic concerns for "racial" and social development. It influenced a range of policies, including not only reproduction but also immigration, economics, and foreign policy. As sex historian Jeffrey Weeks notes: "The task of state policy was to encourage methods to induce a sense of sexual responsibility in the population at large. Theoretically, there were two ways to do this: by encouraging the best to breed, or by discouraging the worst. But in practice, social policy had to be directed at the latter—who...were inevitably seen in class terms" (quoted in Haaland 1993, 78). Goldman saw the effects of moralism and restrictions on women's reproductive freedoms during her work as a midwife in poor neighborhoods (Goldman 1970).

Echoing Tönnies, Goldman suggested that bureaucratization led to instrumental relations between people. People related to one another not on the basis of mutual aid or solidarity but as opportunistic means to an end. A key task for sociological anarchy has been the analysis of alternative relations based on mutual aid in everyday life.

Roots of Sociological Anarchy: Kropotkin, and Mutual Aid

Among the primary historical influences on sociological anarchy, perhaps the most significant is Kropotkin's version of anarcho-communism and, especially, his ideas about mutual aid. Kropotkin was a well-regarded and respected public intellectual whose works were read and whose ideas were engaged with broadly outside of anarchist circles. His articles appeared in such popular publications as *The Times*. In addition he was influential within academic circles and was an esteemed member of numerous academic associations. Among his significant works are: *Fields, Factories, and Workshops* (1899), *Memoirs of a Revolutionist* (1899), *The Conquest of Bread* (1906), *Modern Science and Anarchism* (1912), and *Ethics: Origin and Development* (1924). His most influential work is *Mutual Aid* (1902) a serious rethinking of the place of completion, conflict, and cooperation in evolution.

Kropotkin directed his research and writing against the notion, taken up by social Darwinists, that competition was the central or "natural" factor of group life. Such views were a reflection of life within competitive capitalist social order. In contrast to competition as a "natural law," Kropotkin emphasized human sociability and mutual aid. For Kropotkin:

> Sociability is as much a law of nature as mutual struggle. Of course it would be extremely difficult to estimate, however roughly, the relative numerical importance of both these series of facts. But if we resort to an indirect test, and ask Nature: "Who are the fittest: those who are continually at war with each other, or those who support one another?," we at once see that those animals which acquire habits of mutual aid are undoubtedly the fittest. (1902, 5–6)

In *Mutual Aid* Kropotkin documents the centrality of co-operation within animal and human groups, and links anarchist theory with everyday experience. Kropotkin's definition suggests that anarchism, in part, "would represent an interwoven network, composed of an infinite variety of groups and federations of all sizes and degrees...temporary or more or less permanent...for all possible purposes" (quoted in Ward and Goodway 2003, 94). As Ward (2004, 29) reminds us: "A century ago Kropotkin noted the endless variety of 'friendly societies, the unities of oddfellows, the village and town clubs organised for meeting the doctors' bills' built up by working-class self-help." Both Kropotkin and, to a much lesser extent, Marx, commented on and were inspired by peasant collaboration in various aspects of daily life from the care of communal lands and forests, harvesting, the building of roads, house construction, and dairy production.

Kropotkin's political archeology, and especially his studies of the French Revolution and the Paris Commune, informed his analyses of the Russian revolutions of 1905 to 1917 and colored his warnings to comrades about the possibilities and perils that waited along the different paths of political change (Cleaver 1992b). This remains an important social and political undertaking in the context of crisis and structural adjustment impelled by the forces of capitalist globalization.

> In 1917 Kropotkin saw the dangers in the crisis: both those of reaction and those disguised in the garb of revolution, whether parliamentary or Bolshevik...In 1917 Kropotkin also knew where to look for the power to oppose those dangers and to create the space for the Russian people to craft their own solutions: in the self-activity of workers and peasants...In 1917, as we know, the power of workers to resist both reaction and centralization proved inadequate – partly because the spokespersons of the later cloaked their intentions behind a bright rhetoric of revolution. Today...such rhetoric

is no longer possible and in its place there is only the drab, alienating language of national and supranational state officials. (Cleaver 1992b, 10).

Kropotkin's extensive research into "mutual aid" was motivated by a desire to develop a general understanding of the character of human societies and their processes of evolution. It was partly concerned with providing a sociological critique of the popular views of social Darwinists like Huxley and Spencer. According to Kinna (1995), Kropotkin's *Mutual Aid* was also designed to argue against the authoritarianism of state socialists and the growing interest in Nietzschean individualism. More than that, as Cleaver (1992a; 1992b) notes, Kropotkin's work was aimed at laying the foundation for his anarcho-communist politics by showing a recurring tendency in human societies, as well as in many other animal societies, for individuals to help each other and to cooperate with other members of the species, rather than to compete in a Hobbesian war of all against all.

For Kropotkin, individuals did not create their world in an atomized fashion. Rather, individuality was realized through their social activity. On this matter, Goldman agreed and argued that:

> A certain atmosphere of "belonging," the consciousness of being "at one" with the people and the environment, is more essential to one's feeling of home. This holds good in relation to one's family, the smaller local circles, as well as the larger phase of the life and activities commonly called one's country....Peter Kropotkin has shown what wonderful results this unique force of man's individuality has achieved when strengthened by co-operation with other individualities....He demonstrated that only mutual aid and voluntary co-operation—not the omnipotent, all-devastating state—can create the basis for a free individual and associational life. (1983, 94–95)

In several book-length research works, including *Mutual Aid, The Conquest of Bread* and *Fields, Factories and Workshops*, Kropotkin tried to sketch the manifestation and development of mutual aid historically. What his research suggested to him was that mutual aid was always present in human societies, even if its development was never uniform or the same over different periods or within different societies. At various points, mutual aid was the primary factor of social life while at other times it was submerged beneath forces of competition, conflict, and violence. The key was that, regardless of its form or the adversity of circumstances in which it operated, mutual aid was always there "providing the foundation for recurrent efforts at co-operative self-emancipation from various forms of domination (the state, institutional religion, capitalism)" (Cleaver 1992b, 3).

Kropotkin was not, in a utopian manner, trying to suggest how a new society might or should develop. In his view, these practices were already happening and were appearing in the present. As such, anarchism is not involved in drawing-up social blueprints for the future. This is one reason that anarchists, to this day, have been so reluctant to describe the future "anarchist society." Instead, anarchists have tried to identify and understand social trends or tendencies, even countervailing ones. The focus is resolutely on manifestations of the future (and supposed past) with in the present.

In major works such as *The Conquest of Bread*, Kropotkin sought to detail how the post-capitalist future was already emerging in the here and now. His research in this case was concerned with, and indeed managed to offer, examples of practical cases in the present, which suggested aspects of a post-capitalist society. In this way Kropotkin's work, as with the work of other anarcho-communists, offers something more than simply a proposition. Thus his politics were grounded in ongoing, if under-appreciated, aspects of human societies (Cleaver 1992a; 1992b).

Kropotkin argued that human societies developed through processes involved in the ongoing interplay of what he called the "law of mutual struggle" and the "law of mutual aid." These forces manifested themselves in various ways depending on historical period or social context but they were typically observed in conflict rather than in stasis or equilibrium. This was not a strictly evolutionary schema, since Kropotkin included critically within his view of the interplay between these forces, periods of revolutionary upheaval. Thus, his approach is one that moves beyond strict dualism to offer an integration of tendencies in struggle.

> On the one side were the institutions and behaviors of mutual struggle such as narrow-minded individualism, competition, the concentration of landed and industrial property, capitalist exploitation, the state and war. On the other side were those of mutual aid such as cooperation in production, village folkmotes, communal celebrations, trade unionism and syndicalism, strikes, political and social associations. (Cleaver 1992b, 4)

According to Kropotkin, one or the other force tended to be predominant, depending on the era or instance, but it was his considered opinion that forces of mutual aid were on the rise, even as capitalism appeared triumphant. In fact, industrial development for which capitalism was famous could not be possible without an incredible degree of co-operative labor. Kropotkin argued against capitalist myth-making that presented the rapid growth of industrial development as the result of competition and instead suggested that the scope and efficiency of cooperation were more important factors (see Cleaver 1992a; 1992b). In this his analysis was remarkably close to that of Marx, who indeed saw the mass co-operation of industrial production as a prerequisite for communism.

> Where economists emphasized static comparative advantage, Kropotkin demonstrated the dynamic countertendency toward increasing complexity and interdependence (cooperation) among industries – a development closely associated with the unstoppable international circulation of knowledge and experience. Where the economists (and later the sociologists of work) celebrated the efficacy and productivity of specialization in production, Kropotkin showed how that very productivity was based not on competition but on the interlinked efforts of only formally divided workers. (Cleaver 1992b, 5)

Anarchist sociologists might do well to remember Kropotkin's advice concerning the methods to be followed by anarchist researchers. In his 1887 essay, *Anarchist Communism*, Kropotkin suggests that the anarchist approach differs from that of the utopian: "[The anarchist] studies human society as it is now and was in the past...tries to discover its tendencies, past and present, its growing needs, intellectual and economic, and in his [sic] ideal he [sic] merely points out in which direction evolution goes" (quoted in Cleaver 1992b, 3). Cleaver notes that

> This focus on tendencies, or developing patterns of concrete behavior, differentiated his approach from both early utopians and later Marxist-Leninists by abandoning the Kantian "ought" in favor of the scientific study of what is already coming to be. Neither Fourier nor Owen hesitated to spell out the way they felt society ought to be organized, from cooperatives to *phalansteries*. Nor were Lenin and his Bolshevik allies reluctant to specify, in considerable detail, the way work should be organized (Taylorism and competition) and how social decision-making ought to be arranged (top down through party administration and central planning. (Cleaver 1992b, 3)

Marx's writings offered much less detail than Kropotkin's works when it comes to the issue of working class subjectivity in contrast to the rather extensive analysis Marx provided with regard to capitalist domination. It was only through the decades of work carried out by various autonomist Marxists (such as Cleaver) that a Marxist analysis of working class autonomy developed that came close to a parallel of Kropotkin's work (Cleaver 1992b, 7).

Conclusion

Living examples of the anarchist perspectives on order emerging "spontaneously" out of social circumstances are perhaps most readily and regularly observed under conditions of immediate need or emergency as in times of natural disaster and/or economic crisis, during periods of revolutionary upheaval or during mass events such as festivals. In other cases, anarchists sometimes point to post offices and railway networks as examples of the way in which local groups and associations can combine to provide complex networks of functions without any central authority (Ward 2004). Postal services work as a result of voluntary agreements between different post offices in different countries, without any central world postal authority (Ward 2004). As Ward observes: "Coordination requires neither uniformity nor bureaucracy" (2004: 89).

Unlike utopian thinkers, anarchists exercise extreme caution when discussing "blueprints" of future social relations since they believe that it is always up to those seeking freedom to decide how they desire to live. Still, there are a few features common to anarchist visions of a free society. While anarchists are not in agreement about the means to bring about the future libertarian society, they are clear that means and ends cannot be separated. According to anthropologist David Graeber:

> The moment we stop insisting on viewing all forms of action only by their function in reproducing larger, total, forms of inequality of power, we will also be able to see that anarchist social relations and non-alienated forms of action are all around us. And this is critical because it already [sic] shows that anarchism is, already, and has always been, one of the main bases for human interaction. We self-organize and engage in mutual aid all the time. We always have. (Graeber 2004, 76)

The anarchist future present must, almost by definition, be based upon ongoing experiments in social arrangements, in attempting to address the usual dilemma of maintaining both individual freedoms and social equality (Ehrlich 1996). The revolution is always in the making. These projects make up what the anarchist sociologist Howard Ehrlich calls "anarchist transfer cultures."

> Despite the dominant authoritarian trend in existing society, most contemporary anarchists therefore try and extend spheres of free action in the hope that they will one day become the mainstream of social life. In difficult times, they are, like Paul Goodman, revolutionary conservatives, maintaining older traditions of mutual aid and free enquiry when under threat. In more auspicious moments, they move out from free zones until by their example and wisdom they begin to convert the majority of people to their libertarian vision. (Marshall 1993, 659)

Even more, as many recent anarchist writings suggest, the potential for resistance might be found anywhere in everyday life. If power is exercised everywhere, it might give rise to resistance everywhere. Present-day anarchists like to suggest that a glance across the landscape of contemporary society reveals many groupings which are anarchic in practice if not in ideology.

> Examples include the leaderless small groups developed by radical feminists, coops, clinics, learning networks, media collectives, direct action organizations; the spontaneous groupings that occur in response to disasters, strikes, revolutions and emergencies; community-controlled day-care centers; neighborhood groups; tenant and workplace organizing; and so on. (Ehrlich, Ehrlich, DeLeon, and Morris 1996, 18)

While such examples are rarely explicitly anarchist in ideology, they often operate to provide examples of mutual aid, and non-hierarchical and non-authoritarian modes of living which carry the form or memory of anarchy within them. Often such practices are essential for people's day-to-day survival and coping under the crisis states of capitalism. Ward notes that "the only thing that makes life possible for millions in the United States are its non-capitalist elements....Huge areas of life in the United States, and everywhere else, are built around voluntary and mutual aid organisations" (Ward and Goodway 2003, 105). Yet these necessary relations of everyday anarchy are often minimized within approaches to social order focused on statist institutions and bureaucratic arrangements. A central task of anarchist-sociology is to direct an appropriately serious attention to these facts and observations. With this focus, anarchist-sociology can recapture previous anarchist practices, grow and evolve contemporary anarchist social phenomenon, and aim to achieve broader anarchist goals of social transformation in the future.

CHAPTER THREE

COLIN WARD'S SOCIOLOGICAL ANARCHY

Colin Ward may be one of the few anarchist writers to have a larger reader-ship outside of anarchist circles than within them. This is a testament both to his writing (and the issues he addresses within those writings) and to the rhetorical preferences of contemporary anarchist readers—especially at a time when highly abstract and theoretical post-modern/anarchist hybrids have provided some footing for academic anarchists and their publishers.

Colin Ward is perhaps best known, at least to anarchists, through his third book *Anarchy in Action* which was—until his 2004 contribution to the Oxford Press "Short Introduction" series, *Anarchism: A Very Short Introduction*—his only book explicitly about anarchist theory. Longtime anarchist George Woodcock identified *Anarchy in Action* as one of the most important theoretical works on anarchism and we would have to agree. In fact, we argue that *Anarchy in Action* is an excellent work of radical, prefigurative sociology, too. It is in the pages of that relatively short work that Ward makes explicit his highly distinctive version of anarchism, what might be called an anarchy of everyday life or, more simply, everyday anarchy.

Ward described his approach to anarchism as one that is based on actual experiences or practical examples rather than theories or hypotheses. Ward's anarchism, "far from being a speculative vision of a future society...is a description of a mode of human organization, rooted in the experience of everyday life, which operates side by side with, and in spite of, the dominant authoritarian trends of our society" (Ward 1973: 11). While having no formal, academic background in sociology he argues for the importance of taking a sociological approach to the world. Taking this approach has consequences simultaneously liberatory and practical since "once you begin to look at human society from an anarchist point of view you discover that the alternatives are already there, in the interstices of the dominant power structure. If you want to build a free society, the parts are all at hand" (Ward 1973: 13). As David Goodway suggests, this approach also addresses two seemingly insoluble problems that have long confronted anarchists and socialists alike (Ward and Goodway 2003: 11).

The first is, if anarchism (or socialism) is so highly desirable as well as feasible, how is it that it has never come into being or lasted no longer than a few months (or years). Ward's answer is that anarchism is already partially in existence and that he can show us examples "in action." The second problem is how can humans be taught to become co-operative, thereby enabling a transition from the present order to a co-operative society to be attained. Ward's response here is that humans are naturally co-operative and that current societies and institutions, however capitalist and individualist, would completely fall apart without the integrating powers, even if unvalued, of mutual aid and federation. Nor will social transformation be a matter of climactic revolution, attained in a millennial movement, but rather a prolonged situation of dual power in the age-old struggle between authoritarian and libertarian tendencies, with outright victory for either tendency most improbable. (Ward and Goodway 2003: 11)

The primary historical influences on Ward's everyday anarchy are Peter Kropotkin's anarcho-communism and the libertarian socialism of Gustav Landauer. In *Mutual Aid*, Kropotkin documents the centrality of co-operation within animal and human groups and links anarchist theory with everyday experience. Ward has modestly stated that *Anarchy in Action* is merely an extended contemporary footnote to *Mutual Aid* (Ward and Goodway 2003: 14). As Ward (2004: 29) reminds us: "A century ago Kropotkin noted the endless variety of 'friendly societies, the unities of oddfellows, the village and town clubs organised for meeting the doctors' bills' built up by working-class self-help." Still, Ward goes beyond Kropotkin in the importance he places on co-operative groups in anarchist social transformation. Thus, Ward's anarchism openly draws on Landauer's exhortation that militants prioritize the formation of producers' and consumers' co-operatives. At the same time Ward follows Kropotkin in identifying himself as an anarchist-communist.[1]

The Propagandist

Ward was won to anarchism through his contact with Glasgow anarchists Eddie Shaw, Jimmie Dick and, especially, Frank Leech, during a posting, ironically, with the Army School of Hygiene in 1943. Leech encouraged the young Ward to put together some articles for the London publication *War Commentary—for Anarchism* published by Marie Louise Berneri of the

---

[1] For an anarchist-oriented collection of Ward's writings, please see Wilbert and White (2011).

Freedom Press Group (itself co-founded by Kropotkin) and the material appeared in December of 1943.

Ward notes that this was a time when most of the British left was swept up in a torrent of what he calls "Stalin-worship," in which there was a tacit agreement not to utter criticism of the Soviet Union. Ward suggests that it is difficult for later generations to fully appreciate how deeply the assumptions of the British and Western European intellectuals were constrained by Marxist and Stalinist ideas. Ward explains the left's infatuation with Stalinism during that period as a result of the search for ultimate certainties in sociology and politics. Ward spent much of his life working against similar tendencies, intending to discover comparable ultimate certainties within anarchism.

Ward began his long publishing career in 1946 with a series of nine articles on the postwar squatters' movement in the longstanding anarchist magazine *Freedom*. In 1947, Ward was invited to join *Freedom*'s editorial group. By the early 1950s, the characteristic preoccupations that Ward would emphasize over the next five decades of his writings had emerged: housing and planning, workers' control, and industrial self-organization (Ward and Goodway 2003: 5).

Ward was deeply impacted by the squatters' movements that emerged during the 1940s as homeless families seized empty military camps. Yet his anarchism was so outside of the parameters of mainstream anarchism that in the 1940s, when Ward tried to convince his Freedom Press Group colleagues to print a pamphlet on the squatters' movement "it wasn't thought that this is somehow relevant to anarchism" (Ward and Goodway 2003: 15).

In March 1961, in a compromise response to his arguments that *Freedom* move from weekly production to become a monthly, Ward was assigned the editorship of *Anarchy*, a monthly complement to *Freedom*. Under his editorial guidance, *Anarchy* produced 118 issues until its closing in 1970, with a circulation of more than 2000 copies per issue. Less well known is the fact that Ward often wrote much of each issue of the great journal himself, under a string of pseudonyms or in unsigned articles (Ward and Goodway 2003: 8). The journal reflected Ward's major preoccupations, focusing on housing and squatting, progressive education, and workers' control.

One of the major contributions of the journal *Anarchy*, under Ward's editorship was to take anarchist writing from the status of fringe or marginal commentary and to encourage a broader audience to take anarchist ideas on a variety of topics seriously. By intervening in a credible and engaging manner, beyond easy clichés or prefabricated responses, on matters of public concern *Anarchy* showed that anarchists could offer coherent and relevant responses to key social questions.

For three decades Ward also disseminated this approach to anarchy as a regular contributor to the sociological journal *New Society* and its successor *New Statesman and Society*. For almost a decade, beginning in 1988, Ward contributed a weekly column to that publication. Through this work he was able to spread anarchist ideas more broadly, and among more diverse readerships than most anarchists were able to achieve.

The challenge, which Ward met mostly successfully, was to keep routine and ready-made formulas from intruding on his writings, especially as they gained in longevity and scope.

> I am convinced that the most effective way of conducting anarchist propaganda through the medium of a monthly journal is to take the whole range of partial, fragmentary, but immediate issues in which people *are actually likely to get involved*, and to seek out anarchist solutions, rather than to indulge in windy rhetoric about revolution. A goal that is infinitely remote, said Alexander Herzen, is not a goal at all, but a deception. On the other hand, these preoccupations led to a neglect of a whole range of topics which *Anarchy* has ignored. Where, for example, is a thorough anarchist analysis of economic and industrial changes in this country. (Ward and Goodway 2003: 59)

Through the responses of readers to articles published in *Anarchy*, Ward found that for many people anarchy aptly described the "organized chaos" that people experienced during their daily lives, even at their workplaces. It was this convergence of peoples' everyday experiences and their responses—whether active or in terms of thoughts and feelings—to these experiences with anarchism that informed Ward's work throughout. Recognizing and respecting the fact that many people understood the world in an anarchistic way, even if they had no contact at all with explicitly anarchist theory or with anarchist movements, encouraged Ward to write in a straightforward manner on a variety of issues that were often overlooked within anarchist publications. It also taught him that anarchist ideas were more important than attachment to a specific theoretical body or tradition and that the anarchist writer would find a ready audience, indeed a diversity of audiences, willing to engage with anarchist perspectives if they were presented in a clear language and if they dealt, not necessarily with the "big picture" issues anarchists themselves thought were most important, but rather with the daily concerns people face in going about their lives.

In one of his earlier articles Ward, in reflecting on the condition of anarchist politics, suggests that it was "Because we have failed to formulate
anarchist alternatives in the most prosaic as well as the most important
fields of life, that the very people who could bring to life our own activities
cannot bring themselves to take us seriously" (Ward and Goodway 2003:
57). Taking this approach, Ward, more than most anarchists, came to have
an impact well outside of anarchist or even leftist circles. His views on
issues ranging from education to architecture to children's activities to
planning have been sought by people seeking alternatives to government
initiatives or business-mandated cutbacks. As Ward himself suggests:
"My aim was, as always, to make the anarchist approach a point of view
that was taken seriously in every field of social life. I want anarchist attitudes to be among those that citizens everywhere know about, and cannot
dismiss as an amusing curiosity of the political fringe" (Ward and Goodway
2003: 123).

As one example, Ward became an important influence within planning
circles. He gained recognition as a credible advocate for anarchist
approaches to planning and has been credited with launching a movement in planning that has revived the anarchist visions of planning pio-
neers such as Ebenezer Howard and Patrick Geddes. In his inventive and
widely influential paper "The Do-it-yourself New Town," Ward advocated
"a new concept of building communities, in which the residents themselves would be involved directly in planning, designing and building their
own homes and neighbourhoods. The role of local authorities would be
limited to that of site provision and basic services" (Hardy 1991: 173).
Neighborhood planning is a radical, direct, and meaningful activity. Ward
suggests that "squatters' campaigns, as well as providing a roof for
homeless people, are significant as a symbolic challenge to the concept of
property, and for their effect on the participants" (Ward and Goodway
2003: 73).

Ward's decades-long writings, engaging with anarchism, have done
more than simply refine anarchist ideas, and make them practical and
useful to his wide readership. He has also served—along with other
English-language writers like Paul Goodman and Murray Bookchin (and
maybe C. Wright Mills, Dave Dellinger, and Dorothy Day; see Cornell
2011)—as a bridge between the "golden age" anarchism that ended with
Franco's victory in the Spanish Civil War and the 1960s "new left." Ward
was instrumental in reinterpreting and repackaging classic anarchist ideas
for a modern audience that had been terrorized by world wars, and
had seen the decimation of working-class radicalism via anti-communist

propaganda, rising standards of living, and business unionism. In doing so, Ward also rediscovered and strengthened anarchism's latent sociological character.

The Anarchist Sociologist

The anarchist and popular sex educator Alex Comfort was one of the first to argue that anarchists had much to learn from sociologists. In his work *Delinquency* (1951), Comfort called for anarchism to become a libertarian action sociology.

Ward took this call to heart and he draws much of his inspiration from the sociology of autonomous groups. His writings in the now out-of-print sociology bulletin *Autonomous Groups* contributed to understanding the existing capacities for influencing social change within informal networks such as the Batignolles Group, founders of Impressionism, and the Fabian Society. Notably these groups were incredibly effective, exercising an influence well beyond their numbers.

The autonomous groups that Ward studied or participated in are characterized by "having a secure internal network based on friendship and shared skills, and a series of external networks of contacts in a variety of fields" (Ward 2003: 44). Such autonomous groups are marked by a high degree of individual autonomy within the group, reliance on direct reciprocities in decision-making, for decisions affecting all group members, and the temporary and fluctuating character of leadership. Autonomous groups are distinguished from other organizations who are characterized by "hierarchies of relationships, fixed divisions of labour, and explicit rules and practices" (Ward 2003: 48). Among these autonomous groups, Ward also includes the Freedom Press Group, A.S. Neill's Summerhill School of alternative education, Burgess Hill School, and South London's Peckham Health Centre which offered approaches to social medicine.

As Ward (2003: 48) notes, anarchists traditionally "have conceived of the whole of social organisation as a series of interlocking networks of autonomous groups." Thus it is important that anarchists pay serious attention to the lessons to be learned from successful groups. This focus compensates for a curious blind spot in mainstream North American sociology, which is obsessed with "social problems," but fairly indifferent to studying the practical solutions to such problems (especially as popularly-initiated and decentralized endeavors).

Anarchists address the key issues of "who provides and who decides." Everyday anarchism is about developing ways in which people enable themselves to take control of their lives and participate meaningfully in the decision-making processes that affect them, whether pertaining to education, housing, work, or food. In a contemporary, post-Fordist context, Ward notes that changes in the structure of work, notably so-called lean production, flexibilization, and the institutionalization of precarious labor, have stolen people's time away from the family along with the time that might otherwise be devoted to activities in the community (Ward and Goodway 2003: 107). Of course, this trend has always been a central source of class struggle under capitalism: the struggle over everyday life and the time spent in activities of capitalist value production against the time spent in taking care of ourselves (what some call self-valorization). Ward finds resonance in the research of industrial psychologists who suggest that satisfaction in work is very strongly related to the "span of autonomy," or the proportion of work time in which workers are free to make and act on their own decisions.

Ward has made some important contributions to analyses of the welfare state and its role in the deterioration or destruction of mutual aid in capitalist societies. In discussing the welfare state, Colin Ward sums up its positive and negative aspects in short: "The positive feature of welfare legislation is that, contrary to the capitalist ethic, it is a testament to human solidarity. The negative feature is precisely that it is an arm of the state" (Ward and Goodway 2003: 79). Ward focuses on recent examples, such as holiday camps in Britain, "in which a key role was played by the major organisations of working-class self-help and mutual aid, the co-operative movement and trade unions" (Ward and Goodway 2003: 17). A significant theme in the perspectives of everyday anarchy is "the historic importance of such institutions in the provision of welfare and the maintenance of social solidarity" (Ward and Goodway 2003: 17). Ward points out that the provision of social welfare did not originate from government through the "welfare state." Rather, it emerged in practice "from the vast network of friendly societies and mutual aid organizations that had sprung up through working-class self-help in the 19th century" (Ward 2004: 27). Sam Dolgoff makes the same point with reference to the importance of mutual aid groups for the provision everything from education to elder care within the labor movement in the US. Ward notes that "the only thing that makes life possible for millions in the United States are its non-capitalist elements.... Huge areas of life in the United States, and everywhere else, are built around voluntary and mutual aid organisations" (Ward and Goodway 2003: 105). For example, organizations like self-help groups, credit unions, labor unions, and even Social Security all fall into this broad category.

In numerous works, Ward illustrated how, since the late nineteenth century, "'the tradition of fraternal and autonomous associations springing up from below' has been successively displaced by 'authoritarian institutions directed from above'"(Ward and Goodway 2003: 17). As Ward suggests, this displacement was actively pursued, with often disastrous results, in the development of the social citizenship state: "The great tradition of working-class self-help and mutual aid was written off not just as irrelevant, but as an actual impediment, by the political and professional architects of the welfare state... The contribution that the recipients had to make... was ignored as a mere embarrassment" (quoted in Ward and Goodway 2003: 18). From his research on housing movements, Ward comments on "the initially working-class self-help building societies stripping themselves of the final vestiges of mutuality; and this degeneration has existed alongside a tradition of municipal housing that was adamantly opposed to the principle of dweller control" (Ward and Goodway 2003: 18). Ward's work is directed towards providing useful "pointers to the way ahead if we are to stand any chance of reinstituting the self-organisation and mutual aid that have been lost" (Ward and Goodway 2003: 18).

> It is still an anarchism of present and permanent protest – how could it be anything else in our present peril? But it is one which recognises that the choice between libertarian and authoritarian solutions occurs every day and in every way. And the extent to which we choose, or accept, or are fobbed off with, or lack the imagination and inventiveness to discover alternatives to, authoritarian solutions to small problems is the extent to which we are their powerless victims in big affairs. We are powerless to change the course of events over the nuclear arms race, imperialism and so on, precisely because we have surrendered our power over everything else. (Ward 2003: 55)

Rather than falling into the trap of excessive enthusiasm, Ward is also aware of Errico Malatesta's reminder that anarchists are only one of the forces acting in society and history will move according to the sum of all the forces. Thus, it is necessary for anarchists to "find ways of living among non-anarchists as anarchistically as possible" (Malatesta quoted in Ward and Goodway 2003: 85). Beyond being a reflection on the difficulties facing anarchist organizers in overcoming authoritarian social relations, this is a warning against being satisfied only with subcultural or lifestyle approaches to carving out spaces of anarchy within hierarchical society.

Ward had little time for artsy anarchists concerned with producing avant-garde works "intended to shock the bourgeoisie, without regard for the fact that artists of all sorts have been shocking the bourgeoisie for a century, and that the rest of us find it hard to suppress a yawn"(Ward and

Goodway 2003: 124). At the same time he avoided the trap of sectarianism. His criticisms of other anarchists and their perspectives always played a minor part in his writings and he has publicly offered the view that squabbling among anarchists tends to lessen their relevance to non-anarchist readers. "To the outside world, anarchism, like Trotskyism, makes itself ridiculous because of its ideological subdivisions" (Ward 2003: 41). Similarly Ward was critical of anarchists' preoccupation with anarchist history and in his own works he preferred to emphasize the here-and-now and the immediate future (Ward and Goodway 2003).

This does not mean that he avoids debate on anarchist strategy, tactics, or theory, however. Ward's concern that anarchism develop practical, real world alternatives in the here-and-now has left him with little patience for the emergence of primitivism and anti-civilizationism within anarchism. He comments, with some disdain, on the "sentimental and privileged idealisation of 'wilderness' and the natural environment" that has led many anarchists to abandon involvement in social issues in favor of adopting a stance of "misanthropy towards their fellow humans" (Ward and Goodway 2003: 97). In his view, deep ecology became fashionable among those affluent enough to "get away from it all" and pursue a variety of esoteric and mystical beliefs "as long as the cheques kept flowing into their bank accounts" (2004: 93). Ward suggests that "as ecological awareness spread among the children of the affluent, the national guilt over the genocide of indigenous peoples led to an exaltation of the Noble Savage, and distaste for ordinary mortals who hadn't got the Message (Ward and Goodway 2003: 98).

Ward joined Murray Bookchin (who did likewise in his polemic *Social Anarchism or Lifestyle Anarchism*, albeit with a far more acid tongue) in repudiating these approaches and seeking instead "to confront the abandonment of social concerns in an increasingly divided America" (2004: 94). This, in turn, requires challenging the hierarchical, racist, sexist, class-based state apparatus and its histories of militarism, conquest, and occupation. It is not enough—and, for Ward, simply unhelpful—to cheer on the supposedly impending collapse of civilization, as primitivists are wont to do.

The Reformist?

Some critics might dismiss Ward's work as being "non-revolutionary." To do so is to repeat the mistake, common in much thinking on the left, of conceiving of revolution narrowly as a specific moment of upheaval or seizure of power (usually in terms of the state). Under this sort of myopic view, which insists on a rather abstract opposition between revolution and reform, Ward would be conceived as a reformist. Ward's work recognizes that revolutions do not emerge fully-formed out of nothing. His perspective emphasizes the need, in pre-revolutionary times, for institutions, organizations, and other social relations that can sustain people as well as building capacities for self-defense and struggle. Ward was fond of quoting Paul Goodman on these matters: "The pathos of oppressed people, however, is that, if they break free, they don't know what to do. Not having been autonomous, they don't know what it's like, and before they learn, they have new managers who are not in a hurry to abdicate" (Goodman quoted in Ward 2004: 69).

By taking a more nuanced approach to revolutionary transformation one can understand Ward's work is concerned with the practical development of what Howard Ehrlich (1996) calls revolutionary transfer cultures. Anarchist organizing is built on what Ward calls "social and collective ventures rapidly growing into deeply rooted organizations for welfare and conviviality" (2004: 63). As such, Ward refers to these manifestations of everyday anarchy as "quiet revolutions." All revolutions require considerable "build-up" prior to mass insurrections and the decentralization of power (e.g. the 1917 Russian Revolution and 1936 Spanish Revolution). As argued elsewhere in this book, it is during this time period that new social norms are being created, and socialization is helping to justify and extend these practices throughout the population. Without these "transfer cultures," insurrections will fade into history books as mere riots, not revolutions.

Conclusion

When people have no control over or responsibility for the crucial decisions over important aspects of life, whether regarding housing, education, or work, then these areas of social life become obstacles to personal fulfillment and collective development. Yet, when people are free to make decisions, and contribute to the planning and implementation of decisions involving key areas of daily life, there are improvements in individual and social well-being (Ward and Goodway 2003: 76).

The perspectives and practices of everyday anarchy, in addressing immediate day-to-day concerns, provide an important reminder to revolutionary anarchists that they must offer examples that resonate with people's experiences and needs. Or as Herzen has remarked: "A goal which is infinitely remote is not a goal at all, it is a deception" (quoted in Ward 2004: 32). Thus, constructive, practical anarchy is the most empowering variety available, as it illustrates a positive, fulfilling way forward. Everyday anarchy relies on time-tested anarchist principles of direct action, prefigu-rative politics, and self-management. Ward's anarchist-sociology can serve as a wise sign-post for both anarchists and sociologists alike, to appreciate what is of greatest importance. Such an analysis invariably leads to the critique of major institutions, such as patriarchy and capitalism.

CHAPTER FOUR

THE PERSONAL IS POLITICAL: EMMA GOLDMAN AND FEMINIST SOCIOLOGY

Despite the serious contributions made by anarchists to social analysis and theory, anarchist thinkers and writers have too often been portrayed in a limited fashion as activists or organizers. The dramatic character of many anarchists' lives, and their direct involvement in revolutions and uprisings, has entranced many commentators who have viewed anarchists as radical icons rather than social analysts. Much of the work on anarchist theorists has been biographical in nature focusing on their lives and struggles rather than their contributions to social thought.

Most of the academic work on Emma Goldman has focused overwhelmingly on her life and personal biography—for understandable reasons, since her life history was indeed quite compelling. Attention has been given to her many journeys and her direct involvement in revolutionary upheavals—most notably in Russia in the 1910s and 1920s and Spain during the 1930s (Goldman 1970).

Relatively little attention has been given to Goldman's *ideas*. Those works that have examined Goldman's ideas have come almost exclusively from the realm of political science and have focused on her contributions to anarchist theory. Some few works have also examined Goldman in the context of philosophy—again concerned primarily with anarchist political or ethical philosophy. Where real attention has been given to Goldman's work is in the context of feminist theory and women's history. Feminist theorists have long recognized the contributions of Goldman's work for developing feminist theory and practice.

Yet a closer examination shows that Goldman's work has great relevance for sociology. Goldman was aware of and made regular use of sociological research in her writings on various topics, including birth control, labor markets, and sex work. For example, Goldman is included in an entry within George Ritzer's *Blackwell Encyclopedia of Sociology*, where authors note that "Emma Goldman's contributions to sociology are most evident in her political critiques of major social institutions" (Sandefur and MacLean 2007: 2007). She applied a sociological analysis to personal troubles as well as public issues, including, or especially, those most often treated through the frame of moralism or what she called Puritanism. Thus an examination of Goldman's works offers a useful contribution to sociological history and theory. It also allows for a reappraisal of intersections between anarchism and sociology.

Even more, revisiting Goldman provides a rethinking or reconsideration of early developments and contributions to feminist sociology. Critical or radical feminism is associated with the 1960s movements and movements in the decades since. Goldman shows an early manifestation of a feminist viewpoint in sociology and feminist approaches to social analysis. Goldman's ideas remain important for contemporary feminist analysis as well as for efforts of public sociology and social change. Feminist scholar and social historian Linda Gordon suggests that Goldman more than any other figure should be credited with fusing sex radicalism into a single theory (Haaland 1993, ix). Likewise, Alice Wexler credits Goldman with "going further than most radicals in her understanding of the politics of sex" (1984, 278). This chapter is a reflection of her sociological approach to gendered social problems and other issues of feminist concern.

Personal Troubles and Public Issues

Goldman was an early proponent of the intersection of public views and private deeds. She was a proponent of the notion that "the personal is political," a key tenet of post-1960s feminism. She did not privilege public work over personal engagement. Goldman brought together Kropotkin's theory of mutual cooperation with a theory of individual freedom influenced by Nietzsche and Ibsen. Prefiguring Mills's (1959) writings on the sociological imagination—in which the social factors causing individual troubles are sought—Goldman suggests that a complete anarchist theory should view internal and external factors as complementary (Haaland 1993, 16). Goldman boldly refused the arranged marriage her father had set for her at 16. She defiantly asserted that she would never marry for anything but love (Drinnon 1961, 5). Her own political views drew from, and were revised through, engagement with her own experiences. For years she worked as a nurse and midwife in poor communities of New York City's East Side. As a community organizer, one of her many arrests came in 1916 when she was arrested for delivering a public lecture in which she advocated birth control.

Emma Goldman offered a vision of society in which personal troubles and public issues intersect and develop together. She provides an analysis in which social structures and institutions are moral as well as material. Hers is a nuanced view that moves beyond base/superstructure approaches or perspectives that privilege structure over ideas or the reverse.

Within many versions of early sociological, as well as anarchist, theorizing, knowledge has been viewed as the product of the public sphere. As Haaland notes: "Thus, we are also able to infer that activities situated in the private realm (e.g. sexuality and reproduction) are considered random, arbitrary, and irrelevant and are excluded from the realm of theory or knowledge" (1993, 4). Bureaucracy devalued domestic knowledge, and constructed knowledge, culture, and intellect as separate from the domestic realm. It belonged to the realm of the public—bureaucracy. Knowledge could only be gained through public sphere participation. It was divorced from the realm of instinct, desire, nature, care—the supposed realm of the home and women. As Haaland notes, "to assume that worthwhile knowledge was only attainable in the realm of culture or intellect, was to adopt a patriarchal 'culture' in which instinct was devalued" (1993, 50). Goldman challenges the notions of public reason, or rationality, and private or domestic desire, or irrationality, that mark much of modernist political theory.

Goldman persistently rejected the separation of the domestic and political realms. For Goldman, ideas of sexuality and reproduction are connected, indeed intimately, with political commitments, but these ideas are developed and evolved through lived experience. There is mutual engagement between domestic and political realms rather than separation or bifurcation.

Goldman, significantly, viewed sociology as a means to bring discussion of sexuality "out of the closet," so to speak, of moralism and superstition. She greatly admired social analysts such as Havelock Ellis and Edward Carpenter. As Kissack (2008) notes, Goldman was a voracious reader of Ellis and Carpenter's sexology research, as well as psychologists, sex radicals, and who today we would call "queer" authors. Sexuality was a matter of individual liberty and no one—not the state, Puritanism, or medical authorities—should have the right to constrain people's sexual lives, regardless of the shapes or forms they took. She also included articles defending homosexuality in her journal *Mother Earth* and widely lectured on the topic of homosexuality throughout the United States. Her well-attended lectures during the 1910s exposed thousands of Americans to issues around sexuality, and she was, perhaps, the individual who can claim responsibility for presenting a favorable and supportive view of queer issues to the greatest number of people during this time period in the US.

And Anarchy

Emma Goldman was largely responsible for bringing analysis of sexuality and reproductive labor into anarchist theory. In this she clashed with leading figures such as Kropotkin who viewed matters such as sexuality as beyond the purview of a "political" theory like anarchism. Issues of the family and roles of reproduction within the domestic or household sphere were largely invisible to earlier theories of both sociology and anarchism. For leading male anarchists especially, issues of sexuality were largely avoided as sources of embarrassment. Kropotkin had little interest in issues of feminism or sexual liberation. Indeed, Kropotkin consigned sexuality to the realm of the personal rather than the political. Thus it was not, in his view, a subject for anarchist theory to concern itself with. Proudhon is largely understood to be anti-feminist in his approach (Woodcock 1983).

Early sociological and anarchist theories too often took for granted the patriarchal family as a permanent and unchangeable institution. Significant male anarchist theorists viewed the patriarchal family as an unproblematic, even desirable, institution. Proudhon, for example, viewed patriarchy as a source of support against the intrusions of capital and as a necessary feature of the communal life of peasant producers. The family also served to veil issues of sexuality that were central to issues of power and social control but which were rendered invisible or obscured within anarchism, thus weakening its over approach as a critical theory of social power (Haaland 1993, 1).

Goldman's work marks a shift in anarchist theory away from androcentric theory to what today is called intersectional or integrative theory. Goldman sought to understand and analyze the intersection of social structural issues, politics, and organization along with personal issues of biography or what she called individuality. Thus, her approach is expressive of what Mills defines as a sociological imagination.

Goldman addresses a major gap in Kropotkin's work on mutual aid and human social development: his failure to account for the material specificity of women. In his various works on mutual aid, Kropotkin leaves women largely subsumed within the group and group activities. He discusses the family as a site of mutual aid but avoids the contradictions of power and authority within the family. There is no discussion of, or critique of, the patriarchal family. He does not account for patriarchy as a factor limiting freedom (Haaland 1993, 12). Kropotkin, as suggested above, is too easy on customs and habit and not critical enough of moral compulsion within small scale and face-to-face social settings (Woodcock 1962, 13). Kropotkin viewed questions of organization as separate from issues of desire or individual needs.

Goldman suggested that these were not separate questions. Goldman instead argued for "economic arrangements consisting of 'voluntary production and distribution associations' in which individuals would work in 'harmony with their tastes and desires'" (Haaland 1993, 16). For Goldman, issues of sex, marriage, and reproduction more broadly are, or should be, at the center of anarchist concerns. They are not matters for the margins of social thought. As the sociologist Bonnie Haaland suggests: "Goldman's inclusion of these issues, subsumed within her overall theory of anarchism, meant that anarchism was not to be a theory only for men in the public sphere, it was to be a theory for women (and men) whose public and private lives were not sharply bifurcated" (1993, 22).

Unlike most social theorists of her day, Goldman rejected the "absurd notion of the dualism of the sexes, or that man and woman represent two antagonistic worlds" (1972, 123). As Haaland suggests:

> In this she not only went against the grain of Western philosophy and social organization, but also introduced a revolutionary conception of gender relations and associational life. Goldman placed men and women in the domain where feminist traits have traditionally prevailed...Goldman also rejected the taken-for-granted philosophical proposition that because men and women possess different instincts, they belong in *separate spheres*. (1993, 53)

Goldman sought to overcome the dualism of thought/action and mind/body in her own life. Rather than simply espousing theoretical positions, she sought to make them real, material factors in the world. Custom, habit, and superstition render men and women strangers, even within the close confines of marriage. Goldman argued for a non-hierarchical relationship between men and women.

Against Puritanism: Goldman and Moral Regulation

Anarchists have argued against the "fixed idea" in all spheres of thought and action. Conceptions of life must be movable not immovable. In opposition to sameness and uniformity, anarchists stress variety and diversity. Achieving real emancipation, or even opening the possibility of it, meant overcoming the restraints of tradition, prejudice, and custom that marked *Gemeinschaft* (community) as well moral regulation under conditions of bureaucratic modernity (recall Chapter 2's discussion of *gemeinschaft*).

For Goldman, emancipation is not simply independence from external tyrannies. In her view, what she called the "internal tyrants" pose far greater threats to life and growth. These internal tyrants are ethical and social conventions—the practices and techniques of social and moral regulation. The internal tyrants are voiced publicly in employer wishes, public opinion, and government bureaucracies. They apply an ongoing pressure that must be broken for emancipation to be possible. Real emancipation requires cutting "loose from the weight of prejudices, traditions, and customs" (Goldman 1969, 224). Goldman argues that these constraints impose themselves upon people as much as the structures of economics and politics. Indeed, they too act as barriers to personal and social development, particularly for non-elites. See Chapter 7 for more about social norms and socialization.

Goldman gives the name "Puritanism" to modes and practices of moral regulation and analyzes the ways in which such puritanical approaches serve to restrict, repress, and regulate people in the modern period. Goldman speaks of moral regulation as "the horrors that have turned life into gloom, joy [into] despair, naturalness into disease, honesty and truth into hideous lies and hypocrisies" (1969, 168). For Goldman, Puritanism suggests that life is a curse imposed on people who must seek redemption through constant penance (1969, 167). Against healthy impulses, people must turn away and refuse personal joys.

In the modern era, Puritanism has become entrenched behind states and laws. For Goldman: "Pretending to safeguard the people against 'immorality,' it has impregnated the machinery of government and added to its usurpation of moral guardianship the legal censorship of our views, feelings, and even of our conduct" (1969, 174). Goldman notes the growing expansion of the government and public bureaucrats into the private realms of the people, into their most intimate aspects of life. Puritanism has abandoned "the thumbscrew and rack; but it still has a most pernicious hold on the minds and feelings of the American people" (1969, 169). Government bureaucracy, which dictates notions of good and evil, even in liberal democracies, conditions ideas of purity and vice that had been the monopoly products of religion in other eras.

Repression limits and stunts human development, for societies as for individuals. As Goldman suggests:

> Every stimulus which quickens the imagination and raises the spirits, is as necessary to our life as air. It invigorates the body, and deepens our vision of human fellowship. Without stimuli, in one form or another, creative work is impossible nor indeed the spirit of kindliness and generosity. The fact that

some great geniuses have seen their reflection in the goblet too frequently, does not justify Puritanism in attempting to fetter the whole gamut of human emotions. (1969, 176)

In particular, moral regulation poses a restricted range of options for women. As Goldman suggests: "All these busybodies, moral detectives, jailers of the human spirit, what will they say?...How many emancipated women are brave enough to acknowledge that the voice of love is calling, wildly beating against their breasts, demanding to be heard, to be satisfied" (1969, 221–222). Sexual self-restraint and the regulation of women's sexuality have been imposed on unmarried women with a range of harmful consequences—psychological, social, and physical. Chastity is a key expression of artificial regulation for Goldman. In her view: "The modern idea of chastity, especially in reference to woman, its greatest victim, is but the sensuous exaggeration of our natural impulses" (1969, 171). This concern with moral regulation underlined Goldman's developed analyses and criticisms of both marriage and the panic over the sex trade, which she saw as related by political economic concerns and the exploitation of women. Goldman noted that prostitution is perhaps the greatest triumph of Puritanism, despite the fact that its participants were hounded, imprisoned, and punished. The only solution offered by the state has been and continues to be repression.

Goldman considered the effects of Puritanism on women to represent a crime against humanity. Socially, it has served to disempower and marginalize women. For Goldman: "Puritanism, with its perversion of the significance and functions of the human body, especially in regard to woman, has condemned her to celibacy, or to the indiscriminate breeding of a diseased race, or to prostitution" (1969, 171). Puritanism also influenced social theory, driving concerns over sexuality into the domain of domestic issues, to be avoided or written out of political theory.

Goldman noted the economic as well as social venues affected through the sexual repression of women. She analyzed the intersections of moral regulation and economics in the case of abortions, and the discourses around abortion. As Goldman argued: "Thanks to this Puritanic tyranny, the majority of women soon find themselves at the ebb of their physical resources. Ill and worn, they are utterly unable to give their children even elementary care. That, added to economic pressure, forces many women to risk utmost danger rather than continue to bring forth life" (1969, 172) The illegality of abortion added crucially to the threats against women. As Goldman noted: "Considering the secrecy in which this practice is necessarily shrouded, and the consequent professional inefficiency and neglect,

Puritanism continuously exacts thousands of victims to its own stupidity and hypocrisy" (1969, 172–173). Her analysis in this regard is remarkably contemporary and speaks to ongoing concerns raised within debates over abortion in the current period of Republican-led efforts to roll back even the limited abortion rights of the late twentieth century in the US.

Goldman noted that Puritanism stamped "its approval only on the dullness of middle-class respectability" (1969, 168). Through a range of essays she examines the political economic or class based aspects of moral regulation or Puritanism in various aspects of women's intimate lives and labors.

"Marriage and Love"

One of the social institutions that Goldman targets for critical analysis is marriage. Moral regulation forced free women, including Mary Wollstonecraft and George Eliot, into what Goldman calls "the conventional lie of marriage" (1969, 168). Goldman focuses on marriage not only as practice but as moral enterprise.

For Goldman, popular understandings of marriage and love rest not on facts but on superstition. In her writings on marriage and love, Goldman analyzes the "power of connection" and public opinion. It is these forces, rather than mystical feelings of love, that give marriage its continued power. While marriage can result from love, love almost never results from marriage.

Goldman applied an economic analysis to marriage. In her view:

> Marriage is primarily an economic arrangement, an insurance pact. It differs from the ordinary life insurance agreement only in that it is more binding, more exacting. Its returns are insignificantly small compared with the investments. In taking out an insurance policy one pays for it in dollars and cents, always at liberty to discontinue payments. If, however, woman's premium is a husband, she pays for it with her name, her privacy, her self-respect, her very life, "until death doth part." (1969, 228)

Men also pay this toll, according to Goldman, but because of social inequalities, and their disproportionate effect on women, men are less restricted. The toll paid by men is mostly economic. Thus, men experience some disadvantages, but marriage overwhelmingly privileges them.

Goldman turns to sociological analysis to make her point. She uses statistics on divorce, adultery, and desertion to bolster her analysis. She also makes reference to cultural developments and references to marriage in popular discourses, art, and literature. In this, she notes that "writers are discussing the barrenness, the monotony, the sordidness, the inadequacy of marriage as a factor for harmony and understanding" (1969, 229). In words that prefigure C. Wright Mills, Goldman suggests: "The thoughtful social student will not content himself with the popular superficial excuse for this phenomenon. He will have to dig down deeper into the very life of the sexes to know why marriage proves so disastrous" (1969, 229). Goldman identifies the customs, indeed superstitions, around marriage as factors in delimiting women's knowledge of sex and sexuality. She suggests:

> The prospective wife and mother is kept in complete ignorance of her only asset in the competitive field—sex. Thus she enters into life-long relations with a man only to find herself shocked, repelled, outraged beyond measure by the most natural and healthy instinct, sex. It is safe to say that a large percentage of the unhappiness, misery, distress, and physical suffering of matrimony is due to the criminal ignorance in sex matters that is being extolled as a great virtue. (1969, 231)

Goldman also targets inequality within the marriage relationship. She argues that as the social inequality of women diminishes, through the efforts of women organizing, the durability of the marriage institution will be shaken. With increased freedom for women, marriage will see greater dissolution and shorter duration. Indeed Goldman's assessment is predictive of actual marriage trends over the twentieth and twenty-first centuries in the West. She argues at length:

> At any rate, woman has no soul—what is there to know about her? Besides, the less soul a woman has the greater her asset as a wife, the more readily will she absorb herself in her husband. It is this slavish acquiescence to man's superiority that has kept the marriage institution seemingly intact for so long a period. Now that woman is coming into her own, now that she is actually growing aware of herself as a being outside of the master's grace, the sacred institution of marriage is gradually being undermined, and no amount of sentimental lamentation can stay it. (1969, 230)

Marriage tends to sanction motherhood that is conceived even in hatred or compulsion. At the same time it condemns motherhood conceived in love, ecstasy, or passion. The latter form of motherhood is questioned and the result condemned as "bastard" (1969, 236). Marriage becomes the socially acceptable option for women and moral pressures make marriage the less painful of limited options:

> Time and again it has been conclusively proved that the old matrimonial relation restricted woman to the function of man's servant and the bearer of his children. And yet we find many emancipated women who prefer marriage, with all its deficiencies, to the narrowness of an unmarried life, narrow and unendurable because of the chains of moral and social prejudice that cramp and bind her nature. (1969, 221)

Goldman offers love—by which she means affinity and mutual aid between people as the expression of autonomous and self-determined choices freely arrived at—as an alternative to the regulatory approach represented by marriage. In her view:

> Love, the strongest and deepest element in all life, the harbinger of hope, of joy, of ecstasy; love, the defier of all laws, of all conventions; love, the freest, the most powerful moulder of human destiny; how can such an all-compelling force be synonymous with that poor little State and Church-begotten weed, marriage? (1969, 236)

Love, for Goldman, represents the informal relations, freely engaged, between autonomous individuals. It is an expression of solidarity. Marriage on the other hand represents formal arrangements monitored, policed, sanctioned, and regulated by the state. Goldman argues that it is a form of what contemporary sociology calls "governmentality." Marriage derives from hierarchical relations of authority. Love is a grassroots phenomenon and nurtured from the bottom up.

Love can, of course, suffer its own confinements and distortions. This is particularly so through the romantic constructions of love as devoted to the pursuit of marriage. Love is often directed into a narrow stream of action which is the familiar one of conservation in monogamous relations sanctioned by the state.

Many anarchists up to the present period suggest polyamory and polysexuality as modes of loving expression, mutually self-determined among those directly involved, as alternatives to the hegemonic construction of marriage and exclusivity in relations between people. According to anarchists, these more open forms of relationships are more in keeping with, and accommodating of, human desires. They offer opportunities to avoid the inevitable hypocrisy and repression, and associated feelings of jealousy and possessiveness that accompany the hierarchical institutions of monogamy and marriage.

The hypocrisy of marriage and monogamy and their roles in moral regulation is reflected in another social institution that shadows and, indeed, mirrors them: the sex trade and prostitution.

"The Traffic in Women"

Perhaps the most potent analysis of social problems offered by Goldman involves her searing criticism of moral regulation involving the sex trade and the conditions of sex trade workers. Once again her analysis is drawn from a vital mix of personal experience with the sex trade and sex trade workers, and sociological research. Goldman points out the hypocrisy marking much of the public concern over trafficking and the sex trade. She also questions the legalistic response focused on laws to halt trafficking.

Goldman notes that the attention of reformers has done little for the real victims of the sex trade—exploited sex workers—and adds that this is also the case for workers in other industries. She suggests that prostitution is the condition for all who are compelled to sell their labor (their bodies) for someone else's pleasure (profit or surplus value).

Goldman offers an early analysis of what has come to be known within sociology and criminology as a "moral panic." She notes that such panics inaugurate social crusades that do little to address the real causes of social problems and often make the situation worse for those who are most negatively impacted by the issue at hand. Reforms do not touch upon the real causes of prostitution and trafficking: exploitation and the underpaid labor of women and the restricted labor market opportunities for women, especially poor and working class women. Moral panics help to create a few more political jobs—inspectors, investigators, border security, for example. Panics do not name the underlying sources of the social problem. For Goldman: "It is much more profitable to play the Pharisee, to pretend an outraged morality, than to go to the bottom of things" (1969, 178). For Goldman, going to the root of things requires a sociological rather than moralistic or even psychological approach.

Industrial capitalism limits the labor choices of poor and working class women. The economic inequality experienced by women in relation to men is largely responsible for prostitution. The state response to prostitution has predominantly focused on the regulation and criminalization of women sex trade workers. Far and away the large majority of sex trade workers come from poor and working class backgrounds, rather than even middle strata backgrounds. Most arrive in sex work from want, desperate economic circumstances, family needs, or unpleasant family situations. In the studies of Goldman's day many prostitutes were married. This led Goldman to remark: "Evidently there was not much of a guaranty for their 'safety and purity' in the sanctity of marriage" (1969, 180).

Goldman noted that while prostitution has existed in previous periods of human social history, the Industrial Revolution of the late 19th and early 20th centuries transformed it into a social and economic institution of grand scale. Industrial development, the competitive market, the insecurity of employment, and the breakdown of communal social bonds all contributed to the growth and expansion of prostitution. So too did the concentration and congestion of people in urban centers. The limited range of choices available to poor and working class women in the labor market has been a crucial factor.

Goldman advocated sex education as one means of increasing women's autonomy and increasing the control a woman has over her body and labor. Yet Goldman recognized that open, frank discussion of sex will be opposed by a vocal section of the US population (as indeed it is today). In her view, a lack of sex education makes women vulnerable to exploitation in prostitution and oppression within marriage. Goldman's conclusions have been confirmed by numerous studies on the lack of sex education within contemporary societies. Even more, sex education is a matter of individual liberty for women. They should not be made to conform their desires to stilted conceptions of morality. Public education can play an important role in increasing liberty. For Goldman: "An educated public opinion, freed from the legal and moral hounding of the prostitute, can alone help to ameliorate present conditions. Wilful shutting of eyes and ignoring of the evil as a social factor of modern life, can but aggravate matters" (1969, 194). In her 1915 pamphlet "Why and How the Poor Should Not Have Many Children," Goldman advocated the use of multiple forms of birth control. She also explained practices for safe condom use and offered instructions for homemade contraceptive methods (Haaland 1993, 70). Goldman sought the increased autonomy and self-determination of women through contraception, sex education, and delay or refusal of marriage. Once again, she took up her own challenge. Goldman was arrested and detained for providing sex education materials publicly.

Goldman was also critical of the phenomenon that Shantz (2012) calls supply-side policing of sex work. As she suggests:

> Yet society has not a word of condemnation for the man, while no law is too monstrous to be set in motion against the helpless victim. She is not only preyed upon by those who use her, but she is also absolutely at the mercy of every policeman and miserable detective on the beat, the officials at the station house, the authorities in every prison. (1969, 188)

Goldman goes beyond conventional condemnation of those who procure prostitutes from the general population or pimps themselves, and she probed and questioned the social relations that give rise to the pimp as well as the prostitute. Her social study of the issue shows that the procurer emerges in the US through reform efforts targeting brothels. Following a wave of reform to "abolish vice," brothel keepers as well as sex workers were forced into the streets. Once on the streets, sex workers were subject to fines, bribes, or arrest by police. These actions against them remain the common complaints of sex workers who are advocating decriminalization in the twenty-first century. Criminalization leaves sex workers even more vulnerable and pimps take advantage of the situation to profit themselves. As Goldman notes:

> While comparatively protected in the brothels, where they represented a certain monetary value, the girls now found themselves on the street, absolutely at the mercy of the graft-greedy police. Desperate, needing protection and longing for affection, these girls naturally proved an easy prey for cadets [the "procurers" of prostitutes], themselves the result of the spirit of our commercial age. Thus the cadet system was the direct outgrowth of police persecution, graft, and attempted suppression of prostitution. (1969, 193)

Suppression serves to worsen the problem rather than addressing underlying causes. Legislation has done nothing but drive the practice into secret, hidden venues, making it more dangerous both to women and to society. Similar arguments are made by modern anarchists regarding laws criminalizing certain "illicit" drugs. The more strict the persecution, the worse the resulting social problems.

Social analysis must work to break through convention and moralism. According to Goldman,

> We must rise above our foolish notions of "better than thou," and learn to recognize in the prostitute a product of social conditions. Such a realization will sweep away the attitude of hypocrisy, and insure a greater understanding and more humane treatment. As to a thorough eradication of prostitution, nothing can accomplish that save a complete transvaluation of all accepted values—especially the moral ones—coupled with the abolition of industrial slavery. (1969, 194)

Moralism, and reform impulses, serve to impede or break solidarity that might form between the sex trade worker and the "respectable" woman. Instead of seeing solidarity in the fact of selling their bodies (or being dependent on the income of men), morality denigrates one while conferring a sense of privilege to the other. Goldman spoke even against the Puritanism within socialist and anarchist movements. For Goldman, people need to draw on more expansive, richer experiences.

Beyond Liberal Feminism: The Basis for an Anarchist Feminism

Goldman's perspective remains relevant to feminist theory and concerns of women's emancipation. Goldman leveled strong criticisms against mainstream or liberal notions of women's emancipation, which sought formal freedom and equality through the state. In her view women must emancipate themselves from their so-called emancipation.

Goldman critiqued bureaucracy and legal-rational authority. Rather than a realm of freedom and efficiency, she recognized the oppressive and regulatory aspects of bureaucratic institutions, particularly the state and corporations. The call for equality in the legal-rational bureaucratic realms, as in liberal feminism, serves in effect as an uncritical endorsement of the norms and values of those realms (Haaland 1993, viii).

Institutional changes will not be enough despite the hopes of social reformers and socialists. As Goldman suggested: "The right to vote, or equal civil rights, may be good demands, but true emancipation begins neither at the polls nor in the courts. It begins in woman's soul. History tells us that every oppressed class gained true liberation from its masters through its own efforts" (1969, 224). Goldman rejected the state realm as a sphere for emancipation. Thus, she did not advocate women pursue the "long march through the institutions" of the state as do liberal feminist reformers. Goldman was critical of women reformers who sought to change state institutions from within. She viewed these reformers as "moral custodians" (what contemporary sociologists, like Howard Becker, call "moral entrepreneurs") who were only extending the powers of the state. Rather than improving conditions for women the moral custodians "were acting on moral imperatives to enslave women further" (Haaland 1993, 36). In Goldman's view, the extension of the state would only lead to greater, not lessened, oppression for women or for men. The symbolic gain of the vote would draw women's movements into the domain of the state and bureaucracy where those movements would be corrupted or confined, their vital energies dissipated. Such has, indeed, been the case of labor movements historically, for example, who have been subsumed in social democratic parties or electioneering.

Goldman did not reject the state on the basis, as professed by some feminists, that it is a male realm or a sphere of activity built by men. This is not a call for *women* to stay out of the public realm. It is a call for *all humans* to avoid the state sphere as a realm of participation. As Haaland notes:

> Goldman differed from many of the "maternal" feminists of her day who believed women's higher morality, stemming from their maternal nature, could improve the conditions of the impure State. Instead, she believed that the State was beyond purification and that claims of women's moral virtue only served to enslave them further. (1993, 57)

Women could, of course, be equal to men in the public sphere. But this only made them equal as authoritarians or, worse, oppressors. Ample evidence of this may be seen in recent history, in the cases of Margaret Thatcher, Golda Meir, Indira Gandhi, and others.

As well, Goldman was concerned about the impacts of bureaucratism on the inner life of people who pursued professional careers within bureaucratic state or capitalist institutions. She was aware of the ways in which bureaucracy could deaden or limit human sentiments such as solidarity or mutual aid, and notions of independence or emancipation. The result was the creation of what she called "professional automatons" (Goldman 1972, 173). The bureaucracy converts education and intellectual activity into professions and careers. Men, too, are victimized by the state. The state exerts great pressure on men to conform and comply with regulations and practices. The professional man of the bureaucracy, for Goldman, "has been made an almost complete automaton by our own commercial life" (quoted in Falk 1984, 126). For Goldman, men and women needed to be freed from the limiting conditions of bureaucracy. Goldman did not equate men with the public realm and did not condemn men as men. She sought instead relations of mutual union.

Involvement in the bureaucratic realm might be uplifting for the specific women involved, as in a careerist fashion, but would not uplift other women. The involvement of women in the state would rather extend bureaucratic reach and control, and could harm other women as well as men. On the matter of liberal feminism, Haaland suggests: "Goldman viewed the social philosophy of individualism as a form of indoctrination whereby individuals were encouraged to work hard and achieve in order to improve their own position, while, in fact, they would be improving the position of those possessing economic and political power" (1993, 83). Individualistic notions of mobility and improvement conceal the general social patterns that lack choice and freedom. Neither men nor women gained through the assertions of individualism and success as defined in individual terms. In other words, freedom must be a collective endeavor, or else it is simply anecdotal privilege enjoyed by some. Later, we discuss the limits of individual mobility and the anarchist advocacy of anarchist *autonomy* from hierarchy.

Goldman's feminism does not portray women as in a liberal feminist model. She does not privilege a model of single, childless professionalism in the service of the state. Nor does she advocate the restriction of emotional or sexual expression (Haaland 1993). She is even critical of social activists who prefer indignation and who lack humor. Goldman argued against an emerging Puritanism in women's movements, and cautioned against developing approaches that reactively refused to tolerate men and uncritically rejected motherhood.

Hers is an approach based on solidarity for emancipation, prefiguring third-wave feminist approaches. From Goldman's perspective:

> woman's freedom is closely allied with man's freedom, and many of my so-called emancipated sisters seem to overlook the fact that a child born in freedom needs the love and devotion of each human being about him, man as well as woman. Unfortunately, it is this narrow conception of human relations that has brought about a great tragedy in the lives of modern man and woman. (1969, 219)

Goldman's view of feminism and the state grew out of her anarchism. As Haaland suggests: "Goldman's horror at the artificiality of professional women stemmed from her theory of anarchism which, by definition, rejects the form and substance of those activities falling under the wide purview of what she considered to be 'the State'" (1993, 56). For Goldman, the state is not a sphere for reform. Women cannot remake the state in their own image, nor can the state become a realm of care. The state could not, no matter how hard one might wish or try, become a non-bureaucratic bureaucracy.

According to Goldman, equal suffrage and increased labor opportunities would mean exploitation at less than equal remuneration. This assertion puts Goldman at the leading edge of analyses that identified the peril of the double day for women who work outside of the home. Goldman offers a social and economic analysis of women's emancipation which places class and exploitation at the forefront. No one who sells their labor in capitalist economic systems can be said to be "independent" or "self-supporting."

Goldman is rather harsh in her assessment of economic "freedom" to sell one's labor within a maintained system of exploitation. Speaking of the US economy she says:

> Six million women wage-earners; six million women, who have the equal right with men to be exploited, to be robbed, to go on strike; aye to starve even. Anything more, my lord? Yes, six million wage-workers in every walk of life, from the highest brain work to the most difficult menial labor in the mines and on the railroad tracks; yes, even detectives and policemen. Surely the emancipation is complete. (1969, 232–233)

Goldman is among the earliest to assess the double burden or second-shift that women face in industrial capitalist economies. As she notes, "the home no longer frees her from wage slavery; it only increases her task" (1969, 233). Goldman reports:

> According to the latest statistics submitted before a Committee "on labor and wages, and congestion of population," ten per cent of the wage workers in New York City alone are married, yet they must continue to work at the most poorly paid labor in the world. Add to this horrible aspect the drudgery of housework, and what remains of the protection and glory of the home? (1969, 233)

The dual or split labor market that undervalues women's labor, thus driving down wages for all, goes hand in hand with the institution of marriage that offers both an excuse to exclude women from access to the labor market while providing free labor for the reproduction of the working classes. Goldman's analysis prefigures the works of contemporary socialist feminists who have put forward arguments for wages for housework and the recognition of the social value of household work (Lilley and Shantz 2004).

While recent feminists have turned attention to the social benefits of shared parenting or community care, Goldman made this appeal central to her social analysis in the first decade of the twentieth century. For Haaland: "These claims are that women's freedom is closely allied with men's freedom and that children need to be nurtured by both men and women" (1993, 53). Contemporary social researchers have noted the gains to social relationships under such conditions. As Haaland suggests:

> To the extent that Goldman argued for dual parenting, with both women and men being placed in the realm of community, kinship and family, she offered a revolutionary alternative to the dualism that divides man and women and the responsibility for the giving of care. Some contemporary feminists believe that feminism must call for a "revolution in kinship" in which men would supply the same nurturance as do women. (1993, 54)

Men should assume responsibility as care givers rather than leaving those responsibilities to women. As Haaland suggests:

> Goldman's rejection of such activities when carried out in service to the State, under institutional control and at the expense of the emotional, sexual dimension of human life, speaks to the degree to which Goldman opposed the bifurcation of "mental" from "physical," knowledge" from "feeling," "theory from practice" and, thus, to the degree to which she opposed a truncated womanhood. (1993, 56)

In this, Goldman prefigures postmodern criticisms of the dualism of knowledge and the privileging of professional over colloquial forms, as well as the dichotomized roles of the sexes and the arbitrary nature of "gender" itself.

Conclusion

Some anarchist communists criticized Goldman for her attention to personal issues and individual lived experience. Yet Goldman's work would make fundamental contributions to the development of anarchist theory and feminist sociology. In assessing Goldman's public sociology, Alice Wexler suggests: "Her own radical vision, broader and more encompassing than that of almost anyone else on the left, had shocked, inspired, and educated thousands, both inside and outside the anarchist movement" (1984, 274).

Goldman asserts the potential pleasure of sexuality for women rather than the dangers or fears that authorities present for women in discussions of sexuality. In opposition to other advocates of women's rights, including Suffragettes, Goldman advocated sexual experimentation and variety (Haaland 1993, xii). Repression leads to an inhibition of thought. Sexual repression, for Goldman, causes people to waste time regulating themselves. This draws attention away from more productive and creative pursuits.

Contemporary theorists recognize that sexuality is connected with, indeed embedded in, relations of power, and these relations seek to maintain the social order—in terms of race, class, gender, and sexual preference. Goldman attributed seemingly individual experiences such as frequent unwanted pregnancies to economic and cultural issues, including Puritanism and repressive approaches to sexuality.

Goldman asserted that sex and matters of sexuality more broadly, which her anarchist contemporaries viewed as a private matter, were actually public issues. Goldman sought to affirm the centrality of sexuality to human well-being and worked to achieve an environment suited to free expression of sexuality (according to self-determined needs in mutual association with others). Such recognition of the legitimacy of sexuality would transform those institutions, such as religion, that had denied, repressed, or controlled sexual expression for external purposes. Her anarchism combined the social structural aspects of Kropotkin with concern for internal or psychological issues as discussed by Ellis and Carpenter. Hers was a fundamentally sociological approach and is one that sociology has only belatedly engaged with. Thankfully, recent generations of feminist sociologists have found a rich wealth of resources within Goldman's approach.

Goldman offered an early version of a social approach that rejects universalism and notions of universality in social change, yet which seeks social justice. In many ways, her approach prefigured postmodern writings on situational or tactical approaches to social change. Her analysis also suggests the notions of unity in diversity that characterize postmodern and contemporary ecological approaches.

Hers is also an approach that does not envision a final social peace arrived at in full social positivity. She does not seek a future free of antagonism and does not create a vision of a society enjoying full peace. Goldman viewed freedom and individuality as social processes. From her perspective: "'What I believe' is a process rather than a finality. Finalities are for the gods and governments, not for the human intellect" (1983, 35). At the same time she does imagine a productive arrangement in which differentiation and holism creatively develop together.

It is clear that Goldman is not suggesting a sameness or imposed equality as in some versions of socialism. Goldman asserted the need for individual and collective freedoms to coincide. She sought the basis for a correspondence of the individual and the mass in industrial (or post-industrial) societies. For Goldman: "The problem that confronts us today, and which the nearest future is to solve, is how to be one's self and yet in oneness with others, to feel deeply with all human beings and still retain one's own characteristic qualities" (1969, 213–214). In her view: "Peace or harmony between the sexes and individuals does not necessarily depend on a superficial equalization of human beings; nor does it call for the elimination of individual traits and peculiarities" (1969, 213). In a manner that prefigures C. Wright Mills's (1959) reflections on the sociological imagination, Goldman suggests: "The motto should not be: Forgive one another; rather, Understand one another" (1969, 214). Equality need not mean sameness. Goldman's approach goes beyond difference and equality dualisms. She seeks rather a "unity in diversity." Consequently, Goldman's feminist sociology is a highly useful and informative one that foreshadows contemporary gender scholarship, and points the way forward to a more radical and comprehensive feminist view of emancipation and liberty.

As with her anarchist predecessors—such as the anarchist, but anti-feminist Proudhon—Goldman viewed efforts to achieve broader social freedoms as enmeshed in the struggle against the worst forms of subjugation, such as patriarchy, capitalism, and the prison system. We now turn our attention to a radical, but overlooked contribution of social analysis that focuses on these matters.

CHAPTER FIVE

PROUDHON AND CRIMINOLOGY

Introduction

The work of Pierre-Joseph Proudhon is almost completely overlooked within studies of criminology. Certainly, major texts in criminological theory (Williams and McShane 2004; O'Grady 2007; Miller, Schreck and Tewksbury 2008), including those that address the origins of criminology and the classical criminological theories, make not even a reference to Proudhon's thoughts on social order, crime, and the social response to crime. Notably, even significant works in critical criminology make little or no reference to Proudhon (see Brooks and Schissel 2008; Ferrell, Hayward and Young 2008). This oversight is unwarranted as Proudhon offers important insights on crime and conflict within society. Indeed his analysis anticipates recent writings by Left realist criminologists (see Alvi 2000; DeKeseredy and Perry 2006; Lea 2002; Lea and Young 1984; Young 1994; 1997), who focus on the lack of resources within working class and poor communities and the impact that crime has on further reducing resources within those communities (including by removing caregivers, income earners and mentors through incarceration). At the same time, Proudhon's ideas go beyond recent criminological theories by emphasizing locally self-determined activities rather than appeals to the state that mark much of even critical criminology and have weakened Left realist analyses. Yet these aspects of Proudhon's analysis are largely overlooked or forgotten, both among anarchists and critical criminologists.

Anarchists, as for other radical and revolutionary theorists, have often been excluded from the history of academic disciplines such as sociology and criminology, or, where included, marginalized and muted. This chapter contributes to a re-thinking of the history of criminology. Most accounts of criminology (Schmalleger 2003; Tepperman 2006; White, Haines and Eisler 2009; Winslow and Zhang 2006) suggest its emergence in the classical liberal theories of Cesare Beccarria and Jeremy Bentham or the positivist theories of Cesare Lombroso. Anarchism, if it is mentioned at all in accounts of early criminology, appears only in reference to Lombroso's infamous text *The Anarchists* which presents "the anarchist" as one of the measurable criminal types. These so-called "classical" approaches are presented without peer, as though there were no alternative analyses of crime, power, and social order. Critical approaches to criminology appear much later in the story, largely attributed to students influenced by Marxism and the social movements of the 1960s. Anarchist criminology is left without history, relegated to footnotes as a post-Marxist development of the 1970s.

Even those texts that address anarchism tend to dismiss it as utopian or naïve (see Lanier and Henry 2004). In part this reflects a political bias, and even a class bias, within academia, on behalf of the framers of those disciplines. Beyond any bias, however, is the sense that anarchism, and other radical theories, are idealist in nature, deferring crucial policy questions until some future point, "after the revolution," or in an anarchist society or forsaking short-term pragmatic approaches to social problems in favor of broadly transformative aims, in a way that creates a dualism between the two. In addition, anarchist organizers have sometimes been reluctant to address real world responses to crime, particularly punishment, or offer alternative prescriptions, believing that to do so is to play into the hands of the "law and order" right, wing, or that discussing such issues reinforces regimes of moral regulation and disciplinarity. Indeed, for many anarchists, criminology is probably avoided as a discipline perceived to be about the training of police officers and security guards.

A good part of the disdain that anarchists have for criminology, beyond the choice of some departments to serve primarily as recruiting grounds for police, security guards and lawyers, relates to the dominance of statist approaches within criminological theory. Mainstream and critical criminology alike rest on the assumption that justice is based on social order (Brooks and Schissel 2008; Linden 2008; Miller, Schreck and Tewksbury 2008; Tepperman 2008). Thus the state is most often invoked as the agent *par excellence* of social order and justice is viewed as an outcome of the establishment of order through the state. While debates emerge over the character of the state and its relation to elite interests, with critical criminology emphasizing state reforms, the state in some form is too often invoked as a key player in the maintenance of social order and justice.

For Proudhon, social order is established on the basis of inexorable justice (1888: 103). He provides a compelling, if underappreciated, alternative to the emphasis on distributive justice that marks most of criminology, from the classical period to the present day. His work provides something of an antidote to the authoritarian, mythic conceptions of justice presented by social contract theory and mainstream criminology but also the limited and constrained notions of justice posited by statist critical theory and socialism. His thinking on justice influenced all of his work on social and political issues. More fully appreciating Proudhon gains from closer examination of these under-appreciated aspects of his thought.

The work of Pierre-Joseph Proudhon offers an important contribution to anarchist organizers seeking to develop approaches to understanding crime in capitalist societies and addressing the impacts of crime within working class and poor communities, as well as offering significant insights to students of criminology and sociology seeking alternatives to conventional and radical theories alike. This chapter examines not only Proudhon's critical thoughts on courts and police (and the illegitimacy of such institutions), but explores his views on the causes and solutions to social disorder and suggestions for community-based dispute resolution and responses to crime. It also considers Proudhon's ideas in relation to contemporary discussions of restorative justice and peace-making criminology, situating his work as a precursor to contemporary work in those areas and suggesting that practitioners of those approaches will gain by visiting and engaging with Proudhon's thinking. This makes an important contribution, both to contemporary thinking about crime and causes of crime as well as to anarchist ideas about how to deal with everyday concerns in a practical and critical way and to develop "real world" alternatives to authoritarian social relations.

Proudhon's is an approach that takes social disorder and crime seriously, as immediate concerns that primarily impact the poor and working class, without simultaneously basing itself on increasing repression, punishment, or social exclusion. Proudhon moved beyond utopian notions that crime would disappear in an anarchist society. Instead he preferred to discuss "real world" arrangements, relations of mutualism, that might encourage social harmony. Contrary to the view of anarchism as utopian, Proudhon understood the key issues relating to the emergence of crime are primarily economic rather than political. Thus attempts to address crime appropriately should be economic rather than political.

Focusing on Proudhon the criminologist shows a widely engaged thinker, radical in his approach to social issues and his critique of dominant perspectives, but pragmatic in his concern with actually affecting change in the here-and-now of existing relations. Concerned with issues of social order, he offers analyses that show him to be an important, if overlooked, contributor to sociological and criminological thought. Examining his perspective more closely helps to broaden our understanding of his thoughts and preoccupations, in ways that have too long been overlooked,

Contemporary anarchist criminology is still very much in development, indeed still underdeveloped, often cut off from its roots, presented as a recent phenomenon, which in many ways it is. Yet grappling with an anarchist criminology means engaging more directly and more fully with the history of anarchist writings on crime and social order. Among the most interesting, if largely ignored, examples are Proudhon's thoughts. We should not pass over his works/conception of justice as most criminologists have done. This chapter contributes to a multiple re-assessment of criminology, its origins and its development, highlighting the complex perspectives, in the works of Proudhon, that have been written out of that history. Proudhon's work takes anarchism from the margins of criminology, situating it as a serious opponent of notions of social contract and social order as presented especially within classical theory. Criminologists would do well to take up this call to re/consider Proudhon and criminology.

Dilemmas of Criminology

Reconciling peace and freedom, order and liberty, requires an answer to the problem of community and the relationship of the individual to society. This is the underlying issue that has motivated sociology and criminology from the start. Often overlooked within both disciplines, Pierre-Joseph Proudhon's answer to this problem posed the question of community in a new and unusual way. His approach is both radical and realistic (Ritter 1967: 457). Before examining Proudhon's analyses of crime and punishment, it is perhaps useful to examine criminology and the context within which a pressing need to develop an approach that is both radical but pragmatic has emerged.

For mainstream criminology, from classical the classical theories of Beccaria, Bentham and Lombroso through psychological criminology (Kohlberg 1969) and sociological criminology (Cohen 1955) to contemporary control theory (Gottfredson and Hirschi 1990; Hirschi 1969) and conservative (Wilson 1975) or "broken windows" theories (Kelling and Coles 1996), the problem of community is largely posed and understood as a matter of restoring social order, rather than gaining or preserving freedom. Influenced by Hobbes and his notion of the social contract, such criminologists suggest that people, left to their own devices, will destroy each other in pursuit of their own selfish, aggressive aims. The solution for much of mainstream criminology, and indeed, much of the criminal justice systems of liberal democracies is authoritarian deterrence. Only by threat of punishment can individuals be prevented from acting upon aggressive, selfish desires (Beccaria 1767; Gottredson and Hirschi 1990). The primary institution responsible for, and indeed the one capable of, posing and following through on the threat of punishment is the state (Kelling and Coles 1996). Mainstream criminology is largely incapable of conceiving of a legal reality beyond the purview of the state. For mainstream criminology, justice is impossible in the absence of functioning legal institutions to give rights legitimacy. This approach tends to overlook the alternative of guiding activity into harmonious paths by encouraging and facilitating cooperation and discouraging hostile desires or acts. While this problem has motivated mainstream criminology, too little attention or concern has been given to solving it in a way compatible with demands for liberty and freedom. Any solution must enable people to think and act as they deem necessary.

For critical criminology, any plan for harmonious social action must address the desire for freedom. Otherwise it would certainly fail. Securing freedom is as central as gaining peace. Conservatives are critical of such an approach. From a conservative perspective, situations in which people are free to associate and communicate as they wish will only worsen the very hostility and conflict that needs to be constrained in the maintenance of social order.

Like conservatives, liberals accept that strong political rule is required to maintain social and political order, as conservatives do. For liberals, voluntary government or political arrangements that violate the rule of law undermine community. According to influential early liberal theorist Benjamin Constant: "Arbitrariness in political institutions is the same thing as their destruction; for since political institutions are the body of rules on which individuals must be able to rely in their relations as citizens, there are no political institutions where such rules do not exist" (quoted in Ritter 1967: 464). The rule of law is said to contribute to governmental strength, building common expectations. However, even if the contribution of the rule of law to governmental strength can be shown, it is less clear that such a contribution is made to positive community building. Liberals suggest that the rule of law is a powerful force for social peace but are less attuned to the impact of legal institutions and authorities on the disruption of social peace or their role in the maintenance of social conflict.

Proudhon does not only criticize liberalism from a conservative stand-point as failing to provide sufficiently for order. His criticism of liberal per-spectives comes also from the left on matters of freedom (Ritter 1967; Pepinsky 1978; Kingston-Mann 2006). For liberals, freedom is typically understood as the absence of political control, the freedom to pursue pri-vate self-interests without direct government interference. If government respects the rule of law, a person is free. "To Proudhon, such freedom is entirely inadequate, since a person who enjoys it may still be coerced in numerous ways. Though manipulated socially, exploited economically, censored religiously or repressed legally he would still qualify as free" (Ritter 1967: 468). This perspective is reflected in dominant versions of human rights discourse in which human rights are posed largely in a nega-tive sense as the absence of interference from the state.

Proudhon rejects, in particular, notions of social contract as presented in mainstream criminology, on which people are said to surrender liberty in return for protection from the state. This is the social contract of Hobbes and Rousseau alike and provides the foundation for classical criminology as well as the criminal justice systems of liberal democracies. Government is based on force and the idea that the people consent to its acts, whether individually or collectively, is nothing more than superstition or religion. So too is the notion that the "will of the people" can be known directly through plebiscite, or indirectly, through public opinion (Osgood 1889: 11). These are the fictions of law and social contract. "All laws which I have not accepted I reject as an imposition on my free will" (Proudhon 1969: 138). In opposition to those who offered abstract notions of justice based on mythic concepts such as social contract, Proudhon argued that justice is not the outcome of law. Law is only an expression after the fact of specific interactions and relations of power.

Proudhon rejected notions, as in Locke, that justice is only possible where there is law backed by institutions such as courts and legal profes-sions. Proudhon was aware that any order achieved through rule of law enforced and implemented by compulsion and force is fragile. Compliance is easily withdrawn once the threat of compulsion is removed. Typically people who do not recognize a rule as right will not hold it as being just, and will not call it justice. He highlights the need for meaningful responses to social problems of law and order in the context of criminology domi-nated by notions of law and order founded in state authority. For Proudhon: "If the idea that our form of justice and right is ill-defined, if it is imperfect or even false, it is clear that all our legislative applications will be wrong, our institutions vicious, our politics erroneous, and consequently there will be disorder and chaos" (1840: 26–27). Mainstream criminology exhibits a failure to make the connections between social experience and hostile activities as well as a failure to trace the origins of oppressive acts and desires to inappropriate social institutions. Thus it is largely incapable of offering the changes to these institutions that successful social transformation, and reductions in crime, require.

Proudhon offers an alternative to liberal appeals to universals. Rather than presenting a vision of crime and justice that is applicable in all cases, as adjudicated through the state as the mediator of the social contract, Proudhon provides a vision that is situational, and related to the specific needs and concerns of those involved. In this he anticipates current approaches to restorative justice. The basis of law is the social norms that develop through social interactions over time. Certainly not legal documents or the will of the people or social contract. The claimed neutrality and rationality of the criminal justice system is refused. Indeed, from Proudhon's perspective, the basis of the criminal justice system and criminal justice collapses. No court or institution, distant and outside of relations, holding to abstract universal values can contain justice. Proper social conduct rests in personal conscience or group norms. It is not a dictate of the criminal justice system.

Essential to justice is that the norms in which it is rooted express the aims of people interacting within voluntary relations undertaken in the course of their everyday lives. Justice exists within the context of these voluntary relationships. Justice is defined and redefined by those concerned, in the daily activities of associations on the basis of reciprocity. People actively create justice. This is a participatory, positive, and active conception of justice, rather than a passive, representative, negative one. It is plural rather than universal or singular. Justice is created by people undertaking their own actions. These are characteristics of justice that have been emphasized by proponents of restorative justice, as is discussed below.

For Proudhon, the "people," are a diverse collectivity that acts as a collectivity when concluding contracts directly. They are not the subjects of an abstract social contract. This is a federation, not one collective, but networks of them connected through contractual obligations, rather than an abstract *a priori* "society." Association or federation assumes contracts concluded freely and voluntarily. Such association can be concluded between individuals and between different communities.

Many critical criminologists, who approach similar criticisms as those raised above, fall back on the state as a necessity in modern mass societies.

Proudhon did not substitute state authority with an abstract group authority as Marxist criminology tends to do. The tasks or responsibilities of justice cannot be turned over to the state or a criminal justice system. Neither
can they be deferred to future societies. Proudhon's is a perspective that
places responsibility on people based on their own situations, needs, and
experiences.

Critical theorists focus not on a social contract but similarly on an
abstract social agreement expressed through general notions of solidarity
or class unity derived largely through the state (or party), though now a
workers' state. Critical theories again turn their analysis primarily to the
state as the agent of social change and social order. For much of critical
criminology, attention is directed towards reform of the state such that its
focus on non-elite crimes or "street crimes" is shifted towards elite or corporate crimes and criminals (Rieman 2006; Simon 2007). Thus it remains
a largely reactive critique of the limits, biases, or excesses of the state
rather than opposition to the state *per se*.

The criticisms of the current criminal justice system are that resources
are badly or inefficiently deployed towards working class crimes while corporate or elite crimes, which are much more harmful, go unchecked.
Critical criminology is based largely around calls to reform that state and
criminal justice system or, less frequently, to take over the state and direct
it on a working class basis (either through gradual reforms and elections,
or through revolutionary actions).

Yet there are few approaches beyond these roughly reformist and revolutionary poles, both of which see the response to crime centered in the
state and dependent upon state actions. This leaves critics to claim that
critical criminology avoids the real, everyday concerns of non-elites who
are the ones primarily victimized by non-elites or "street crimes." Even
those who have made profound contributions in critical criminology criticize its overall idealism and preference for sweeping social change in the
future to serious alternatives that address concerns about crime (Young
1994; 1997).

Proudhon presents what is, despite his reputation among revolutionary socialists, a more grounded approach to the state, social order, inequality, and justice than critical criminology offers. He did not turn to a "social
contract," law, or social order founded in the state as a response to these
ills. He did not seek the typical responses of critical criminologists,
either state reform or collective enterprise or appeals to solidarity,
to address these issues. Thus Proudhon offers an approach that, if
overlooked or unrecognized, is unique in posing a perspective on

understandings of crime, justice, and punishment that moves beyond both mainstream and critical approaches.

Proudhon's Mutualist Criminology

Few writers have dealt as systematically and deliberately with both sides of the problem of community – order and freedom – as Proudhon (Ritter 1967: 467; Pepinsky 1978). Proudhon wrestles with examining and understanding the conditions under which community can be established that is both liberating and harmonious, and he frames the problem of community as one of securing peace with freedom. He finds fault with conservatism for its failure to meet the demand of liberty. The first condition of successful communal rebirth is the satisfaction of the demand of liberty.

For Proudhon, the state, nor any other individual institution, is no guarantor of justice. Instead, he refers to the active belief in reciprocity and mutual interest, the same belief that motivates a shopkeeper to accept a banknote. Order is not the result of some initiative by a singular entity or individual, but results from the social organization of relations themselves (1858). The only rules that must be obeyed are those that people have actively adopted themselves, or that they agree with. For Proudhon: "As long as I have not wanted this law, as long as I have not assented to it, voted for it or signed it, it binds me to nothing, it does not exist" (1923: 313). Proudhon objects to laws in the formal sense as opposed to agreements or "contracts" freely entered between individuals. Agreements are the personal state of the individual (1923: 313). This is a synallagmatic relationship in which each party is obliged to the other (1923: 320–21; 1979). It is commutative as the exchange involves goods of equal value (1923: 320–21; 1979)

In contrast to the approaches of distributive justice that dominate criminological debates and criminal justice system practices as well, Proudhon saw the foundations of a more just social order in commutative justice. Commutative justice as advocated and outlined by Proudhon is significantly distinct from the notions of justice and liberty maintained within varieties of social contract theory as in Hobbes, Locke, and Rousseau. Even more, it is distinct from the distributive justice advocated by proponents of critical criminology, who seek a re-allocation of state administered resources through reforms to the criminal justice system, such that more resources be deployed in punishing corporate criminals, for example.

The underlying problem with social contract theory, apart from its basis in a vague myth, was that the social contract subjected the individual to the state, demanding that she or he abandon their specific will or conscience to the universal regulation of the sovereign power (1923). Within social contract based systems of justice, people do not contract actively and directly with their fellows, devising, revising, and carrying out obligations and responsibilities through engagement with each other. Instead, their interactions are directed or mediated through an external, ever distant third party. If one is injured or harmed by a neighbor or acquaintance the issue is not resolved through people's own actions. This can make for lazy and deferential relations in which people turn to police, the government, or security firms to address issues rather than working proactively to avoid or resolve problems. The greater fear or concern is that over time people become accustomed to relying on government authorities, becoming distant and distrustful of their neighbors and associates. This can contribute to relations of fear and insecurity, which reinforce a dependence on external authorities.[1]

Social contract approaches, for Proudhon, contribute to this breakdown of social relations and the social bonds that unite people. Under social contract theories such as Rousseau it is, at the end of the day, the state that is sovereign rather than the individual who is promised liberty and equality (1923: 113). In the end, both social contract and Marxist approaches lack trust in the capacity of individuals to act responsibly as autonomous agents (1923). Within Rousseau's system, Proudhon argues, "no association or special meeting of citizens can be permitted, because it would be a State within a State, a government within a government" (1923: 119). The distinction between distributive and commutative justice is particularly important concerning the economic rights and privileges of working class people. Under systems of distributive justice, governments set themselves as the guardians of their citizens. Thus, for Proudhon, the outcome of distributive justice is of "a *superior* granting to *inferiors* what is coming to each one" (1923: 112). In a social order based on distributive justice, working people are expected to contribute the products of their labor to an impersonal general store that is re-distributed by the State. Proudhon offered his theory of commutative justice as an alternative to systems of distributive justice that dominate capitalist and some socialist perspectives and practices alike.

---

[1] This is a principal argument made by Kropotkin to explain how the State had begun to supplant people's tendencies towards mutual aid (Kropotkin 2006).

As noted above, his perspective excludes the State as a third party to all contracts between people. It is the free agreements that individuals enter into with other individuals "which would result in society" (1923: 112). For Proudhon, entering into personal contracts

> is an act whereby two or several individuals agree to organize among themselves for a definite purpose and time, that industrial power which we have called exchange; and in consequence have obligated themselves to each other, and reciprocally guaranteed a certain amount of services, products, advantages, duties, etc., which they are in a position to obtain and give to each other; recognizing that they are otherwise perfectly independent, whether for consumption or production. (1923: 113)

This is a much different conceptualization than is typically presented within notions of social contract. In Proudhon's perspective, people are thus responsible in dealing with each other. Proudhon defined justice as "the recognition of the equality between another's personality and our own" (1876: 231). Society, justice, and equality would become equivalent terms. Force would not be resorted to in a context regulated by reason and persuasion. The recognition of the other holds an important place in Proudhon's thinking on justice under anarchy. This recognition of the other, combined with *equité*, or social proportionality, would allow for development of a better form of society (Osgood 1889: 3). In his words: "Turned to myself, the respect for human dignity forms what I call my right; turn to my fellows it becomes my duty" (quoted in Douglas 1929: 792). For Proudhon: "Reciprocity, in creation, is the principle of existence. In the social order, reciprocity is the principle of social reality, the formula of justice" (1927: 48). In conditions of free exchange, the options for each individual in a contract is likely to be marked by reciprocity as each individual is able to put itself in the other's position, to understand their experiences and needs, and reach a mutual agreement that will reconcile the individual interests of each.

Proudhon makes the distinction between crime as harmful, anti-social behavior and deviance, or the violation of conventions and rules of ruling majorities, not related to the maintenance of social security and solidarity (Yarros 1936: 475). No one should be punished simply for refusing to work with the larger community. Every individual has a right to ignore the state and do as he or she wishes as long as the equal liberty of others is not infringed upon (1923: 313). Rules result from this sort of on-going active engagement. There is always room for disobedience, if one did not participate in developing the rules.

The overall perspective through which Proudhon addresses such questions is mutualism. Mutualism is a social and economic theory, most often associated with anarchism, which traces its roots to Proudhon's writings. In place of political institutions, Proudhon advocated economic organizations based upon principles of mutualism in labor and exchange, through co-operatives and "People's Banks," as means towards that end. The consequences of this reorganization of social life include the limiting of constraint, the reduction of repressive methods, and the convergence of individual and collective interests. This Proudhon calls "the state of total liberty" or anarchy, and suggests that it is the only context in which "laws" operate spontaneously without invoking command and control.

Proudhon's perspective on social conflict, misery, and crime proposes that "individuals and groups, unimpeded by hierarchy, law or market, bargain directly with each other for the things *they* want, without any intermediaries, until they arrive at mutually acceptable terms of agreement" (Ritter 1967: 470). This approach offers Proudhon the basis for liberation from external coercion. "A bargainer, unlike a trader in a market, a member of a social class, or a subject of a state, does not submit to externally imposed regulation. Instead, he makes the rules he submits to himself, by negotiating acceptable terms of agreement" (Ritter 1967: 470). Mutualists follow Proudhon in envisioning future social organizations as economic rather than political. They see society as organized around free federations of producers, both rural and urban. Any co-ordination of efforts must be voluntary and reasoned.

A distinction is sometimes drawn between individualist anarchism, with its emphasis on individual liberty and personal transformation, or communist anarchism, with its emphasis on equality and collective mobilization for broad social change. Mutualism is often viewed as a mid-level perspective between these two approaches. Individualist anarchism places greater emphasis on personal freedom to act unfettered by the constraints of social mores and norms. While placing less emphasis on the individual, and emphasizing co-operative labor, mutualism also differs from social anarchism in its distrust of large-scale social institutions, especially the mass organizing for radical or revolutionary social change preferred by socialists and social anarchists, and exemplified in mass labor unions or social democratic political parties.

Mutualism is, for Proudhon, the law of economic justice. The realization of this law effects economic equilibrium and, more importantly, social harmony:

> What, in fact, is mutualism? A form of justice...in virtue of which members of society, of whatever rank, fortune, or condition, corporations or individuals, families or towns, industrial workers, farmers, or public functionaries – all reciprocally promise and guarantee service for service, credit for credit,

pledge for pledge,...value for value, information for information, good faith
for good faith, truth for truth, liberty for liberty, and property for property.
(Proudhon 1924: 203–204)

In Nolan's words, departing from economic justice and frugality has meant
"the repudiation of equality amongst the members of the community with
the growth of *'parasitisme*, inequality of instruction' and the 'false distribution' of the products of labor" (Noland 1970: 301). This departure results
from greed and avarice, the pursuit of pleasure and ease, selfishness and
special privilege. It results in the disruption of economic equilibrium and
social harmony. The social cost of inequality, disequilibrium, and injustice
is pauperism. Pauperism not only engenders social and economic misery,
it also promotes corruption and class conflict and, even more, "engenders
tyranny in the State" (Noland 1970: 302).

Property is not a natural right, but is guaranteed and upheld by the
state. The two institutions are correlative and reciprocally dependent
(Proudhon 1840). The chief function of the state is that of policing in
service of the protection of property. "The state, which is organized
force, legalizes rent, profit, interest, and protects property owners
while they plunder the rest of society" (Osgood 1889: 6). This is the source
of poverty to which the mass of society are condemned. Property is the
source of crime. The seeming paradox "property is theft," for which
Proudhon is perhaps best known, sums up his thoughts on the problem
of human misery. Laborers fall into debt and become more dependent
on their employer the more they produce. The tenant pays for his or
her land several times over but never owns it. The interest paid by the
borrower far exceeds the capital, but the debt remains unpaid (Osgood
1889: 6).

Proudhon argued that vice and crime, rather than being the cause of
social antagonisms and poverty as popularly believed, are caused by social
antagonisms and poverty. This is a central reason why he considered state
order to be "artificial, contradictory and ineffective," thereby engendering
"oppression, poverty and crime" (1969b: 53). In his view the constitution of
societies under states was strictly anomalous. Furthermore, "public and
international law, together with all the varieties of representative government, must likewise be false, since they are based upon the principle of
individual ownership of property" (1969b: 54). The inequalities and injus-
tices in modern society are due to legalized robbery. Proudhon's theory of
property led him to see that the state acts as the servants and protectors of
the thieves. Its main purpose is to protect them from expropriation by
those whom they have robbed. As well, it impedes the construction of

effective and voluntary cooperation within society. For Proudhon, juris-
prudence, far from representing "codified reason" is nothing more than
"simply a compilation of legal and official titles for robbery, that is for
property" (1969b: 54). Authority is incapable of serving as a proper basis
for constituting social relations, he argued; rather, the citizen must be governed by reason alone, and only those "unworthy and lacking in self-
respect" would accept any rule beyond their own free will. Proudhon
suggested that economic justice and equality would remove most of the
causes of crime.

Mainstream criminologists are constantly applying palliatives. There is
only one remedy, the destruction of inequality at its source. The task of
society, the goal of humanity, is the realization of economic and social
justice. To achieve social peace and harmony within society requires
bringing an end to pauperism by removing its fundamental causes, primarily economic inequality or disequilibrium. In a transformed, just social
order, political institutions would be absorbed into the economic institutions (Proudhon 1923).

Mutualists are less concerned with private property than with the
monopoly control of property by corporate interests backed by the state.
They argue that a large proportion of the wealth created through social
and technological development in a market economy becomes concentrated in the hands of monopolists by way of economic rents. This
concentrated, unearned, and unproductive, wealth is the primary cause of
poverty in capitalist economies. Collecting private profit by restricting
access to natural resources, is made even worse given that productive
activity, such as industrial works, were burdened by taxes while land values were not. Natural resources are the product of nature rather than
human labor or initiative, and as such should not provide the basis by
which individuals acquire revenues. Nature as the common heritage of
all humanity must be made a common property of society as a whole.

For mutualists everyone is entitled to the products of their directly
applied labor, through individually or collectively controlled means of
production, and payment should reflect socially produced value.
Mutualists advocate for an exchange economy unsupported by the state
force or laws that allow and protect concentrated wealth under capitalist
so-called "free trade" economies. Under mutualist relations, this includes
a labor market in which people choose, without coercion, to work for
others, for themselves, or co-operatively. A mutual credit bank provided
money to facilitate this scheme. Unlike communism, which advocates
exchange on the basis of the maxim "from each according to ability, to

each according to need," mutualism advocates trade on the basis of equivalent amounts of labor. This is a key point that distinguishes Proudhon's
perspective from anarchist communists and collectivists.

The saving of wealth allowed by the abolition of interest through the
People's Banks would be so great, and the stimulus given to production so
strong, that all public and private debts could be paid off quickly (Osgood
1889: 17). Taxation could be reduced and finally abolished as the expense
of administering government was lessened. The resulting property enjoyed
by all classes would be abounding and permanent (Osgood 1889: 17). As a
result, poverty, the cause of crime, would also lessen. Courts and police
administrations would no longer be necessary. With the extension of the
new relations among nations, internal well-being would be enhanced and
wars would be less likely to break out. Entire departments of finance, justice and police, and foreign affairs would gradually disappear (Osgood
1889: 17).

A major threat to the operation of a society of negotiators is an inequality of power among them. Proudhon recognizes that bargaining degener-
ates into violence where the strong are able to impose terms on the weak,
and thus he argues that members of a peaceful and free society must be
relatively equal in power (Ritter 1967). An equality of negotiators could
lead to stalemate, however, in which "a feeble, more or less precarious
society will result" (Proudhon 1927: 133–134). Stalemate can itself lead to
conflict as frustrated negotiators try to win by force what they could not
gain through agreement (Ritter 1967: 471). Proudhon responds partly by
arguing that social units should be diverse as well as equal. Diversity in
quality will increase the incentive to negotiate by offering the possibility
for each side to gain qualitatively unique advantages (Ritter 1967). This
mix of equality of status with diversity of type is part of what Proudhon
means by a mutualist society.

Within the context of a mutualist society, guarantees of the acceptance
of commutative justice, of the acceptance of the rule of each according to
productivity, is difficult to provide. The orthodox legal and political mechanisms are not available (Ritter 1967). In response, Proudhon refers to his
awareness of the psychological effects of social organization. Society
should be organized such that its members internalize the commutative
norm. People are wicked and ignorant because they have been forced to
be, directly or indirectly. Through the mechanism of the state they have
been subjected to the will of others or are able to transfer the evil impacts
of their acts to another (Osgood 1889: 10). If the mature individual were
freed from repression and compulsion, and came to know that he or she is

responsible alone for his or her acts and must alone bear their consequences, they would be thrifty, prudent and energetic, seeing and following their highest interests. This may sound similar to the classical liberal view of crime except that, for Proudhon, the state is nowhere a mechanism for punishment and coercion of society's members and the law is not used as deterrence. Similarly, the utilitarianism underlying law, which allows the majority to harm the minority, is absent. Unlike laws, there is no compulsion forcing someone to fulfill a contract or remain in an association longer than their conscience dictates.

Still this might be achieved through social pressure. Social censure and boycott are means for encouraging people to live up to their commitment. Thus, while external restraints of law and government are eliminated, people are not fully liberated since they are subjected to social pressures. While these social pressures are better hidden than legal and political pressures, they are not necessarily less coercive of action or will (Ritter 1967). Anyone who has lived in closed communities of religious fundamentalism can attest to this fact. Some would argue that social pressures are even more coercive than formal mechanisms of control—in part because their agents are in closer proximity and present on a daily basis. The informal forces at work under mutualism may echo the insularity, surveillance, and condemnation of traditional rural communities rather than real freedom.

One might well argue that this is still better than the coercion and punishment available to the state is regularly wielded against nonconformists. Even more, such pressures would lack the concentration of resources, the monopoly of force, wielded by the state. Indeed, a mutualist might well suggest that the duty of the individual to act their conscience, knowing that the result will bring no physical harm, is an aspect of freedom. Surely in a free society one will still be required to show the courage of their convictions, even though it meets with scorn and disapproval. Freedom is not synonymous with convenience or comfort.

The state obtains much of its power, certainly its ideological power, to the extent that people obey it and acknowledge it. The state is provided with power when people view its institutions and ends as legitimate, and act accordingly. For Proudhon, the revolution that would change social order fundamentally is not political and has little if anything to do with the overthrow of existing governmental apparatuses (Reichert 1967: 859). It has even less to do with the taking over of those apparatuses by non-elites, as Marxists have advocated. Authority is overthrown when people no longer obey its commands. Reaching this point means that people must first enter into new relationships with others.

Mutualists understand anarchism not as a revolutionary establishment of something new, a leap into the unknown, or as a break with the present. Rather, they regard anarchism as the realization of anti-authoritarian practices of mutual aid and solidarity that are already present in society but which have been overshadowed by state authority. Revolution occurs as people become enlightened and thus comes through their own participation in civic affairs. The role of anarchism, then, is, in many ways pedagogical. The apparatuses of government are destroyed when enough people are convinced of the futility of trying to reform society through the use of political power. As Paul Goodman suggested (as cited in Ward 1996), anarchism is the extension of spheres of freedom until they make up the majority of social life. Starting from this perspective, mutualists seek to develop non-authoritarian and non-hierarchical relations in the here-and-now of everyday life.

Mutualist anarchism, unlike that of anarchist communism, is based on gradual, non-violent, rather than revolutionary, social and cultural change. In place of force, Benjamin Tucker advocated the liberation of the individual's creative capacities. Tucker looked to gradual enlightenment through alternative institutions, schools, cooperative banks, and workers' associations as practical means to enact change. Social change, for Tucker, required personal transformation first and foremost but at the same time, while rejecting force, which he termed domination, Tucker did assert the right of individuals and groups to defend themselves.

Revolutions fail where they only substitute one form of government for another. A real revolution, for Proudhon, abolishes government and institutes in its place the rule of reason. Revolution is a permanent attempt to establish justice. Society determines whether it will be gradual and peaceful, or violent (Osgood 1889: 7).

Proudhon's Bank of the People, which could make industrial loans to workers' cooperatives without interest, was eclipsed in the age of mass production and mechanization. It might make some sense, however, in an age of re-artisanilization and service economies. Especially in a period in which the major capitalist banks are in crisis, closing, and seeking government hand-outs. The state as a source of aid and support has been deeply questioned in terms of its service to working class and poor people, small businesses, and small farmers. Mutual banks and cooperative producers' associations become once again more attractive and compelling alternatives to corporations, multinational chain stores, and chain banks. Proudhon's notions of People's Banks and local currencies have returned in the form of LETS (Local Exchange and Trade Systems). In North America, 19th Century mutualist communes, such as those of Benjamin

Tucker, find echoes in the autonomous zones and squat communities of the present day. Recent and contemporary theorists who present versions of mutualism include Paul Goodman, Colin Ward, and Kevin Carson.

Proudhon believed that political corruption and capitalist tyranny will undermine respect for law and confidence in government. A determined group of anarchists might, through persistent agitation, be able to contribute to the process of nullifying law. With real world alternatives, experienced in practice, it might no longer be possible to enforce obedience to law (Osgood 1889: 24).

The banishment of crime will be realized, not by increasing the political bonds that unite society or increasing administrative machinery and strengthening tendencies towards centralization, as even socialists urge, but rather by decentralization, removing political bonds. The pragmatic approach is to act now to prevent suffering rather than waiting for the revolution. Prospects for change are believed to be most likely in the advocacy of short-term policy changes that effect economic improvement in the here-and-now, while improving justice conditions for the poor and working classes.

Punitive vs. Restorative Justice

Most criminological theory, including versions of Marxist criminology (Quinney 1974; 1980; Reiman 2006) and Left realism (Alvi 2000; DeKeseredy 2000), views punishment as a protection against crime. As deterrence retribution, punishment is presented as a primary means for controlling social misconduct and wrongdoing.

In *De la Justice dans la Révolution et dans l'Église*, Proudhon calls for the "complete abolition of the supposed right to punish, which is nothing but the emphatic violation of an individual's dignity" (quoted in Ritter 1975: 70). Proudhon opposed utilitarianism and thus is unimpressed by appeals to consequences as justifications for punishment. He rejects punishment as coercive and external. Indeed, Proudhon calls for "the complete, immediate, abolition of courts and tribunals, without any substitution or transition"; this, he says, is "one of the prime necessities of the Revolution" (1969a: 260). In calling for abolition, Proudhon suggests that state courts, tribunals, and judges are illegitimate because the supposed social contract on which they rest is fraudulent, a myth perpetrated by authority to rationalize privilege and injustice. Those brought before such courts and tribunals have made no contractual agreement. There is no written, reciprocal obligation, signed by their hand that would give the courts any of the authority they claim. Authentically voluntary contracts are the only basis of legitimate "laws." For Proudhon, where there has been no contract, there can be neither crime nor misdemeanor before the courts (Spangler 2007).

Although Proudhon rejects punishment as coercive and external, Ritter (1975: 69) argues that Proudhon ultimately recommends controlling crime through punishment, largely as a means of incapacitating offenders such that they might be constrained from committing additional crimes. Yet Ritter makes this argument through a quite broad definition of punishment "to designate suffering imposed on an offender by a legally unauthorized person for a nonlegal defence" (1975: 70). He recognizes that his definition of punishment is removed from common usage and even places the term in quotation marks. Proudhon refused to grant to any authority that it should judge, and after judging that it should punish. Addressing crime does not mean an acceptance of government and the machinery of repression.

Nonlegal punishment is possible, as Ritter notes, as in non-statist societies when wrongdoing is treated not by legally authorized officials but by the individuals affected. Of course, practices like shunning and excommunication can be considered punishment. An anarchist society is certainly barred from using legal punishment. Nonlegal punishment would be possible, however, and Proudhon does offer some examples of it.

For Proudhon, the definition of punishment includes only that which is imposed by an authority. Acts of passion, vengeance or self-defense are not punishment since the actor lacks the authority required to punish. Anyone can harm another, but a punisher must be authorized (Ritter 1975: 71). This does not mean that this authority is conferred by law. While authority is required as a condition of punishment, those with nonlegal as well as legal authorization may both punish. For Ritter (1975 72): "By insisting that a punisher needs (nonlegal) authority, the anarchists show that despite their unclarity on how it is conferred, authority for them is a logical requirement of punishment."

Additionally, for an act to count as punishment, it must be in response to a misdeed. Thus Proudhon distinguishes acts of war from punishment on the grounds that those harmed in war need not have done wrong. No matter how much one might suffer, that suffering cannot be called punishment if he or she has not misbehaved.

Proudhon consistently and regularly identifies punishment with vengeance, seeing it not as a means to any positive social end. Even where it is a comprehensible "reaction of outraged conscience to immorality, he often argued that it is misguided and unreflective" (Harbold 1976: 237). His overarching view was that the criminal was a "scapegoat, charged with the sins of Israel," a position he claimed in his *System of Economic Contradictions* (Harbold 1976: 237).

Proudhon, as for other anarchists, views censure as an anarchist substitute for punishment. For Proudhon: "Police action, whether by instituted officials or the censure of public opinion, is both unlikely to be effective and an attack on human dignity, because it denies liberty" (Harbold 1976: 238).

As well, voluntary reparation, and social encouragement of such reparation, play important parts in Proudhon's thinking on how anarchists might deal with wrongdoing. Indeed, as for contemporary advocates of restorative justice, Proudhon believed that reparation carried a "powerful reformative effect" (Ritter 1975: 80). Proudhon did allow for the possibility of arbitration, leading towards restitution for assaults upon life:

> I understand that these men who are at war with their fellows should be summoned and compelled to repair the damage they have caused, to bear the cost of injury which they have occasioned; and, up to a certain point, to pay a fine in addition, for the reproach and insecurity of which they are one of the causes, with more or less premeditation. (Proudhon quoted in Spangler 2007)

However, restitution and dispute resolution were the only legitimate functions of authentic justice for Proudhon (Spangler 2007). Punishment was not.

> But that beyond this, these same people should be shut up, under the pretext of reforming them, in one of those dens of violence, stigmatized, put in irons, tortured in body and soul, guillotined, or, what is even worse, placed, at the expiration of their term, under the surveillance of the police, whose inevitable revelations will pursue them wherever they may have taken refuge; once again I deny, in the most absolute manner, that anything in society or in conscience or in reason can authorize such tyranny. (Proudhon quoted in Spangler 2007)

On this basis, justice, springing from liberty, will no longer be based on and reflect vengeance. Rather, justice will consist merely of reparation. The process of such reparation will involve, not the institutions of the state and its courts, but at most the participation of mutually agreeable arbitrators, selected by the parties to a dispute on a voluntary basis. Thus, for Proudhon: "Moreover the machinery of lawsuits then will reduce itself to a simple meeting of witnesses; no intermediary between the plaintiff and defendant, between the claimant and the debtor, will be needed except the friends whom they have asked to arbitrate" (quoted in Spangler 2007). Members of anarchist society would regard each other on the basis of respect. Anyone who violates this respect might experience not only the criticism of his or her peers but internal feelings of remorse (Ritter 1975). Such feelings will be more powerful, for Proudhon, where those harmed do not respond by making the offender suffer, but instead ask him or her to act to repair the damage caused through material compensation and/or performing altruistic and virtuous acts (Ritter 1975: 80).

> If they made him suffer, they themselves would break the rules of respect. Understanding this, the offender might lose his commitment to these rules and feel resentment, not remorse. But if those whom he has harmed ask for reparation, they remain true to the standards they share with him and give him a chance to redeem himself by showing he too can abide by the rules. (Ritter 1975: 80–81)

Material and moral reparation thus serve something of a rehabilitative function since, for Proudhon, it allows the offender to win back the respect lost through commission of the crime. Reparation also allows the offender to regain self-esteem. "Knowing that he is respected by his fellows despite his misdeed, he feels contrite. Respecting himself again after a period of self-hate, he fears a relapse. Both feelings are reformative, making him less likely to commit further crimes" (Ritter 1975: 81). Such experiences have been regular features of restorative and peacemaking approaches to justice.

Proudhon does allow that in periods before the achievement of pure liberty, or anarchy, some "punishment" may be deemed necessary by a society's members where they view immediate abolition as unsafe. If one becomes aggressive or invasive, violating the principle of equal freedom, punishment and restraint might be deemed justifiable by those involved (Yarros 1936: 475). This punishment, however, should be circumscribed and sparingly applied. Offenders should do no more than "repair the damage they have caused, bear the costs they have occasioned, and pay a limited fine in addition for the scandal and insecurity which they have more or less deliberately helped produce" (Proudhon 1924: 312). Government, for Proudhon, means controlling the non-aggressive and non-invasive, and that punishing someone for injuring others is not to govern them.

While there are ambiguities and contradictions in Proudhon's thinking on punishment, this reflects the fact that there are no easy answers to such questions and much will be worked out, renovated, and discarded through practice. Proudhon, like all other criminological thinkers offers a framework for understanding crime and deviance, social roots, and possible responses rather than complete programs.

Some have suggested that Proudhon specified private courts and private police as alternatives (Spangler 2007). This conclusion is drawn from Proudhon's suggestion of the "absorption of government by the economic organism" in the *General Idea of the Revolution in the Nineteenth Century*. Confusion on this matter arises, however, because commentators such as Spangler (2007) and Ritter (1975) conclude that, by the economic organism, Proudhon could only have meant the capitalist market and nothing else.

A proper reading of Proudhon's work shows that he "reject[s] the orthodox methods of social control—law, government, the market and social hierarchy—on the ground that they are unacceptably coercive" (Ritter 1967: 469). Those who submit to such rules, he argued, are not free. "The trader on a market, the member of a social class and the subject of a state all obey directives imposed on them from without. Hence, if men are to be free to act as they think fit, they must be emancipated from the regulation of market, hierarchy and law" (Ritter 1967: 470). So-called market "freedom" is no freedom at all. The capitalist market, which favors monopoly and the concentration of wealth, is only possible precisely because it is supported and sustained by the state.

For Proudhon, organized police power violates basic principles of individual freedom. Such organized power must deny the individual the right to regulate and discipline themselves. People who have been coerced into order over a period of time become accustomed to force and eventually lose the capacity to order themselves, becoming dependent on authorities. Crime and punishment, for Proudhon, "are certainly manifestations and consequences of injustice in social life, but those punished are not peculiarly responsible, nor will their punishment cure the evil. At its best, like all religious thought and institutions, punishment is a powerful, symbolic representation of the moral problem" (Harbold 1976: 237–238).

All crimes are subject to the "law of compensation," for Proudhon. More effective than abolishing punishment, which could lead to an outbreak of private vengeance, is seeking the "security of citizens" (Harbold 1976: 238). Punishment can be suppressed only in so far as crime can be prevented. For Proudhon, the great, persistent problem is the reconciliation of liberty and justice.

The punitive society, according to Proudhon, creates crime and punishment by its maintenance of special privileges and its lack of mutuality. Positive anarchy is an alternative to punitive society, in which penal discipline is "replaced by the morality of justice" (Harbold 1976: 238). This is fostered through the nurturing of extensive opportunities for all through mutualist social arrangements which enlarge rather than limit liberty. "In place of the law that disposes, orders, punishes, repairs, you have the Idea that does not command but gives life" (Harbold 1976: 238). Necessary is the substitution of an economic and social regime for the governmental and militaristic. By this Proudhon means an organization of economic forces based on agreement, operating according to the principle of reciprocity. This requires the abolition of the state, and transfer of control of social interests to individuals and their voluntary associations.

In place of political institutions and administration Proudhon advocated economic organizations based upon principles of mutualism in labor and exchange, through voluntary co-operatives and "People's Banks," as means towards that end. The consequences of this reorganization of social life include not only the limiting of constraint, the reduction of repressive methods, and the convergence of individual and collective interests, but it also prepared the ground for addressing crime and developing social security in a non-authoritarian way. (1969: 92).

Beyond Left Realism: Towards a Radical But Practical Criminology

Radical criminologists have primarily opposed the criminal justice system rather than concerning themselves with questions of order or providing supports for the working class victims of crime (Miller, Schreck and Tewksbury 2008: 183). Thus, they are vulnerable to criticisms that they have little concern about questions of order and security that trouble many in working class and poor communities. Where radical theorists have chosen to avoid such issues, or to postpone their consideration until some point "after the revolution", they have weakened the relevance of critical approaches.

Among the criminological theories that has most actively attempted to overcome this dilemma is Left realism. Left realism emerged in the 1980s, initiated largely through the work of one-time anarchist Jock Young. Left realism was offered simultaneously as a critique of both the law and order agenda of the New Right and the "left idealism" of much of radical criminology.

For Young, much of critical criminology was idealistic because it overlooked the day-to-day realities and concerns of non-elites, who were the ones most victimized by crime, in favor of a theoretical or abstract privileging of broad revolutionary politics and sweeping, long-term social change. Such a theoretical perspective ignored or downplayed the concerns of working-class people and communities who faced victimization in their own communities. Those isolated and marginalized at the bottom of the power structure are politically powerless to change their situation. Instead frustration and anger is expressed in abusing each other and their communities, rather than the elites who gain from inequality. Crime becomes an unjust, individualistic "solution" to the experience of injustice among people who lack means of solving the problem of relative deprivation (Lanier and Henry 2004).

Left realists are critical of "armchair sociologists," anarchists, and Marxists, who are content to wait for a revolution to create significant changes rather than affect change themselves, right now. Aware of the harm done to working class people by crime, and recognizing the ways in which crime harms the quality of urban community life for the working class and poor, is important for radical criminologists and organizers alike if they are to connect with people in those communities.

Left idealism's nearly exclusive focus on corporate crime and its romantic celebrations of street criminals as working class heroes (Lanier and Henry 2004; O'Grady 2007) ignores the day-to-day concerns of working-class people, especially working class crime victims. Left realists prefer not to wait for after the socialist revolution before implementing policies that reduce the suffering from crime caused by capitalism and its agencies of social control. To do so throws the real world policy debate into the corner of the right-wing law and order forces. Left realists note that the abstract, utopian approach of Left criminology, and its avoidance of real concerns of the working class victims of crime has allowed New Right criminology, and criminal justice system advocates to dominate the discussion and set the terms of criminal justice system discourse. For Left realists this has contributed to the swing towards "law and order" policies over the last few decades, using public perceptions and fears of crime to implement to punitive measures, such as mandatory sentences, longer sentences and more prisons to "get tough on crime." In place of tougher sentences and more prisons, left realists advocate community involvement.

Unfortunately, in attempting to develop short-term, practical responses to crime, left realists' policies have included community policing or citizen involvement on police boards. Elsewhere they have advocated for job creation or retraining programs, such as a police-run "squeegee work mobilization program" that tried to provide alternatives to squeegeeing for youth by training them to repair bikes. Left realists seek to provide "equal justice" to the powerless, largely through state protection, community policing and neighborhood watch programs. Police, in their view, should be democratized and subject to community control. The criminal justice system should be restructured rather than abolished for Left realists. They join liberals in believing that the law can provide the structurally powerless with real gains. These policies, however, leave the oppressive structures of capitalism intact, even strengthening the state. Criminal justice system reform, without accompanying structural changes away from capitalism is reinforcing of capitalist structures of exploitation.

Proudhon's thinking on justice also serves as an important alternative to socialist approaches in criminology that place fraternity or solidarity ahead of concerns for justice. Of socialists, he asks: "Why will they never understand, that fraternity can only be established by justice; that justice alone, the condition, means and law of liberty and fraternity, must be the object of our study" (134, n. 20). Even more Proudhon writes that "social order is established upon the basis of inexorable justice, and not at all upon the paradisaical sentiments of fraternity, self-sacrifice, and love, to the exercise of which so many honourable socialists are now endeavouring now to stimulate the people" (134, n. 21). One might compare this with the criticisms of socialist criminology and Jock Young's insistence on the need for a Left realist approach.

Proudhon displays a similar disdain for revolutionary rhetoric and appeals to solidarity or fraternity. Unlike some Marxists who place fraternity and equality ahead of justice (as a bourgeois concept), Proudhon saw justice as a central part of social progress in the here and now of everyday life. Justice is not a future outcome of socialism or communism, but is effective now. Unlike Left realism, he did not turn to the state as part of any solution.

While anarchists have been generally criticized for offering utopian responses to questions of crime and conflict (see Lanier and Henry 2004), the writings of Proudhon offer a useful starting point for a criminology that is both radical and pragmatic. His discussions of mutualism and restitution have much to offer radical criminology as well as anarchist community organizers dealing with approaches to crime in exploited and oppressed communities.

Proudhon and Restorative Justice

Proudhon's work is an important, if generally overlooked, precursor to those approaches in criminology, such as restorative justice and peacemaking criminology, that express the value of collective efficacy or "social capital," in which strong community networks of social support and informal social control contribute to reducing occurrences of crime (Lanier and Henry 2004; O' Grady 2004; Williams and McShane 2004). Indeed his approach to crime bears a striking resemblance to themes that animate what is broadly called restorative justice.

Restorative justice, while a relatively recent, and still somewhat marginal, component of modern criminal justice systems, has long been part of efforts to respond to and prevent crime within a variety of local communities. It emphasizes effective practices for dealing with crime, based on consensual, interactive, and participatory, rather than more familiar adversarial models of justice, based on retribution and punishment, that make up the overwhelming part of criminal justice system practice. Restorative justice is concerned with rebuilding relationships after an offence, rather than driving a wedge between offenders and the community as occurs within criminal justice systems in capitalist liberal democracies. Restorative justice allows victims, offenders, and the community to address the harms done by crime, such that the community, rather than being further torn apart and pitted against itself, might be repaired. Rather than imposing decisions about winners and losers in an adversarial system, restorative justice seeks to facilitate dialogue among those affected (Lanier and Henry 2004: 332). All parties with a stake in the offence come together to deal collectively with it. As Sarre (2003: 98) explains:

> A restorative system of criminal justice endeavors to listen to, and appease, aggrieved parties to conflict and to restore, as far as possible, right relationships between antagonists. In restorative justice models crime is defined as a violation of one person by another, the focus is on problem solving, dialogue and restitution (where possible), mutuality, the repair of social injury and the possibilities of repentance and forgiveness.

While conventional criminal justice focuses on the offence to the state by individuals and does little to deal with the consequences to the community and its members, restorative justice emphasizes rebuilding community trust and "social capital" as means to defend against future conflicts and offences. As Brennan (2003: 2008) suggests: "Restorative justice builds on social capital because it decentralizes the offense from merely the act of an offender breaking the law, to a breach in a community's trust in its members. This in turn allows the community along with the offender and victim to *collectively* look for a resolution." Rather than simply assigning blame, it allows for understanding and an opportunity to address issues that give rise to crime within specific communities.

Restorative justice acts on a range of general principles. First is the view that both victim and the community have been harmed by an offender's actions and this causes a disequilibrium that must be addressed to restore relations, lest more social harm be done. This requires some restoration of relations. Counter to traditional criminal justice system approaches, offenders as well as victims and the community have a stake in a successful outcome of this process. Second, those who have offended have some obligation to address the harm they have caused. Third, restorative justice emphasizes the healing of both victim and offender. Victims need information, understanding, safety and social support. Unlike the standard criminal justice system, offenders' needs must also be addressed, including social security, health care, possible treatment for addictions, or counseling.

Providing community support for offenders benefits all in the community as well as representing fairness in the practice of justice. Restorative justice offers the prospect of escaping the "zero-sum game" of the traditional criminal justice system, whereby what is said to benefit victims must hurt offenders. In restorative justice, victim, community, and offender all stand to gain in their own ways.

Such an approach differs greatly from the dominant emphasis of the criminal justice system and its institutions. Proponents of restorative justice note that punishment-centered models of crime control are both ineffective and costly, both in human and resource terms. Prisons are wildly expensive systems for containing and managing people who have been targeted for criminalization, but, even more, incarceration has long been shown to offer few positive or constructive outcomes for those who are so punished. This is a point that is in keeping with Proudhon's discussion of the ways in which non-participatory, non-consensual punishments breed resentment and contempt in those subjected to it. The result of such approaches, as Proudhon notes, is more often the pursuit of vengeance rather than justice.

Harsh prison sentences, at most, provide victims of crime with a sense of revenge or vindication. Punishment models do little to assist or support victims who may have been multiply impacted by a criminal event or events. Systems oriented primarily towards punishing offenders offer little to those who have been victimized by crime.

Restorative justice is no utopian wish. In fact it has been attempted within several jurisdictions to deal even with extremely violent crimes. Research suggests that restorative justice shows clear effectiveness, both in terms of offender accountability and victim healing (Umbreit, Coates, Vos and Brown 2002).

Similarly, peacemaking criminology argues that the idea of making war on crime needs to be replaced with the idea of making peace on crime. Bracewell identifies the motivating themes of peacemaking criminology as follows: "(1) connectedness to each other and to our environment and the need for reconciliation; (2) caring for each other in a nurturing way as a primary objective in corrections; and (3) mindfulness, meaning the cultivation of inner peace" (Lanier and Henry 2004: 330).

> As opposed to the war on crime perspective, the peacemaking perspective has the potential to provide lasting solutions to the problems that lead individuals to commit violations of law. The war on crime perspective, with its emphasis on punishment and retribution ensures that offenders will strive only to commit their crimes in a more efficient manner so as not to get caught. The peacemaking perspective on the other hand, seeks to address the conditions of society that foster crime and to address the problems of the individual offender. Additionally the peacemaking perspective seeks to understand and respond to the concerns of victims. (Fuller 2003: 88)

Instead of escalating the violence in an already violent society by treating violence and conflict with state violence and conflict, through police and penal sanctions, society needs to de-escalate violence (Lanier and Henry 2004). Practices of conciliation, mediation and dispute settlement become preferable options. Peacemaking criminologists, like anarchist-influenced Hal Pepinsky, argue that reducing violence requires people's direct involvement in democratic practices. By this he means "a genuine participation by all in life decisions that is only achievable in a decentralized, nonhierarchical social structure" (Lanier and Henry 2004: 330).

Conclusion

Proudhon in no way believed that social life could be spontaneously peaceful. For Proudhon, human life consists of antinomies without end. In *La Guerre et la Paix* Proudhon asserts that conflict and antagonism are "the law of social life" as well as "the universal law of nature and humanity" (Noland 1970: 294). Against the wishes of classical criminology, which in keeping with its liberal capitalist vision of humanity, poses humans as rational calculating actors, and some "scientific" socialist or Marxist criminology, humans are illogical and contradictory, an incoherent assemblage, simultaneously spontaneity and reflection, automaton and free, angel and brute (Noland 1970: 292). Agitation and antagonism in human history, including war, provide the impetus for the decomposition and re-composition of society. It is the *elan* which drove social existence "to create little by little

harmony and liberty on this earth" (Noland 1970: 296). Thus there is no
social solution that can, once and for all, guarantee either order or freedom.
For Proudhon: "Mere political reform is not enough, because the clash of
wills, which is socially determined, will continue unabated" (Ritter: 468).
This is a point that is often denied by criminologists, mainstream and critical, who search for a final end to criminal activity and social wrongdoing,
and criticize those, like anarchists, who are unwilling or unable to offer hard
and fast "solutions" to the question of crime.

Government, for Proudhon, asserts an impossible harmony between
individual and common interests. At the same time this perspective makes
clear that, despite the charges leveled at anarchists, Proudhon was no utopian. He did not naively believe that a final or universal program, worked
out in his head, could easily overcome the contradictory and conflictual
character of human life.

Proposals that ignore the social and psychological root causes of conflict will fail to secure peace for Proudhon. Efforts towards harmonious
actions must consider the impact of institutions on people's wills.
Institutions must offer support for harmonious volition (Ritter 1967;
Osgood 1889; Pepinsky 1978). Those who ignore this contribution are led
down the fruitless path of seeking social peace by political means. This is
as true for Marxist revolutionaries as it is for liberal democrats.

To secure social peace through institutional reform means the development of social organizations that harmonize people's wills, yet commitment to total liberation means such harmonization is permissible only if
personal autonomy is maintained. For Proudhon, social ills could only disappear if the state and all of its institutions were removed from society.
Property and the state are bound together as one, for Proudhon. Regardless
of the form that government takes, its nature is inequality, misery, and
injustice.

As discussed above, in place of political institutions Proudhon advocated economic organizations based upon principles of mutualism in
labor and exchange, through co-operatives and "People's Banks," as means
towards that end. The consequences of this reorganization of social life
include the limiting of constraint, the reduction of repressive methods,
and the convergence of individual and collective interests (1969: 92).
Proudhon calls this "the state of total liberty" or anarchy, and suggests that
it is the only context in which "laws" operate spontaneously without
invoking command and control.

Proudhon's efforts attempted to reconcile a realist awareness that order
requires social reorganization, with a conviction that external, coercive

interference with thought and action is unacceptable. While not completely successful, his efforts show the difficulties of realistically rebuilding community on a libertarian basis. His work highlights the difficulties and obstacles to developing an approach to community order that is both radical and realistic. This is the challenge of a practical or pragmatic anarchism. It is also a challenge to a critical criminology: addressing the immediate and short-range real world concerns of non-elites who are the ones most often affected by crime in capitalist societies.

These questions posed by Proudhon are still crucial today, as anarchists and sociologists alike have focused their attentions on the multi-faceted forms of domination that afflict modern societies. A practical, realist effort to address social re-organization must confront these many challenges.

CHAPTER SIX

AN ANARCHIST VIEW OF STRATIFICATION, INEQUALITY, AND DOMINATION

Introduction

Sociologists and anarchists share convergent and divergent interests in issues of social inequality. A principal subject of sociological study is social inequalities. In fact, one could argue it is the prevailing, contemporary theme running through most of the discipline. All social phenomena are unequally patterned and distributed. The quest of the sociologist is often to explore the ways in which groups of people are unequal. Yet, there are considerable weaknesses in the usual, liberal, sociological treatment of social inequality. For example, in practice, greater income is not necessarily desirable. Although correlated with happiness, greater income itself does not *guarantee* joy, satisfaction, or autonomy. Improving people's prestige, for example occupational status, does not make a better world, since prestige is itself an elite-creating characteristic. Even increasing the (Weberian-defined) power of the poor over the rich does not suggest the way forward to a more equal world, just a slightly different arrangement of inequality.[1] It is possible to have objectively impoverished people who actually have a great deal of freedom. Thus, someone with low income, part-time work, lots of spare-time, and a big garden is technically disadvantaged compared to someone with middle- or high-income, overtime work, no spare-time, and no garden. Quantity of resources does not equate to freedom.

Anarchists are principally and generally motivated by the presence of social inequality and domination to take action. The philosophy of anarchism rests upon a critique of hierarchical institutions and social patterns and, thus, anarchism directly targets these phenomena for radical transformation. While inequality is considered a serious problem by anarchists, inequality is actually seen a symptom of hierarchy and relationships of domination. Consequently, anarchists claim that raising incomes or

---

[1] Or, to respond to Marxist claims, the dictatorship of the proletariat still implies a dictatorship, just with a different group in-charge.

extending authoritarian power to disadvantaged groups (e.g. electing a Black man president) is not an appropriate solution, and anarchists instead focus upon fostering self-management, autonomy, and mutual aid.

For the purposes of this chapter we borrow both sociological and anarchist definitions of "inequality" and "domination." Inequality is the gap between the resources or lived experiences that people of various groups have; for example, class inequality may be represented by the gap between income, wealth, or occupational status. Domination refers to patterns of unequal relationships that are executed within hierarchies. We rely heavily upon the anarchist assumption that domination precedes and results in inequality, and that domination is a far broader phenomenon than usually presumed. According to Bookchin (2005), hierarchy is

> the cultural, traditional and psychological systems of obedience and command, not merely the economic and political systems to which the terms class and State most appropriately refer. Accordingly, hierarchy and domination could easily continue to exist in a "classless" or "Stateless" society. I refer to the domination of the young by the old, of women by men, of one ethnic group by another, of "masses" by bureaucrats who profess to speak in their "higher social interest," of countryside by town, and in a more subtle psychological sense, of body by mind, of spirit by a shallow instrumental rationality, and of nature by society and technology. Indeed, classless but hierarchical societies exist today (and they existed more covertly in the past); yet the people who live in them neither enjoy freedom, nor do they exercise control over their lives. (68)

This chapter draws upon anarchist and sociological ideas about inequality and domination, with the goal of finding common ground and an agreeable synthesis. We explore sociology and anarchism's common interests in inequality and domination, and formulate a contemporary, sociologically-informed anarchist theory of these phenomena. We consider anarchist contributions to understanding inequality and domination, as well as some of the more anarchistic ideas offered by sociologists. Based upon these two parallel threads, we propose some general observations that we believe can serve as the foundation for a future "grand theory of domination." We then apply these propositions to three major subjects of scholarly study on inequality: class, gender, and race. By considering these different forms of inequality, it becomes clear that dynamics of domination are utterly entangled with class, gender, and race inequality, and that domination is a far more complicated and intractable phenomenon that most sociologists give it credit for. Consequently, there are many ethical problems for empathetic scholars who seek to study inequality and domination, but do not involve themselves in activities to subvert, resist, and undermine these phenomena. Anarchists have not only criticized scholarly inaction—which is often based upon the morally-relative grounds of "objectivity"—but direct their social, political, and economic activities towards the remediation of domination, using a variety of strategies. Anarchists actively try to eliminate domination and authoritarian power, and thus reduce inequality. We begin the next section by providing a brief selection of classical anarchist views on inequality.

Anarchists and Domination

The modern anarchist movement originally emerged in the chaos of the European industrial revolution. The changing character of domination—from feudal, religious, and aristocratic forms of domination to capitalist, parliamentary, and bureaucratic domination—was the impetus for early anarchist critiques.[2] Most anarchist writers spoke of not just material inequality stemming from capitalist growth, but also tyranny rooted in the solidifying nation-state. The first self-identified anarchist of the modern era, Joseph-Pierre Proudhon (1969) identified the multitude of ways in which government harmed individuals:

> To be governed is to be kept in sight, inspected, spied upon, directed, law-driven, numbered, enrolled, indoctrinated, preached at, controlled, estimated, valued, censured, commanded, by creatures who have neither the right, nor the wisdom, nor the virtue to do so.... To be governed is to be at every operation, at every transaction, noted, registered, enrolled, taxed, stamped, measured, numbered, assessed, licensed, authorized, admonished, forbidden, reformed, corrected, punished. It is, under the pretext of public utility, and in the name of the general interest, to be placed under contribution, trained, ransomed, exploited, monopolized, extorted, squeezed, mystified, robbed; then, at the slightest resistance, the first word of complaint, to be repressed, fined, despised, harassed, tracked, abused, clubbed, disarmed, choked, imprisoned, judged, condemned, shot, deported, sacrificed, sold, betrayed; and, to crown all, mocked, ridiculed, outraged, dishonored. That is government; that is its justice; that is its morality. (294)

States facilitated many things, including armed protection of private property and the guaranteed transfer of wealth across generations. Mikhail

---

[2] Purkis (2004) has noted that anarchism and sociology developed during the same time period, and out of a similar concern for the central and peripheral consequences of the Industrial Revolution sweeping Northern and Western Europe in the late-1800s.

Bakunin presciently noted the inter-generational barriers to class mobility and their severe consequences when he wrote:

> ... as long as *inheritance* is in effect, there will be *hereditary* economic inequality, not the natural inequality of individuals but the artificial inequality of classes—and this will necessarily always lead to the hereditary inequality of the development and cultivation of mental faculties, and continue to be the source and the consecration of all political and social inequalities. (cited in Dolgoff 1972, 126, original emphasis)

Early anarchists were also remarkably attuned to non-political and non-economic forms of inequality, including those related to gender, race and ethnicity, sexuality, nationality, and many others. For example, American anarchist Voltairine de Cleyre (2004) wrote sarcastically of the attitudes and efforts of men to suppress women:

> [The] highest idea for woman was serfhood to husband and children, in the present mockery called "home." Stay at home, ye malcontents! Be patient, obedient, submissive! Darn our socks, mend our shirts, wash our dishes, get our meals, wait on us and *mind the children*! Your fine voices are not to delight in public nor yourselves; your inventive genius is not to work, your fine art taste is not to be cultivated, your business faculties are not to be developed; you made the great mistake of being born with them, suffer for your folly! You are *women*! therefore housekeepers, servants, waiters, and child's nurses! (98, original emphasis)

Likewise, Rudolf Rocker (1998) challenged the very assumptions about racial differences and racial superiority (even foreshadowing contemporary ideas about the social construction of race):

> ... it becomes clear that pure races are nowhere to be found, in fact, have in all probability never existed ... how defective still is our knowledge of the inner processes of heredity, [that] one cannot avoid the conclusion that every attempt to erect on such uncertain premises a theory which allegedly reveals to us the deeper meaning of all historical events and enables its exponents infallibly to judge the worth of the moral, mental and cultural qualities of the different human groups must become either senseless play-acting or clownish mischief. (317)

Anarchists—including Benjamin Tucker, Emma Goldman, and Alexander Berkman—also held the distinction of being some of the very first groups of "allies" to speak on behalf of homosexuals in the United States, long before the Stonewall Riot of 1969. Sexuality was considered an expression of personal liberty, and people are free to express their desires, attractions, love, and care for whomever they wish, regardless of sex and gender (Kissack 2008).

Given the above, common examples, it is clear that varied forms of social inequality and domination were and still are regular subjects of anarchist writers and activists. As such, early anarchists already had developed a keen sociological concern—while rarely citing Comte, Simmel, Durkheim, or Weber—that was radically manifested in their political activity and commitment to overturn these various systems of domination.

Sociological Theory and Anarchism

Unlike the regular discussion of social inequality and domination amongst anarchists, sociologists have rarely grappled with anarchist theory, except tangentially (via random, esoteric mention) or out of fear (see Harney 2002). Therefore, few anarchist insights have influenced sociological ideas about inequality and domination. Some of sociology's independently-derived ideas *do* reflect anarchist sentiments, although Marxism and feminism have had a far greater influence on sociological ideas of inequality. Here, we take note of a handful of somewhat arbitrary sociological thinkers who can contribute building blocks for an anarchist-sociologist view of inequality and domination. The anarchistic qualities of these contributions were surely unintentional and we do not mean to imply that the following sociologists *were* anarchists—or even that they would appreciate their ideas being used in this way. Quite to the contrary! These sociologists have advanced ideas, which are sympathetic to anarchist concerns about inequality and domination, including large organizational size and bureaucratization, authority relationships, the comprehensive domination of everyday life by "the system," and the multi-faceted nature of hierarchies.

The writings of Robert Michels,[3] particularly *Political Parties* (1962), contain an anarchist allergy to large organizations and centralized power. Inequality exists *within* organizations, and the power deficit between "leader" and "follower" swells as the organization grows. Group democracy becomes increasingly susceptible to manipulation and self-management lessens with greater membership. Member input, control, and flexibility exist in inverse proportion to organizational rigidity and the distance of leadership from the rank-and-file. Therefore, the growing scale of human

---

[3] It has been suggested that Michels was a revolutionary syndicalist, holding views compatible to anarcho-syndicalism during his early years. However, he apparently turned towards Italian-style fascism later in life.

organization introduces and increases domination. Incidentally, anarchists have long since understood this—for example, Ehrlich (1996) notes the anarchist preference for deliberately small organizations that helps to retain directly democratic and egalitarian characteristics.

Marx argued that the foundation of inequality came from property relations. Ralf Dahrendorf (1959) responded that authority relations create inequality *and* property relations. Property exists and may be owned by some, because people in certain institutions have the authority to enforce this claim upon the rest of society. The inequality found in society comes from social structures and organizations that favor some participants over others, namely "order givers" over the "order takers." For example, in a work organization like a corporation, owners (Marx's "bourgeoisie") give orders to managers, who in-turn give orders to workers (the "proletariat"). The managers are in a contradictory position in this system, as they have incredible control over the day-to-day functioning of corporations, but do not own them. In fact, most manifested labor conflict takes place between worker and management, not worker and owner (who are often invisible). The conflict between worker and management cannot be explained by ownership of the means of production, but rather by who has authority over whom. Consequently, inequality exists in any relationship between people in different positions of authority. There are many (if not infinite) potential positions in a stratification system, which indicates the complexity of inequality—it is not just "us against them." Instead, there are many half-allies and half-enemies. Dahrendorf's analysis may be applied to all manner of situations: children and often wives as the order takers of patriarchal male order givers, or in relations between citizens and police. The means of production is irrelevant in these situations, while authority—the ability to have one's orders followed—is paramount. Dahrendorf's work represents an important improvement over earlier views of inequality. Here, inequality is an indicator—a canary in a coal mine—suggesting the presence of some form of domination. Inequality is thus a symptom of the problem of domination, not itself the problem.

Critical theorists, such as Jürgen Habermas (1985), have argued that the modern world is dehumanizing and is the source for vast domination. Large systems—notably bureaucracies, the state, consumer capitalism, and mass media—"colonize" the "life world" of people's everyday lived experiences. In the process, "democracy" becomes mediated through the scientific manipulation of public opinion. Civil participation is reduced due to the influence of money and power upon the public sphere.

Importantly, Habermas argues for the use of reason (not mere positivism) for emancipatory purposes, a praxis that is rooted in a social reality that clearly takes the side of society's dominated, values participatory democracy, and expresses a utopian vision for society. True communicative action is necessary to cut-through all the domination in society, so people can articulate their interests and find a collaborative way forward.

Black feminists have been vocal critics of early attempts to understand major forms of inequality (like class, gender, and race). Sociologists like Patricia Hill-Collins have argued that a "matrix of domination" exists wherein various forms of inequality affect individuals in divergent ways, depending on their own position in the matrix, as well as other life factors, including time and space (Collins 1991). Collins—and others like Angela Davis, Audrey Lorde, and Barbara Smith—observe that the lives of women in the feminist movement during the 1960s and 1970s were not the same. The interests, opportunities, resources, privileges, and overall position in hierarchies were very different. For example, white women tended to have greater opportunities than black women (and other women of color), middle-class and affluent women greater resources than poor women, and straight women greater privileges than lesbians. Consequently, to speak of an "essential" womanhood is to ignore than multitude of ways in which women are different, both privileged and disadvantaged (Harris 1990). bell hooks (1981) expands upon these ideas by identifying a "white supremacist capitalist patriarchy" that intersects to create the hierarchies of the matrix. However, hooks observes avenues of resistance: by "coming to voice" women (and other dominated groups) can articulate their own experiences and discover others with whom they can collectively struggle towards freedom (hooks 1989). In this respect, hooks reflects the anarchist practice of identifying domination and seeking alternative forms of social organization.

None of the above social theorists encapsulate an explicitly anarchist view of inequality and domination. Still, each of the above echoes important anarchist *concerns*, which, taken together, suggest key areas of overlap between anarchism and sociology. Consequently, anarchists have made criticisms of excessively large organizations, authoritarian power, how massive institutions structure everyday life to perpetuate inequality, and the multiplicative hierarchies affecting all people. Next, we illustrate how anarchist-sociologists can use these sociological observations, combined with classic anarchist ideas on inequality and domination, to create a systematic anarchist theory.

An Anarchist Grand Theory of Domination

Brian Martin (2007), writing in the scholarly peer-reviewed journal *Anarchist Studies*, claimed that certain anarchist theories are in need of further development, including "a high-level grand theory of domination, oppression, inequality and/or hierarchy... A grand theory of domination would be a specific anarchist contribution" (108). While there are numerous sociological critics of grand theory (e.g. Mills 1959, Merton 1968), this task may be reasonable given the radical character of anarchism and the centrality of inequality and domination to its theoretical lens. With anarchism, it is meaningful to speak of a comprehensive theory to describe patterns of domination, since the philosophy treats these patterns as enduring phenomena in the recent human epoch, and these patterns are the ultimate consequence of hierarchical institutions and authority.

Grand theory aims to explain a large amount of how the world works, and its conclusions are not dependent upon time or place for qualification. Consequently, a grand theory needs to be universally robust in its explanatory power. Anarchism has tended to assert a broad, comprehensive argument that hierarchy creates domination and inequality. Below, we describe key anarchist assumptions and observations about domination. Each may serve as a proposition needing verification from further evidence—a task that we undertake later in this chapter.

Proposition 1: Domination is Based Upon the Successful Use of Hierarchical Power.

Hierarchy in human relations is an overwhelmingly negative and dehumanizing force. The "power over" that some possess is the foundation of domination. As Hartung (1983) notes, "Anarchism generically begins with the assumption that patterns of domination—including classism, racism, sexism and heterosexism—can be traced to the hierarchical imposition of authority" (89). Each form of domination in society derives from institutionalized hierarchies where some use their privileged positions to wield power at the expense of others. For example, exploitation is the result of some people (e.g. capitalists) employing economic power within a capitalist economy, dominating those with less power (e.g. workers)—thus resulting in class inequality. Hierarchical power needs to be properly deployed in order for it to be effective and thus dominate others. This successful use often requires a mixture of legitimacy, hegemonic force, impressiveness, and unanimity. In order to end domination, hierarchy needs to be removed.

Proposition 2: Domination Results in Negative Consequences for Individuals.

Domination diminishes desirable states of being, harms individuals, and limits human potential. The process of domination robs the dominated of agency and choice, autonomy, empowerment, self-identity and self-esteem, freedom, self-determination, and personal safety. Individuals, and the groups they are in, are harmed in their present condition, sometimes through hardship, deprivation, or violence (whether physical, mental, or emotional). Domination also stunts human potential by restricting possibilities, curtailing dreams, crushing ambitions, and causing people to put up with poor conditions.

Proposition 3: Domination Results in Negative Consequences for Society.

Domination is a severely anti-social phenomenon. The practice of domination taints human relationships and interactions, causing manipulation, tension, distrust, malice, revenge, danger, and violence. Consequently, domination pollutes society and degrades its overall cooperative potential. Even people who are in very advantageous positions are negatively impacted by missing opportunities for broader friendships, experiences, and perspectives. Since social relationships and interactions are the meaningful fabric of daily life, it is important to reduce domination for the good of all people.

Proposition 4: Inequality Takes Many Forms, More Than we Can Identify or Comfortably Analyze at Once.

In addition to major forms of social inequality—such as class, gender, and race—others can always be identified. In fact, new forms of inequality are regularly being "discovered," noticed, and articulated. This "multidimensionalism" is an important trend in the study of inequality (Grusky and Szelényi 2007). For example, recently added forms being studied in the field of sociology—but by no means new in the real world—include sexuality, spatial location, information access, age, nationality, ability status, and others. Even race and gender are themselves relatively new research subjects in mainstream North American sociology, since most sociologists in the first half of the Twentieth Century were highly-educated White men who did not appreciate forms of inequality that they did not personally face. It is highly likely that societies will identify new forms of inequality in the future. In addition, inequality forms in other societies are likely different and unfamiliar to foreign observers. Understanding the varied forms of inequality helps to understand the world more accurately and thus we can formulate appropriate solutions to problems. Two other forms of domination that have received greater focus in recent years exist outside of inter-human relations: the domination of nature and the domination of non-human animals.

Proposition 5: The Privileged do not Have an Ethical "Right" to Their Privileges.

Existing social structures and relations are not natural, biologically-determined, or ordained by god. Thus, potential dominators do not "deserve" their power and authority, or the privileges that accompany them. No person or group should dominate any other person or group. However, privileges do not always need to be taken from the privileged, but sometimes privileges merely need to be extended to the disadvantaged. For example, academic professors with job tenure should not have their privileging tenures taken away from them, but rather comparable tenure ought to be offered to all occupations so that other people can share the same privileges as professors. Or, men should not be stripped of the respect society offers them, but women ought to be extended comparable respect to raise them to the same level of men. Consequently, privileges may not be monopolized by some to the detriment of others, but need expansion to benefit all. Ultimately, everyone—both disadvantaged and privileged—has an interest in fighting domination. The individuals who benefit most from systems of domination also could benefit (although in different ways and to a somewhat lesser extent) from the elimination of those very systems. For example, patriarchy and machismo can be viewed as social diseases that actively destroy men, as well as women.

Proposition 6: Certain Disadvantaged Groups Will Regularly (Although not Always) Resist Domination.

Domination is not a mere one-way street, with those receiving disadvantage and absorbing the actions of dominators quietly: it is sensible to presume there will be attempts by dominated persons to engage in reciprocal force. Resistance is a "natural"—or at least expected—consequence of domination and disadvantage. Domination creates desires, emotions, and goals within dominated communities that can and will clash with various hierarchies. People who are disadvantaged and deprived will likewise seek redress and a means to improvement. Ensuing conflicts may lead such communities and individuals to attempt to counter their subordination. Additionally, the ways and extent to which inequality harms people is partially dependent upon the resistance offered by those in disadvantaged positions. But, it is difficult (if not impossible) to predict in advance who will revolt, where, and when. It is usually difficult for others to identify and notice the feelings, conditions, and deprivations that some people are experiencing. Indeed, the factors that will make a certain group "snap" may confuse observers. For example, those in revolt may seem in some respects privileged, like students or middle-class Blacks in the 1960s. Therefore, analysis of a revolt is always easier in retrospect. But, why do people not *always* resist when injustice is present? Some groups are highly unlikely to resist domination (e.g. young children or people with substantial intellectual disabilities) in any organized capacity. For others, why is resistance rare?

Anarchist-sociologists seek to determine the factors that contribute to revolt in order to help *enable* more rebellion. "Resistance" is also a broad term, and may look orderly or chaotic, reformist or revolutionary. Protest could take the form of pressuring for legislative or policy-oriented changes that will help the disadvantaged. Protest could also attempt to directly stop some sort of domination from occurring. Other forms of radical protest may aim to acquire, grow, and expand the means of self-empowerment. Resistance could even be represented by anti-social behaviors like crime or sub-cultural separatism. In every case, however, resistance is the act of the disadvantaged against their position in a hierarchy, whether fully conceived of as such or not.

We argue that these six propositions are a fairly conservative starting point for an anarchist-sociological view of domination. To test the veracity of these assumptions, we apply these propositions to three major, enduring forms of inequality studied most everywhere in contemporary sociology. Since grand theories must be robust and generalizable by their very nature, it is important to apply this theory to a diverse array of inequalities, not just one or two in isolation.

Class, Gender, Race, and Hierarchy

Surprisingly, we have met and read the writings of numerous sociologists and anarchists that claim that *one* of these major forms of inequality—class, gender, and race—are the central or ultimate forms, trumping the others. Sometimes this prioritization is a subtle implication one senses by the words used, but in other instances people have plainly claimed the supposed omnipresence of one form over others. While the character of these inequality forms has changed overtime and is not the same in all places, it is improper to dismiss some forms at the expense of others. Authors and activists tend to make interesting and good arguments, but the fact that these three forms of inequality are continuously argued over and on behalf of is an indication that they are all formidable and not "minor" in respect to others. Different, yes, but not more or less important. To rank the importance of one form is to begin the exclusion of others, regardless of the empirical validity of the original argument. Decades of recent sociological research, as well as the far longer experience of social movements rooted in struggle against these forms of domination, illustrates just how complex and deep-rooted each form is in modern societies.[4]

As the aforementioned black feminists caution, care should be taken to not "essentialize" one group's experience as the normative experience of all others. For example, the experience of all men is not that of complete or total dominators. Black men and working-class men are disadvantaged in certain aspects of their lives, thus differentiating them from upper-class White men. Considering the impact of all forms of domination illustrates the multiplicative effect of disadvantage upon people. Then, individual conditions of disadvantage unique to one's own life may be considered. Sociology considers average patterns between human groups, and generalizes those experiences and positions of disadvantage or privilege. Even averages, though, ignore differences since not all people share the exact same characteristics and conditions of those in their group.

In the following discussion, we apply the six propositions offered above, in light of the dynamics of class, gender, and race inequality. As such, we explore an anarchist interpretation of these three major forms of inequality of interest to sociologists. Like sociologists, we argue that these are irreducible forms that are influenced by each other, but are still independent. Unlike many sociologists, however, we emphasize how an analysis based on mere inequality between "haves" and "have nots" often misses the hierarchy and authority relationships inherent in each. Also, we argue it is

---

[4] Ironically, often (but not always) the person making this claim is from a disadvantaged category within this form of inequality. People still have problems seeing other forms of inequality as important if they do not face them personally, although the experience with one form of inequality often attunes them to noticing other forms.

important to note the shortcomings in efforts to "equalize" income, wealth, or resources between groups, and how anarchists aim to eliminate the entire hierarchical mechanisms underpinning each form of inequality. The following attempts to be as culturally-independent as possible, but it is unavoidable that the examples given are more descriptive of realities in North America.[5] We discuss the concepts of class, gender, and race in alphabetical order.

Class

Class inequality is premised upon the hierarchical institution of capitalism that allows an owner class to give orders to middle- and working-classes. Power is thus rooted in economic relations of exploitation. Sometimes capitalists do not give middle-class managers and professionals direct orders, and, due to socialization that causes them to identify with the owner classes, these middle-classes run society on behalf of capitalist interests. Capitalists *do not* have the unquestioned right to their inherited wealth, luxurious lifestyles, or inexpensive laborers to boss around. Class domination results in negative consequences for those in the lowest class strata, consequences ranging from exhaustion and alienation to ill-health and low self-esteem. Yet, it is not just the working classes who suffer under capitalism—although they clearly suffer *most*—since class domination also creates desperation, jealousy, property crimes, and other phenomena that adversely affect everyone in society.

While class societies are often legitimated by myths of class mobility, it is very debatable how much mobility actually exists, how regular such mobility is, and whether existent mobility improves the overall state of affairs for all in a society. Mobility is usually aided by various forms of capital (economic, social, or cultural). But, since capital is monopolized by those who are already at the top of the class hierarchy, the wealthy can transmit capital to their children and thereby recreate class hierarchy.

Capitalism is premised upon having workers under the control of managers and owners. Whether these workers are in the same society, or live overseas, some group must be in a disadvantaged position, thus experiencing a lack of empowerment, efficacy, autonomy, and self-management. Tinkering with symptoms like class inequality without addressing capitalism is bound to be a still-born or failing endeavor. Also, debate about the

---

[5] We encourage others to extend this analysis to geographically- and culturally-variant conditions.

extent of a society's class mobility is largely a shell-game. Consequently, efforts like improving mobility, forming business unions and collective bargaining units, social welfare programs administered by the state, or progressive taxation of the wealthy do not change the fundamental relationships in capitalism between upper-, middle-, and working-classes. Anarchists have been very forthright with their demand for working-class power, by any means necessary, especially insofar as these efforts further the dismantling of capitalism. The labor movement has been the phenomenon to most seriously and vigilantly challenge capitalism, particularly through the mass actions of workers and their allies, using a variety of tactics ranging from protest and strikes to sabotage and factory seizures.

Ultimately, class inequality can only be eliminated by removing the hierarchical relationships between classes, not just creating maximum and minimum wage laws, or allowing workers and managers the chance to sit-down at a table to discuss grievances. Instead, workers need to control not only the means of production, but also the decision-making apparatus necessary to work. This emphasis differentiates anarchists from social-democrats' efforts to narrow wage differentials, state socialist systems that collectivize productive power and give control to bureaucrats or technicians, and unionists that seek greater say in the workplace without possessing ultimate ownership of their efforts.

Class inequality not only involves unequal power relations between owners, management, and workers, but also union bureaucracy, government regulators, and all others who can intervene within the workplace. If politicians, party officials, specialists, or union officials are in the position to make decisions on behalf of workers, then workers cannot completely and directly control the things that matter greatly to the lived experience of class inequality. However, this does not foreclose the principal ways in which workers have traditionally used the labor movement to gain political and economic power in the past—through syndicalist unions democratically-run by all members. Anarcho-syndicalism has been the radical response to the problems of capitalism for working people seeking to express cross-industry solidarity, manage their own labor, and remain autonomous from both their [soon to be former] bosses and parasitic union leadership (Schmidt and van der Walt 2009).

Anarchists have also tended to reject any work done for the benefit of authority figures. Consequently, in a capitalist society, anarchists desire freedom from the necessity to "work." The motivation to work in capitalist society is not for creativity, self-expression, or joy, but survival—people need money in order to buy food in order to live (etcetera). Work is forced upon people and anarchists have often advocated "zero-work" beyond that immediately necessary to survive or that done for creative, community-building. In this zero-work conception of anarchism (expressed most eloquently by Bob Black's *The Abolition of Work*), class *mobility within* the capitalist system is less desirable than *autonomy from* the entire class system. True worker self-management is achieved by being able to choose whether one labors or not, for whom, and how.

Gender

Inequalities between men and women predate class inequalities, as they are rooted in the multiple millennia-old institution of patriarchy (literally: father rule). Power is derived from sexual relationships and gendered roles. Here, hierarchy is ordered in a way as to benefit men over women, elder men over younger men, and heteronormative performance over non-heterosexual behavior. Anarchists recognize that, like all other forms of social domination, these arrangements are not biologically-determined, but created by unequal interactions between those with and without power in human societies. Many past societies have had more egalitarian social orders between sexes, illustrating that the present order can be changed by human initiative and struggle.

Gender is the socially-constructed characteristics attached to perceived biological sex that lead males to be socialized in a masculine fashion and females to be socialized in a feminine fashion. In Western, industrialized societies these forms of gender socialization help to exaggerate any meaningful biological differences (the main differences pertaining to reproduction, average size, etc.) and justify unequal behavioral patterns. It is perfectly possible for men to adopt so-called "feminine" characteristics and be compassionate, nurturing, and sociable. In fact, anarchists suggest that one way to improve the level of mutual aid, cooperation, and solidarity is to emphasize these traits over the competitive, aggressive, and dominating traits of masculinity. Men are clearly capable of such preferable behaviors, but are socialized to act in ways that perpetuate a variety of forms of domination. Other supposedly "masculine" characteristics like bravery or courage are appropriate for all people, and are obviously not only held by men.

Beyond the gender inequality created by patriarchy, the very categories of female and male, feminine and masculine are socially-constructed. Patriarchy—along with heteronormativity—compels doctors and parents to force children into one sex or gender category of the other. Especially in the case of children with sex ambiguous characteristics, the drive is even more aggressive to clearly emphasize—through surgery or performance—one binary position over the other. Patriarchy thus serves to subjugate transsexuals, transgender people, and even those with more "normative" attributes to standards that force individuals into predetermined acceptable behaviors and identities. Heteronormativity is not a subset of patriarchy, but a somewhat autonomous institution, although a sibling-instantiation, of sex/gender/sexuality domination.

Domination results in negative consequences for women and female-bodied people, such as a taken-for-granted-ness, sexual abuse and rape, and objectification. But, gender domination also impacts men and the broader society, too, especially through widespread machismo and violence. Gender inequality manifests itself in numerous realms. Perhaps the most intimate domain is the family, where there are clearly gendered roles that hold women accountable for the majority of housework and child-rearing. Patriarchy also enables men to be in greater control over family resources and thus to make major strategic decisions independent of women's input. Gender domination is a major factor within amorous relationships, witnessed by domestic battery, sexual assault, rape, and other forms of sexual manipulation and control that men wield over women—again due to their gendered socialization, greater resources, independence, and physical size. Men do not have an inherent right to unrestricted sexual access to women, or the right to free house-cleaners, cooks, and babysitters.

Outside of the family and domestic sphere, gender inequality disadvantages women in the workplace as they are relegated to low-ranking jobs where they do "female-gendered" work that is less well-paid, creative, and under their own control. Culturally, women are regularly viewed as the sole figures responsible for child care. And, due to their "feminine" characteristics, women find themselves the subject of paternalism where men speak and act on their behalf.

Unlike the sociological ideas of class mobility, there is no real upward mobility for women in society, except as a result of the in-roads made by the liberal feminist movement. Also, unlike Marxian views of class revolution, overturning the gender hierarchy to establish women on top and men on the bottom does not produce a desirable outcome. Anarchists and feminists have been clear advocates of removing barriers between men and women, empowering women to exercise more self-determination, and blocking the avenues by which men may dominate. Plainly put: anarchists do not advocate merely eliminating male privileges, but expanding the realm of freedom to include female participation in and possession of those privileges. By doing so, the range of freedom does not merely increase, but also changes character to include freedom that tolerates others, enables cooperation and solidarity, and reduces the potential for power over others. Pro-feminist men are important allies in the struggle for greater gender equality in so far as they defect from male privilege. But, equally important is the need for women to openly embrace radical feminist consciousness, not only by witnessing their own subjugation to patriarchy and how inaction perpetuates it, but also the empowerment gained by assuming a feminist identity. However, feminism is not enough to end gender domination, especially if feminism is only liberal in character and premised upon women having equal representation in other hierarchical institutions like capitalism or the state. To exist within such institutions founded upon hierarchy and domination, women must usually adopt masculine traits of domination, competition, and aggression. A greater presence of women within hierarchies does not achieve true gender equality, nor liberation. Having a woman president or CEO does not change the fundamental nature of the hierarchical state or corporation.

Race

Racial inequality results from the exercise of racially-determined power—in many contemporary societies this indicates a hierarchy based upon White supremacy. Race is understood to be the artificially-created categories based upon perceived (and supposed) biological differences between groups of people. These categories are actually socially-constructed and have little to do with genetics (despite popular belief). Consequently, "race" is a fluid idea and has more to do with prevailing arrangements of power than with any substantive differences. For example, in the United States, race has been legally-created to offer privileges (political, economic, and social) to some people and not others. The state—through legislation and court decisions—has created one group ("Whites") as a superior group, benefiting from the best access to political power, property ownership, legal protection, social status, and so forth. At the same time, other groups—namely Native Americans and African slaves—were denied access to these resources, as were most incoming immigrant groups. Race is premised upon the hierarchical institution of White supremacy, which creates a steep strata of races, with White Protestants at the top. Yet, this arrangement is no more "god-given," natural, or inevitable than class or gender hierarchies—as changing legal interpretations of racial categories has clearly shown (López 1996).

While "race" describes artificially propped-up dimensions, it still has a real-world salience. Racial minorities, although not in any way inherently inferior, have received fewer privileges in all societies than have dominant races. Specifically, White supremacy results in negative consequences for individual racial minorities, including shame, targeted profiling, and fewer life chances.

The problems of White supremacy are considered by anarchists to be wider than just "racism" (prejudicial attitudes of superiority by dominant group members). Individual racists are—on the whole—rather insignificant in comparison to massive, institutionalized racism. Therefore, a true analysis of racial inequality would have to include all the institutions that perpetuate racial inequality: housing markets, the "criminal justice system" (aka "deviance response processes"), law enforcement, exploitative corporations, government policies, etc. Even during modern times where supposed "civil rights" exist in law books, there is *de facto* racism and racial inequality rooted in centuries of past discriminatory practices. Racist ideologies perpetuate many of these practices and help to justify inequality as somehow the "natural" consequence of minority stupidity, laziness, or ineptitude. In actual fact, White supremacy is the villain that creates racial inequality.

Minority groups deserve racial autonomy from dominant groups, whether through increased collective power, broadened rights and freedoms, or through independence (in a cultural, spatial, or political sense). To the extent that conditions and experiences have improved for minorities, it has only been through the in-roads created by anti-racist and civil-rights movements (which include national liberation organizations). The individual mobility of a few individual minority group members is not heralded by anarchists as an end to White supremacy or racial inequality, but merely as evidence demonstrating the flexibility of capitalism and the state. In the end, collective struggle in movements is the true means of eliminating White supremacy, whether through race-conscious education and action, or through racial disobedience or race riots.

Ultimately, these three forms of inequality and domination could be expanded to other categories, such as ability, age, sexual orientation, and others. In countries outside of the United States, inequality may rest upon still other factors, such as religion, nationality or citizenship, language, indigenous status, region of residence, caste, or any of an increasingly wide array of factors. Regardless of the form of domination, how are we to understand and study the broader phenomenon in societies?

The Analysis of Domination

The first analytical task for an anarchist-sociology is to distinguish between a plethora of varied, but closely related concepts, including authority, difference, disadvantage, discrimination, domination, exploitation, hierarchy, inequality, oppression, power, prejudice, privilege, stratification, and subordination. Regardless of the specific definition, the overall commonality to all these terms is the notion of *variation*, almost universally, variation that separates people into groups that lead more enjoyable, comfortable, self-managed, and commanding lives, and groups that do not. While all of the above terms are important to both sociologists and anarchists, we will focus below on the nuances between inequality and dominance.

We argue that inequality, the everyday subject matter of sociology—really its analytical "bread-and-butter"—is actually the result or symptom of other phenomena, namely relationships of domination. For example, status inequality often stems from the domination that professionals have over so-called "non-skilled" occupations. Power inequality derives from the domination of elected "representatives" over civilians and the masses. And hierarchy is the crucible that molds relationships of domination. The ordered, ranks of command and obedience synonymous with hierarchy can be found in all sorts of organizations and structures throughout most societies. Hierarchies of corporations, religions, families, non-profit organizations, schools and universities, armies, and states often straightforwardly and unambiguously define and create the relationships of domination that lead to social inequalities. Thus, anarchists seeking to eliminate class inequality do not aspire to simply raise the poorest workers' paltry wages, but instead target domination in the workplace and the larger hierarchy of capitalism. A simplistic model that explains the generation of these phenomena is presented in Figure 1 below.

To more fully understand the role domination has in generating inequality, it is important to appreciate its complexity. Domination is not a simple or standard phenomenon. In fact, domination can take many forms and can be practiced by many different types of actors. Individuals can dominate others using their greater strength or resources (e.g. muscular people or the rich). Individuals who reside in certain positions or occupations can dominate others (e.g. military generals, managers at factories, border patrol guards, government bureaucrats). Organizations and institutions can dominate (e.g. police squads, schools, private corporations, patriarchy).

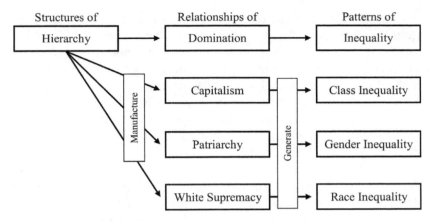

Figure 1. Processes of domination and inequality.

Formal and informal policies can dominate others depending on who is targeted, how policies are enforced, and how sanctions are meted out (e.g. Jim Crow segregation, conscription laws). Normative practices of society can dominate those who are disadvantaged (e.g. rituals of avoidance between unequal parties; see Graeber 2007). Thus, random individuals, as well as the institutions and organizations—that include individuals who reside in certain positions and carry out policies, and create normative practices—all may manifest dominating behaviors and patterns.

Structurally, multiple hierarchies regularly interact with each other, creating an "interlocking" quality. Thus, a mother does not only face the domination of patriarchal behaviors, attitudes, and interactions as a woman, but also the capitalist mandate to work in order to earn "a living" and provide for her children since everything in society has a monetary value and is not free for her to use. Or, immigrants regularly must deal with their outsider racial or ethnic status in the face of White supremacy (or other forms of racism, depending on the societal context), as well as the threat of state capture and violence if they are caught violating a law (or even crossing a border). In other words, inequality results from multiple forms of hierarchical domination and the multi-dimensional character of these forms add layers of disadvantage, restraint, and punishment upon those who find themselves at the bottom of such hierarchies.

The systems of interlocking domination have not always looked the same, nor have they involved a static hierarchy. Institutions and their resultant patterns change. Historical examples of institutions and positions that have existed as centers of power—but which would seem foreign and strange to many today—include pharaohs, conquistadors, industrialists, aristocrats, warlords, chieftains, plantation owners, kings, mafia dons, socialist party leaders, technocratic experts, army captains, emperors, and tax-collectors. The range is very broad, but each assumes localized flavors based in spatial and temporal conditions.

Domination also varies depending on the scale of analysis. Thus, depending on the level that one looks, unequal relationships may be different or be rooted in completely different stratification systems. For example, on a macro-level of major institutions, there are relations of domination between a political ruling class and citizens, owners and workers, cultural icons and everyday people, or religious leaders and laity. Within the meso-level, there is often restricted access to organization membership and resources, as well as privileged positions within organizations. Micro-level, individual relationships can vary between older and younger, husband and wife. Within micro-level situations or interactions, there is inequality between the experienced and the new, extrovert and introvert, or the bully and meek.

Curiously, in many stratification systems, even dominators have obligations. For example, according to Weber (1978), *noblesse oblige* mandated that feudal lords protect serfs from external threats (e.g. invasion). Likewise, patriarchs must provide for families. Police must, in most societies, also "help" people, too (of course the regularity of such practices may vary). Additionally, consistent hostility is not necessarily guaranteed between the dominated and dominator. Slave and slave-master, or worker and boss may even develop "friendly" relationships. But neither obligation nor politeness changes the domination inherent in these relationships, not does it mean that those in positions of dominators are themselves "oppressed" by their obligations. Dominators may even complain about those under their yolk for not appreciating them. Anarchism argues that the ultimate obligation for a dominator who cares about "their" oppressed, is to free them from their subjugated positions.

Additionally, embedded in all relations of domination is a dialectical need that each position has for the other. Consider any such relationship centered on different forms of power. For example, consider the power of parents over children, police over citizens, boss over worker, celebrities over the un-famous, officials over voters, officers over soldiers, clergy over laity, experts over the unskilled, or teachers over students. In each, those in the dominated position (less power) often need or identify with those in the dominant position (more power). Sometimes the whole reason why they are in the subordinated position is due to this need (e.g. children need parental protection and other necessities, laity seek religious guidance, voters want leaders, the unskilled want help, or students require knowledge), whether perceived or real. Consequently, this results in patterns of dependency or identification with one's dominators. Yet, the reverse is true of the dominators: their position of privilege is premised upon needing the presence of those they dominate. Without subordinated workers there are no bosses, if the un-famous do not watch-out for "greatness" there can be no celebrities, elected officials need voters to put them there, and teachers need students to listen to them. Dominators perceive themselves to be indispensable and may construct an identity for themselves based upon their position of privilege (in respect to others) rather than based on their own intrinsic characteristics. Thus, the very relationship of domination creates adherents who need the unequal relationship to define themselves by. This need illustrates some of the formidable challenges in convincing people to avoid, undermine, or overturn domination.

Hierarchy does not necessarily imply a simple analysis, either, dialectical or otherwise. Just having power (via money, force, and solidarity forms) does not necessarily mean that one's will can easily be achieved (Collins 1992). There are multiple restraints on unbridled violence, coercion, bribery, etc. Efficiency and obedience suffers in the end, and thus authority figures do not benefit from repeatedly and fully exercising their power. Often force must merely remain a possibility that others are aware of or fear. Still, if the powerful have the capacity to exercise this authority, then it creates or reifies relations of domination and will cause the disadvantaged to modify their behaviors and aspirations.

Not only are hierarchical institutions responsible for creating domination and inequality, but the inter-personal relationships and situational rituals regularly performed replicate inequality. For example, everyday conversations reinforce and reassure people of the morality and correctness of inequality, and thus the unnecessity of challenging social norms (see Chapter 7). These domination-perpetuating patterns can also be found within radical collectives (even amongst anarchists) that aim to do away with formal mechanisms of inequality along the lines of class, gender, or race. Hierarchical practices, dynamics, or characteristics exist here, even with prohibitions against such forms of discrimination. Informal hierarchies may exist or emerge in the absence of formal mechanisms for power-sharing (Freeman 2002). Or insider cliques of people who all know each other may keep at others at the periphery—or make them to feel like they are unwelcome or that their ideas are unworthy. Those experienced with collective decision-making process are more able assert themselves than the inexperienced, as are those who are loud, extroverted, and politically-suave. Even the time constraints placed upon meeting length and decision-making can create rushed decisions that may cause deference towards some participants. Mansbridge (1979) found evidence for these patterns, especially based upon human capital like education and class level: members with working-class parents were significantly less likely to report that they had "high power" in activist cooperatives or satisfaction in organizational decisions. Education level was also positively correlated with satisfaction regarding organizational decisions (thus greater education predicted more satisfaction). All of these dynamics demonstrate some of the challenges involved in eliminating forms of domination, even in organizations that are ideologically committed to such a mission. Yet, it is one thing to be aware of such problems and a completely different matter to formulate strategies to end domination, as anarchists aspire to do.

Against the Mere Study of Domination

Anarchist-sociologists argue that domination and inequality should not just be studied, but also actively opposed. Study is (maybe) a good first step, but then domination must be reacted and responded to. Large numbers of sociologists share this position, too (e.g. so-called "public sociologists"). The world-renowned academic linguist (and anarchist) Noam Chomsky (2005) discusses how such a critique must be followed by action:

> I think it only makes sense to *seek out and identify structures of authority, hierarchy, and domination in every aspect of life, and to challenge them*; unless a justification for them can be given, they are illegitimate, and should be dismantled, to increase the scope of human freedom. That includes political power, ownership and management, relations among men and women, parents and children, our control over the fate of future generations (the basic moral imperative behind the environmental movement, in my view), and much else. Naturally this means a challenge to the huge institutions of coercion and control: the state, the unaccountable private tyrannies that control most of the domestic and international economy, and so on. But not only these. That is what I have always understood to be the essence of anarchism: the conviction that the burden of proof has to be placed on authority, and that *it should be dismantled if that burden cannot be met*. (178, emphasis added)

Thus, according to Chomsky, the task is to first understand domination and inequality and then do away with their manifestations. Anarchist-sociology is interested in the study *and* transformation of society.

But, what is problematic with pure study, which is the usual endpoint for most sociologists? Studying inequality (and those who are dominated) turns the phenomenon (and the people affected by it) into *objects* of inquiry, thus abstracting and fetishizing the dominated and their needs. The distance implicit in research (with the exception, maybe, of militant ethnographic research methods) creates a crucial disjunction, and further dominates the dominated and privileges the already privileged.

Scholarship feeds the career of academics and policy-makers—thus keeping hierarchical systems like universities and governmental agencies humming along without challenge. Research is conducted in such a fashion that it serves the interests of academics' careers. The placement of articles in academic journals or presentation at conferences does little to reach those most immediately impacted by hierarchy and domination. In fact, most research exaggerates that social distance, not only in the forum chosen, but also the esoteric and jargon-laden delivery. Even if such research could have liberatory potential for the dominated, it cannot reach them (especially in an unfiltered form) as it is sequestered away in the archives of the Ivory Tower (Martin 1998b).

Dominated people need ammunition in their hands to fight back against oppressive power and hierarchy. Research on inequality and injustice can provide this firepower, but who will wield the weapons? To the extent that research is used at all, the traditional scholarly peer-review process within the world of academic journals has tended to only further enable the agency of politicians, policy-makers, and bureaucrats. According to Saul Alinsky (1972), the father of modern community organizing (and a once-aspiring sociologist), speaks to this troubling and lop-sided disconnect:

> As an undergraduate, I took a lot of courses in sociology, and I was astounded by all the horse manure they were handing out about poverty and slums, playing down the suffering and deprivation, glossing over the misery and despair. I mean, Christ, I'd lived in a slum, I could see through all their complacent academic jargon to the realities. It was at that time that I developed a deep suspicion of academicians in general and sociologists in particular, with a few notable exceptions.... So I realized how far removed the self-styled social sciences are from the realities of everyday existence, which is particularly unfortunate today, because that tribe of head-counters has an inordinate influence on our so-called antipoverty program. Asking a sociologist to solve a problem is like prescribing an enema for diarrhea. (para. 1–2)

Who determines what weapons should be available and how useful or lib-eratory they should be? Presently, the isolated researcher, operating within the confines of academia and only influenced by peers, makes these deci-sions. The resources, intellectual toolkits, and expertise are generally not made available to dominated communities; when studied, the dominated usually find themselves to be research objects poked and probed in ways they do not necessarily control, value, or benefit from.

So, who should use research findings to oppose inequality and how should that opposition be manifested? Should non-dominated indi-viduals (e.g. straight, White middle-class men) be advocates or spokesper-sons for dominated groups? How about academics who are themselves members of disadvantaged groups? How exactly should any academics contribute and in what ways? When academics attempt to answer this question—as we are presently trying to do—we exercise not only our privileged positions, but also impose our own preferences, world-views, and biases.

These issues are important since they inform the question of who ought to act to eliminate inequality. Anarchists strongly claim that people must be active agents in their own liberation. Consequently, the liberal claim that the welfare state will help the poor is not just troublesome, but incor-rect. When the state acts it is taking away the important, empowering experience that the poor could—and should—be having. The state is not necessarily acting how the poor would choose to. There is also ample evidence (e.g. Piven and Cloward 1993) suggesting that social welfare policies—even if well-intended (itself debatable)—serve to squelch revo-lutionary action and social disorder that could overturn hierarchical insti-tutions. Once rebellious disruption diminishes, the welfare state retracts its "generous" assistance, thrusting the disadvantaged back into a position of austerity and want.

While assistance to the disadvantaged from well-read and researched state, technocratic, and intellectual figures can be perhaps helpful in the immediacy, it has negative long-term consequences. According to anar-chist theory, saviors should not be trusted (or at least *entrusted* with one's future). One needs to save oneself. Even "altruistic" saviors—such as char-ismatic social movement leaders—are problematic as they rob people of their autonomy, confidence, experiences, and right to rebel. Instead, anar-chism argues for the immediate and direct action of the disadvantaged to oppose domination and inequality, action that does not rely on authority to create a more equal and just society. Authority figures who can hierar-chically grant assistance create new forms of inequality; according to anarchism, one form of authority should not replace another (even if they represent a more benign and "kind" form).

The capacities of the folks at the bottom of the pile should not be over-looked or discounted. Academic viewpoints often diminish the agency of the disadvantaged, and instead present such people as objects in need of improvement. The fundamental problem with this view is that many people know full-well they are in positions of domination: it does not take advanced education to be aware that one has a boss, is at risk of dispropor-tionate violence from certain people around them or police, or that one is subject to laws made by politicians. Indeed, disadvantaged peoples often know they are being dominated and actively utilize their agency (however limited) to rectify their situation. In particular, "organic intellectuals" and grassroots activists who are members of disadvantaged communities already "get it." Even though some acts originating from these communi-ties may sometimes be piecemeal or individualist in nature, they are no less important or meaningful than the acts of benevolent scholars of inequality.

Anarchist Strategies to Eliminate Domination

If domination and inequality are not just curious subjects of study, but actually concrete problems warranting solutions, then what do anarchists propose be done about them? As opposed to a mere analytical philosophy, anarchism is also a practical framework for taking action. However, anar-chist praxis does not lead to mass prescriptions, nor recommend a "one size fits all" model for overcoming domination. Instead, anarchists suggest key values—autonomy, mutual aid, solidarity, anti-authoritarianism, self-management, etc.—that can provide the means to both justice and free-dom. Anarchists also work with disadvantaged groups to aid them in their conflicts with hierarchy. There are a number of key approaches that anar-chists pursue in this quest: propaganda, collective struggle, organizational examples, and dual power.

Propaganda is designed to openly challenge authority and to provoke dialogue with a dominated population. This challenge puts authority fig-ures "on notice," forcing them to either fulfill anarchist's critique of them by continuing their domination or to change in order to retain their legiti-macy. Propaganda is a way to inform people—via a succinct, compelling medium—that there is a problem worthy of attention and response. Thus, propaganda serves an "educational" function, which even if only successful at impacting isolated individuals, can still be transformative for such folks. Also, an anti-authoritarian spirit of rebellion is manifested in anarchist propaganda. This rebelliousness seeks to empower those in disadvantaged positions in society and to let them know they are not alone in their conditions and struggle. If propaganda is widespread, people may believe there is a growing trend toward change emerging, thus raising their expectations and radicalizing demands. The dialogue that emerges between anarchist propaganda and dominated populations helps to circulate and rejuvenate radical ideas. Without such ideas in circulation, people have to rediscover them on their own, which is very challenging in a mainstream of doctrinaire media and schooling. If radical ideas are brought to wider audiences, the interest in social change may be heightened thus causing greater challenge to the systems of domination in a given society.

Once anarchist ideas have taken root in individuals, collective action is possible. The adoption of propaganda by individuals is often enhanced by consciousness-raising, where people figure out their place in a stratification system, alongside other participants (which we referred to as the "anarchist imagination" in Chapter 1). This shared experience leads people to consider future courses of action. For example, mass protest is a mutually-reinforcing activity that helps people to know they are not isolated in their disadvantaged positions. People can shake their fists, express anger, and gain confidence in the process. Direct action not only "gets the goods" (as the Industrial Workers of the World used to say), but allows people to learn more about how the intricacies of domination work within the institutions they fight as well as inequalities that may emerge in their own communities of resistance. Collective struggle serves as experiential learning that helps people to develop skills and acquire the knowledge that inequality can be lessened and domination overthrown. Through collective action, people can develop their own collaborative solutions to domination.

Collective struggle has taken countless forms within anarchism. Many organizations clearly define goals targeting inequality. Anarchists frame inequality as an important target in the struggle for liberation. To take a random example, the Burning River Revolutionary Anarchist Collective (BRRAC) of Cleveland, Ohio declared their opposition to capitalism, the nation-state, the oppression of women, white supremacy, and heterosexism (among other things). BRRAC articulated strategies of collective struggle, including self-defense, dual power (to be described below), criticism/self-criticism, and solidarity (BRRAC 2002). Other organizations also utilize similar "intersectional" critiques of domination.

A variety of "anarchistic franchise organizations" (AFOs)—anarchist inspired groupings with the same name, yet no centralized coordination—are premised upon redressing inequality and overcoming domination through direct action empowerment. AFOs like Food Not Bombs, Anti-Racist Action, Anarchist People of Color, and Bash Back!. Each organization focuses upon at least one form of domination, as viewed through a prefigurative practice. Thus, Food Not Bombs targets some of the most severe symptoms of capitalism—homelessness, poverty, hunger—and addresses these ills by sharing free food with housing-insecure people. Both Anti-Racist Action (ARA) and Anarchist People of Color (APOC) critique White supremacy as a major problem that leads to police brutality, fascist organizing, and even racism internal to radical movements. ARA and APOC have embraced and integrated an intersectional analysis to their original critique based on racial hierarchy, by adding support for radical feminist critiques of patriarchy and heterosexism. ARA practices confrontational strategies—usually in the streets—while APOC organizes to create a free space within the anarchist movement for anarchists who are members of disadvantaged groups and who experience a variety of forms of discrimination. Last, a new AFO called Bash Back! (BB!) composed of anti-authoritarian transgender and queer activists critiques and acts against not just heteronormativity and heterosexism in mainstream society, but also what BB! calls an "assimilation strategy" by the reform-oriented gay rights movement.

One final anarchist strategy for eliminating domination is through the creation of "dual power." Originally coined by Lenin, anarchists have broadened dual power to refer to deliberate attempts to challenge hierarchical power through the meaningful creation of egalitarian social organizations that can substitute for hierarchical forms of organization. For example, instead of having political policies created by national bodies of wealthy, elected officials, decisions could be crafted by directly democratic neighborhood assemblies. Or, instead of the provision of food by large agribusiness corporations and chain supermarkets, people could create vast networks of food co-operatives, community-supported agricultures, and community gardens. If an alternative gains enough momentum and share within a society compared to a hierarchical institution with comparable provisions, then a situation of "dual power" has been reached. In this situation, the alternative is ideally positioned to overtake the ultimately less efficient, less democratic, and less just version, thereby saturating society with the more egalitarian alternative. According to Mumm (1998), anarchist dual power strategy involves community organizing and popular education, as well as the founding of viable alternative economic projects and other institutions.

All of these strategies for eliminating domination present a uniquely anarchist vision, especially dual power. Paul Goodman wrote "A free society cannot be the substitution of a "new order" for the old order; it is the extension of spheres of free action until they make up most of social life" (quoted in Ward 1996: 18). Thus, the process of revolution is unlikely to be a spontaneous throwing off of all forms of domination by disadvantaged groups, but rather the somewhat incremental (although clearly rebellious) proliferation and expansion of pockets of freedom. If the social norms backing major institutions can be modified (see Chapter 7 for more on this), and the form and practice of these institutions changed, egalitarian relations can become the insurgent standard. Dual power is seen as a way to force the state (and other hierarchical institutions) to either enact progressive reform to improve people's lives and self-determination or to eventually "wither away" in the face of grassroots alternatives founded upon cooperation, horizontalism, and egalitarianism.

Dialectical Challenges to Progress

These strategies struggle with a number of dialectical challenges, which are not easily resolved by change agents. First, the strategic issue of reform versus revolution. Should one apply considerable effort in a local matter of social injustice that may have only a limited scope of impact (even if a successful campaign), or channel energy into building for long-term and more radical change? While the latter is ultimately more desirable, to ignore the former conflicts risks the possibility of losing ground in an already imbalanced playing field of injustice, as well as missing the opportunity to engage with folks in day-to-day struggle on big-picture, revolutionary ideas. Put another way, this dialectic involves the contradictions between reactive politics and prefigurative politics. Anarchists warn that people ignore immediate struggles to their own detriment, but also caution against the trappings of reformism and the exhaustion induced by treading water. While always cognizant of the need to stop on-going domination (e.g. the so-called "social problems" emphasized by sociologists), anarchist-sociologists argue for the importance of also focusing upon how such forms of domination could be avoided in the future.[6]

---

[6] Or, as one activist puts it: "Let's take time to sit-down together with our colored-pens and crayons to draw-out our vision!"

A second dialectic challenge is posed by the reactions to past domination and atrocity: consolation versus reconciliation. It is important for dominated peoples to be comfortable in the present, to have apologies for past wrongs, and to have the sympathies of others for their plight. For instance, the consolation extended by the US government for its genocidal actions (which was not put in such strong—or accurate—language, of course) against indigenous peoples is good and meaningful. But is it "enough"? Does it constitute justice? Does it help indigenous peoples in any substantial way? As the saying goes, "talk is cheap." Sometimes an "apology" is a rather bad outcome, since it gives the illusion that an unjust situation has been rectified; i.e. "What is their problem? We already apologized for all that stuff from the past!" Barring the outcome of dramatic separation—which is unlikely for most disadvantaged groups, particularly for women from men—dominated peoples should be able (if they choose) to live with or alongside their [hopefully, former] dominators. If the crimes of past atrocity (e.g. slavery, relocation, or forced sterilization) or the hopefully soon-to-be-ended crimes (e.g. class exploitation, sexual violence, or discrimination) can put an end to the disadvantaged position of the dominated, does that truly solve their problems? Domination tends to leave a residue, which creates a multi-generational disadvantage that needs to be intervened upon. Consider the example of South Africa's formal efforts in the aftermath of Apartheid: a "truth and reconciliation" committee investigated past crimes and sought ways to bring victim and perpetrator together, not unlike restorative justice aims to do (as discussed previously in Chapter 5).

Lastly, there is a strategic, dialectical conundrum posed by the complex sources of hierarchy's power. Hierarchies are premised upon legal rules, social tradition, and unreflective practice. Yet, the easiest way to "attack" a hierarchy is on moral grounds: it is unethical, wrong, and unjust. In fact, such a moral argument is often not difficult to make and even get quick agreement from others (even people who may benefit from such hierarchies). The immoral basis of hierarchy is likely the easiest claim to make, and, consequently, the least effective. Surely it is necessary to eliminate support for the values that undergird hierarchy, but this alone does not undo hierarchy's power. Removing the legal structures to hierarchy is a formidable challenge and even more difficult if no ethical claim has been made against these structures. Tradition can be changed, but it takes dedicated efforts to shift cultural priorities and to reconfigure socialization. And, it is very possible—especially in the midst of great bureaucracies—for a scary inertia to take hold and for immoral acts to continue even in the absence of moral argument for them (witness the *de jure* illegality of racial discrimination in the United States, which exists alongside commonplace, *de facto* discrimination). Although hierarchy is often depicted as a ladder or a pyramid, it is not as easily undone as pushing over a ladder or detonating a pyramid with dynamite (especially via mere moralizing). Hierarchy's complexity aids its staying-power, and provides great challenge to anarchists and others who aim to ultimately up-end it. The inertia of hierarchical norms helps to perpetuate such domination, as well as inhibits efforts to eliminate domination, a topic explored next in Chapter 7.

CHAPTER SEVEN

VIOLATING NORMS, RE-SOCIALIZING SOCIETY

Introduction

Despite the best intentions and efforts of revolutionaries, revolution is difficult and atypical. Even "successful" revolutions seem to eventually relapse into hierarchy. This raises some important questions about the impediments to social revolution. What restrains most members of society from fomenting and joining revolutions, or even having an interest in such rare occurrences? What causes counter-revolutionary tendencies to rear their heads after revolutionary situations emerge?

The macro-level changes that accompanies revolution—economic, political, cultural—are important structural considerations. Revolutionaries attempt to change the conditions under which people work and produce, make decisions and cooperate, and reflect values and ways of living. While these are all important transformations, it is equally necessary to appreciate how major institutions are also "constructed" by people's everyday actions. For example, worker self-management is not merely declared by radical unionists, but also enacted by worker's actions on a day-to-day basis, negotiating tasks, hours, and protocols. Norms are the guidelines that help people execute their roles within organizations, interact with each other, and carry-on their lives. Without norms to suggest the most conducive behavior in a given situation, chaos would result. But, what sorts of norms exist and are followed: those that reinforce domination and order-following, or norms that facilitate anti-authoritarianism and mutual aid? We ought to appreciate the importance that these "taken-for-granted," shared understandings have for society and for revolution. This chapter employs the radical anarchist ideas of social order to analyze the systemic barriers to revolutionary transformation. As such, we synthesize anarchist and sociological ideas regarding norms, socialization, and social change.

Norms would be as integral to a revolutionary society as they are to the perpetuation of hierarchical society. Although norms may be roughly understood as social "rules," this should not be contradictory to anarchism. Rules are based on ideas and understandings, and are not necessarily "bad" according to anarchists if such rules are collectively agreed upon. In all likelihood, anarchists would positively evaluate rules that were collectively and democratically agreed-upon; traffic signs are an example, since those rules are not designed to discriminate against anyone who must obey such signs (although one could make a case that such discrimination may still occur). Another example is speaking only during one's turn in meetings and withholding one's additional comments until after everyone else in attendance has the opportunity to contribute. Ultimately, people rely heavily upon such guidelines, even if very informal, or shared understandings that can enable behavior that is respectful towards others' individuality. Anarchism—and other justice-oriented, liberatory movements—aim to help restructure society by changing norms. Therefore, for anarchists, it is less important and empowering, and shorter-lasting to merely protest and lobby for social change. As Catholic Worker founders and anarchists Peter Maurin and Dorothy Day were fond of saying: "we must make the kind of society in which it is easier for people to be good" (cited in Day 1954, 217).

This chapter grapples with some of the central issues related to norms, socialization, and revolutionary transformation, as seen through an anarchist-lens. We argue that social movements that struggle for revolutionary change will fall short unless the deep-seated issue of socialization to hierarchical norms is considered. To make this explicitly-anarchist case, we will use examples from Western societies, primarily (but not exclusively) the United States, although a comparable analysis could be formulated for many other culturally-distinct societies. First, we consider how norms play a role in reinforcing inequality and hierarchy, key anarchist concerns. Second, socialization in hierarchical societies tends to insure wide-spread adoption and adherence to norms by replicating norm-obedience. Third, many theoretical problems stem from practices that deviate from normative behavior, including the notion of rebellion and deviance. Fourth, we take into account some of the great challenges that impede the creation of less hierarchical norms. Finally, we summarize contemporary anarchist efforts to re-socialize people and present these current and potential activities as vital, revolutionary efforts.

Norms Reinforcing Inequality and Hierarchy

In *The Struggle to Be Human*, Tifft and Sullivan (1980) write: "In reality, the miseries of humankind cannot simply be laid at the statehouse doors of elites or mandarins, for we, our ideas and our constructed relationships, our acceptance of the hierarchy, are the state" (155). Put differently, we cannot simply blame others for all manner of abuse, violence, and social problems, but we must also consider our own role in perpetuating such things. Appreciating how all of our actions contribute to inequality and the perpetuation of hierarchy is an empowering step to overturning these norms throughout society.

Consider a popular, tongue-in-cheek slogan sometimes used by anti-authoritarians: "kill the cop inside your head!" This refers to curbing the very behaviors, ideas, values, or desires that, in other contexts, one might harshly decry. Removing authoritarianism from your own consciousness and actions is clearly a good start. But, authoritarian norms (police-like behavior, in this case) do not merely reside in us as individuals, but within the collective knowledge and practice of a society. Norms can prop-up those "miseries of humankind" just as norms are those very cops loitering in our heads. Thus, this metaphorical "cop" must also be killed within everyone else's head (or within "enough" people), too, in order to truly change society.

Not all norms are synonymous with the practice of law enforcement, though, and norms vary in terms of their revolutionary values. For example, they can be *bad*—deference to the powerful, husbands "speaking for" their wives, or bullying physically-weaker people for personal gain. Or some norms can be *good*—greetings of various kinds, empathy, or sharing excess possessions. An explicitly anarchist-sociology ought to pay attention to the creation and expansion of *better* norms, thus far only adhered to within certain radical sub-cultures—orientation towards collectivity, distrust of those in authority, "twinkling" (waggling fingers in agreement) during meetings, self-organizing into affinity groups prior to protests, or positive advocacy of efforts to foster social change. Norms of these various types saturate our social lives and are almost always invisible to members of a given culture or subculture, except when the norms are transgressed upon.

But, what exactly are norms? They include, but not are limited to, laws, conventions, morals, mores, folkways, customs, and rules. Norms can be understood by comparison to their etymological cousins: what is "normal," "normative," or "the norm." They refer to the generally taken-for-granted assumptions that guide everyday life. According to Gibbs (1965), a norm is a collective evaluation of behavior in terms of what it ought to be, a collective expectation of what behavior will be, and particular reactions to behavior, including attempts to apply sanctions or induce a particular kind of conduct. There are four noteworthy aspects of norms (Jasso and Opp 1997) that have bearing upon an anarchist critique. Although norms suggest a general uniformity within a society, the following aspects describe the ways in which norms may differ from each other.

According to Jasso and Opp (1997), the first aspect of norms is polarity. Do norms encourage or discourage behaviors? This aspect describes the terms in which a norm is socially framed. Prescriptive norms suggest which behaviors people should, must, or ought to do, such as being polite towards others or extending solidarity to those acting upon congruent values. Anarchists follow norms that mandate support for people resisting tyranny. Proscriptive norms indicate behaviors that one should not engage in, such as not interrupting others who are speaking or not treating some people better than others based on status. A hierarchical society is apt to have proscriptive norms controlling a wide-range of behaviors, while anarchist society would have these types of norms to the extent that regulated behavior would harm people and other lifeforms. The more restrictive a society, the more likely proscriptive norms are more plentiful and dominant.

A second aspect of norms is conditionality. Do norms hold under all circumstances? Anarchists argue that people of all social classes, groups, and statuses ought to be unconditionally treated the same. Treatment should not depend upon whether the other person is a neighbor, police officer, coworker, or president. However, in practice, anarchists *do* conditionally treat people differently—those with hierarchical positions of authority are routinely challenged, while mutual aid is offered to those lacking those same positions. A prominent, unconditional anarchist norm is that each individual ought to have the ultimate right to decide their own destiny or fate.

The third aspect of norms, according to Jasso and Opp, is intensity. To what degree do people subscribe to norms? For example, anarchists may practice "security culture" and not share activism details with outsiders (such as with other affinity groups or cells). This norm may not be strictly adhered to by everyone. Some people may share certain details with others or even foolishly divulge more details than they should, while others may not even mention their group's decisions and actions. With the norm of security culture, intensity varies considerably, especially on less sensitive, risky, or illegal activities. But, other anarchist norms are bound to be strictly adhered to: distrust of politicians or police, for example. Even anarchists who attempt to understand why authority figures say and do things, do not trust authority figures' motivations. Thus, anarchists intensely adhere to the norm of "distrust authority."

The last aspect of norms is consensus. Do all members of society share a norm? There is clearly great difference between anarchists and mainstream society in the area of consensus. For example, whether US Presidents should be revered and supported likely varies widely in a given population—thus there is no broad consensus about respecting, liking, or trusting politicians. There is usually less ambiguity and greater consensus regarding other matters such as child abuse, murder, and lying. All societal groups share a consensus in supporting proscriptive norms against these types of things. Taken together, these four aspects of norms summarize the different types of norms and the concerns involved in norm analysis.

Norms guide people's behaviors in situations so as to relieve them of having to stop and consider the consequences of their actions in every single situation and in every single moment. Consequently, norms simplify complex situations, but also routinize the status quo. By endorsing the status quo, norms perpetuate inequalities, without even drawing attention to domination. Thus, norms lead people to treat others unequally, even unconsciously. For example, people regularly treat the homeless as undeserving, people in a workplace give and take orders (depending on their position in the hierarchy), and others adopt and follow the official edicts of leaders. Or, in the words of the infamous American structural functionalist, Talcott Parsons (1968): "Soldiers should obey the orders of their commanding officers," ostensibly to fulfill military efficiency, "national security," and achieve "an end in itself" (75). Pro-status quo norms may not all be the deliberate creation of elites, but such norms tend to—at the very least—provide latent support for elites. Hurd (2005) attempts to describe the ways in which such hierarchies are perpetuated:

> ... people who invest social rules with hefty normative power work at lousy jobs, stay in lousy marriages, and permit themselves only the most conventional pursuits... And people who invest legal rules with an authority that out-distances the wisdom of those rules become complicit in the injustices perpetuated in the name of law." (75)

While this analysis appreciates the consequences of hierarchical norms, it also ignores the fact that laws are not held in-place by accidental foolishness, but by those with power and the acquiescence of those subjugated by such laws. But norms are broader than laws. If norms (and obedience to them) construct and replicate the unequal character of a society on a daily basis, then changing norms could change that society. Thus, introducing anarchist norms would be a revolutionary effort.

Norms are held in place by a complex of rewards and sanctions. First, proper adherence to hegemonic norms is rewarded by most societal members. Rewards provide positive affirmation, incentive, and approval for status quo norm adherence. External rewards may be the nodding support of bystanders, a raise in salary in the workplace, or verbal recognition for doing "what one is supposed to do." Internal rewards can include a positive feeling for doing what one should and the comfort of knowing your actions are approved by others. Second, deviance from accepted norms is usually met with various forms of sanctions. Non-normative behavior is subtly or unsubtly punished in order to rein-in that behavior to normative standards. For example, external sanctions can range from receiving dirty-looks and verbal criticism to physical confrontation, attack, and arrest. Internal sanctions may be the guilty feelings or shame one has when violating a norm. This complex of rewards and sanctions works to reward norm adherence and punish deviance. The consequence of this system is that most people tend to self-regulate their behaviors to receive rewards and avoid sanctions. Rewards and sanctions—whether regular occurrences or based on reputation—are apt to make norm-following the norm and make strong laws less necessary.

An Anarchist View of Norms

The prevalence of laws in a society may indicate the degree to which people are not trusted to self-regulate or the extent to which there is disagreement about proper behavior. According to Amster (2003), "external, written laws represents an abdication of the individual's capacity for moral self-direction and responsibility—an essential element of a social order without institutional coercion" (13). As such, anarchists and pro-justice movements should pursue a revolutionary, but non-law-based, social order. Norms are not simply codified in laws, but are *performed* in everyday life, just as Judith Butler considers gender to be a performance that most people unconsciously do (Butler 1990).[1] Consequently, it is crucial for people to become conscious about the social construction of norms and then voluntarily *choose* to perform differently, in order to modify the social order. But being reflexive about norms is not enough to constitute an anarchist strategy. Anarchists have advocated trusting people to develop *better* norms in times of need and revolutionary fervor, as Colin Ward has argued with his theory of "spontaneous order." People are more

---

[1] Also see West and Zimmerman's (1987) notion of "doing gender" as the regularized process of displaying and performing gender status.

apt to practice anti-authoritarian and egalitarian norms when "order" is not externally imposed upon them. Anarchistic social performance thus sees more intuitive, empowering, and productive norms as a priority in a future anarchist society (Ward 1996).

Norms take a variety of forms, each which may be non-law-based and range in terms of seriousness and rarity. First, taboos refer to any shocking act that is almost unheard of in a society—these acts may occur, but they are incredible rare and society harshly sanctions those who commit such acts. Common examples of taboos are incest and cannibalism. Second, mores are norms that are deeply rooted in a society's shared morals and value system. To violate a more is to transgress upon the commonly-held values of a society. For example, the norm against stealing or murder is a more.[2] Last, a folkway is a typical, less-severe norm that governs general and everyday actions. As the most routine type of norm, it is also the most regularly encountered and broken. Avoiding the violation of a taboo or more is something that most people do not and need not regularly consider. All of these three types of norms are sometimes codified into laws, but they need not be. These types of norms are sometimes fluid and may change given the situation, location, or personnel involved.

A dramatic change in the nature of present taboos, mores, and folkways is necessary to radically transform society. What are defined as these three types of norms would change accordingly. In an anarchist society norms that anarchists would consider to be unfortunate and semi-regular would be expected to almost disappear. For example, murder would be a taboo or nearly unheard of, since it would so deeply offend our sensibilities that it would not be tolerated. Also, the understanding of what is "ethical" would change to include stronger anarchist values. Thus, discrimination and domination would become violations of social mores, as opposed to behaviors typically *endorsed* by folkways. Finally, practices that are presently rare would become expected. Solidarity and mutual aid would be a folkway and a regular occurrence. Contradictory norms could and probably would exist from community-to-community, regarding behavior in a given situation, as anarchism suggests that people could define their own locally-relevant norms.

The quest of anarchists would likely be to differentiate between anarchist-compatible, "desirable" norms and non-anarchist, "undesirable" norms. At present, it is clear that many societal norms are premised upon

---

[2] Of course, exceptions are abound with norms. Murder may generally be a serious violation of a more, except during war, in self-defense, or sometimes in the case of revenge.

negative, anti-solidaritous relations. Paul Goodman (quoted in Stoehr 1994) wrote about the many hierarchical structures that anarchism aims to overturn and replace with other social arrangements and behaviors:

> Anarchism is grounded in a rather definite proposition: that valuable behavior occurs only by the free and direct response of individuals or voluntary groups to the conditions presented by the historical environment. It claims that in most human affairs, whether political, economic, military, religious, moral, pedagogic, or cultural, more harm than good results from coercion, top-down direction, central authority, bureaucracy, jails, conscription, states, pre-ordained standardization, excessive planning, etc. (13)

Thus, spreading "desirable norms" and reducing "undesirable norms" would require attacking, reducing, and hopefully eliminating all of those hierarchical institutions and norms, and building ways for people to be free, direct, and voluntary. For Proudhon, this meant creating norms of "justice" (Hall 1971). This is both a simple and not-so-simple matter; simple in that anyone can do this work to whatever degree they are capable, but not-so-simple because it eventually requires continuous and longer-term efforts to be successful. As Purchase (1994) writes, "Revolution is the result of billions upon billions of revolutionary actions by millions upon millions of separate people, all of whom are striving, however vaguely, toward a new social order" (153). In this view, revolution is not merely an abrasive disruption in society, but also a slow, tempered process. Consequently, some anarchists have used the term "evolutionary" change, sometimes combining it with revolution: "social r/evolution." The question of how desirable or undesirable norms come to eventually be respected in the first place is an important matter, one explained by the process of socialization.

Socialization: Creating and Reinforcing Adherence to Norms

Where do these norms come from and how are they created? Both questions may be addressed through one answer: socialization. Sociologists—and anarchists, for that matter—tend to assume that people are not born as monsters or altruists. Something must happen that will enable and foster some inclinations, while suppressing and stunting others. Socialization is the learning, training, and absorption of norms, values, and skills. Socialization is a process that happens throughout one's life and is conducted by influential "agents" who socialize people (e.g. family, peers, school, media, work). Some of this socialization is very formal and deliberate, as in schools, while other socialization is indirect—as with peers—where we adopt practices without having to be instructed to do so.

Unfortunately, socialization is not only pursued hierarchically, but it also creates hierarchical outcomes. Gordon (2007) sees the implicit hierarchy in this process: "Regimes of domination are the overarching context that anarchists see as conditioning people's socialization and background assumptions about social norms, explaining why people *fall into* certain patterns of behaviour and have expectations that contribute to the perpetuation of dominatory relationships" (38, emphasis in the original). For example, people are generally socialized to not view themselves as capable of solving their own problems and to thus become dependent upon "leaders." Consequently, people fall into the practice (thus supporting the norm) of putting faith in various leaders, like prime ministers, priests, and bosses. Although the quickest and most efficient solution might be personal or collective action, many people often seek to indirectly convince an authority figure to do something on their behalf. Socialization often emphasizes the importance of exercising *minimal* influence over the selection of these leaders (i.e. through voting, talking individually with your boss). We become convinced of the importance of these rituals and their accompanying dependency.

Socialization makes our limited agency seem more important than it really is, and diverts attention and energy from more holistic and systemic solutions to problems. But, this is not to discount people's self-efficacy or their actual agency. According to the non-anarchist, but popular-amongst-anarchists Foucault (1978), power "is produced from one moment to the next, at every point, or rather in every relation from one point to another" (93), but *resistance* exists everywhere, too. Accordingly, there are infinite chances for contesting existing unequal power relations. More specifically, consider how children in contemporary societies are usually taught to look to police for assistance in conflicts, not to themselves and their immediate communities. Yet, Russian anarchist Peter Kropotkin held that coercive means of social control (such as police and prisons) were only necessary in unequal societies. These institutions could be done away with and communities could be *more* empowered to deal with anti-social deviance, through greater solidarity against aggressors, as well as "fraternal treatment and moral support" of such persons (cited in Baldwin 1968, 233). Thus, people do have agency, but hierarchical institutions tend to discourage awareness of agency's potential.

Socialization is done during important transitions during one's lifetime, in preparation for new roles or experiences. Many socialization agents are manifestly designed to acclimate (or socialize) us to hierarchical norms and help to integrate us into existing, unequal power structures. These agents tend to encourage conformity and deference to authority (including the agents themselves). A principle agent of socialization is the family. Children grow-up hierarchical largely due to parental influence. Parents socialize their children in ways similar to their own childhood socialization. Patriarchy plays a large part in this socialization process as children are raised to blindly obey their parents, particularly their fathers. Families thus socialize children to accept binary gender roles, which are more predictable, conform to ideology, and keeps parents free from external criticisms. Peers conduct themselves in similar ways, although their pressure involves group conformity, and the socialization does not occur as early in life and is less instrumental than in the family.[3] The influence of the family is a formidable, conservative challenge to those who desire radical social change. Parents tend to adopt the same hierarchically-oriented parenting techniques that their parents used with them. While child rebellion against parents has been a long-standing, multi-generational theme in the modern era, there is much debate about how wide-spread and permanent such rebellion is. Most rebellion ultimately results in minor changes only. It is easy to rebel at a young age, but difficult to engage in long-term resistance to the centripetal power of one's familial socialization.

School is often the first institutions that children enter once leaving the protective realm of family. Education is ostensibly intended to help youth and broaden their horizons, but this tends to not be the result in most cases. Instead, formal schooling tends to foster nationalism and patriotism, instill obedience to bosses, and numb curiosity, critical thinking, and (ironically) a desire to learn. According to Spring (1998),

> The content of what is taught depends on who controls society. But the power of the school extends beyond its propagandistic role. The socialization process of the school shapes a particular type of character which meets the needs of the dominant power within the society. For [anarchist] critics like Godwin and Ferrer, the socialization process of the school molds citizens who will submit to the authority of the state and function as loyal workers in the new industrial society. And the socialization process schools people into an acceptance of their social position and makes them dependent upon an irrationally organized consumer society. (30–31)

---

[3] However, if one's peers are radical, socialization could take counter-normative directions.

Consequently, schools provide corporations and governments with passive workers and nationalistic citizens. This occurs because universities usually train teachers and school administrators in hierarchical teaching methods, do not provide counter-examples to emulate, and advocate a school structure that "requires" discipline.

A final example of a socialization agent is the mass media. Much modern media serves as distraction and mystification, by redirecting attention from matters that immediately affect people and seeking to entertain audiences without challenging them. Much media is, in fact, advertising, which prioritizes fulfillment through material consumption, encourages people to view themselves as mere consumers in an "abstract" marketplace, and actively lies and deceives audiences. Media socializes people in this way because most of it is a for-profit industry or a state-managed organization. Thus, certain hierarchical socialization practices are central. Corporate and state-based news omits important facts and issues, constrains debate, establishes limited priorities, focuses on arbitrariness, leaders, or gore, and ignores social movements and alternatives (c.f. Herman and Chomsky 1988). "Safe" content is presented that is designed to not turn-off some audiences (especially advertisers and ruling elites). Ideas and in-depth reporting that might challenge the hegemonic control over such information is deliberately excluded.

In the final analysis, these socialization methods seem to be relatively effective in maintaining a social order based on hierarchy, domination, and inequality. The success of these methods raises the question of what makes people susceptible to hierarchical socialization? Fundamentally, agents of socialization are protected due to tradition, how things have "always been done." Revolutionaries try to find pro-active solutions that rob authoritarians and hierarchical norms of their attractiveness, authority, power, and upper-hand. In a future anarchist society, we still might have these or similar agents participating in socialization, but conducting themselves in a radically different fashion. Specifically, non-hierarchical socialization would modify or remove socializing agents' comfort zones, experience, ideological safety, and privileged statuses.

Condemning authoritarians and their socialization efforts is clearly not enough. While anarchists may want to quickly condemn authoritarians for their actions, it is important to know what has led authoritarians to act this way. What would be required to prevent them from hierarchically socializing in the future? Perhaps stripping hierarchical socializers of some of their unwarranted authority and sanctioning their socialization efforts could curtail their impact and facilitate greater positive deviance throughout society. Before appraising the prospects for doing these things, the diverse problems associated with deviance must first be considered.

The Problem(s) With "Deviance"

Socialization sometimes fails—the target does not correctly or completely internalize what is expected of them by socialization agents. Socialization also backfires sometimes—children rebel against their parents, students resist their teachers, peers disagree or avoid each other, and spectators critique the mass media. In such situations, socialization to dominant, hierarchical norms constitutes deviance. The deviance could be seen to represent conscious or unconscious resistance to not only socialization agents, but also broader, hierarchical systems.

Disobeying a norm is termed "deviance" and deviance is thus often seen as the flip-side to norms.[4] As many norms are hierarchical, deviance also has a multi-faceted relationship with the hierarchies described above. Deviance can be seen as a consequence of hierarchy in three different ways. First, deviance can be produced directly by hierarchy; all sorts of crimes of poverty (e.g. theft, drug-dealing, etc.) are the result of a hierarchical society and people having to bend or break laws to survive inequality. Second, deviance is sometimes a reaction to hierarchy; riots and revolutions that take place—commonly considered "deviance"—are often reactions against inequality, injustice, and tyranny. Third, deviance is also regularly enacted in the name of hierarchies; although people often decry such deviance, spousal and child abuse are committed as a consequence of patriarchy, wars as a consequence of states, and worker abuse as a consequence of capitalism.

Deviance, like norms, can exist within subcultures, too. In anarchist circles, particular behaviors—normative in the mainstream—would be considered deviant. Anarchist deviance could involve strong-handed leadership, homophobia, patriarchy, White supremacy, classism, violence and sexual assault, sectarianism, or support for mainstream political figures. Anarchists attempt to eliminate such deviance from their own anarchist circles as well as larger society.

---

[4] It should be noted that this is only one of four different perspectives on classifying norms. According to Spreitzer and Sonenshein (2004), deviance can be statistical (outlier behavior), supraconforming (extreme or addictive adherence to norms), reactive (labeling by an observing audience), or normative (departure from a norm). The latter is the common meaning used here.

Anarchism may be seen as "positive deviance." As a non-normative or counter-normative practice, anarchism emphasizes behaviors that do not replicate hierarchical forms of social relations, yet without the usual negative consequences. As with crimes, poverty, and the like, anarchist resistance—including mutual aid, collectives, political graffiti, militant street protests and blockades—is often portrayed as deviant, but may simultaneously be seen as empowering. Akin to how "do-gooding" is understood as positive deviance, anarchism also has a positive, progressive orientation in its attempts to create a better world. Within Heckert's (1998) typology of positive deviance, anarchism most comfortably fits into the categories of altruism and innovation, involving voluntary action on behalf of others (without hope for reward) and creating new ways of doing things in society, respectively. Through such counter-normative practices, anarchists modify the typical expectations for social action, replacing them with extraordinary and principled forms. Thus, depending on one's values and vantage point, anarchism could be considered "positive" deviance.

However, anarchism is rarely regarded as positive deviance. More often, societies consider anarchist actions to be negative deviance. In fact, it is common in most societies to view the advocacy of anarchism as criminal, and most states have willingly repressed anarchists throughout their histories. Consequently, the "deviant" label is applied to anarchists within the media, by states, corporations, and wealthy elites. The deviant label usually takes more colorful and libelous forms: violent, chaotic, nihilistic, dog-eat-dog, cutthroat, murderous, misanthropic, etc.[5] Today labels are comparably loaded in character: eco-terrorist (Beck 2007) and anarchist-criminal (Borum and Tilby 2005). Systematic campaigns of anti-anarchist propaganda have been conducted over time, in many countries. Using the US as an example, turn of the century periodicals ran attack-stories (Hong 1992) as did corporate television in the 1980s (McLeod and Hertog 1992). The "deviant anarchist" stereotype benefits those who own and direct society. Theoretically, anarchism's survival and proliferation could eventually offer an alternative that would threaten the control the powerful wield. Therefore, the powerful need a "wicked-person" caricature and stereotype by which to frighten the population away from anarchist norms. In doing so, corporations and the state help

---

[5] A recent case of the popular usage of "anarchy" to refer to chaos is during the ensuing disaster following Hurricane Katrina hitting the Gulf of Mexico region in 2005 (Stock 2007).

to justify large police forces, increased surveillance, and regular threats of violence against (supposedly-deserving) deviants.

These are only the problems that stem from the hierarchical-wielding of the "deviant" label. Still other challenges stand in the way of re-socializing people in the practice of anti-authoritarian norms.

Barriers to Plotting an Anarchist Course

Most efforts to change one's prior socialization occur within hierarchically organized settings, called "total institutions." For example, someone who has failed to properly adhere to established laws, as a consequence of a mental disability, may be sentenced to a mental hospital or asylum.[6] Within this total institution, an inmate's daily life is systematically structured by staff in an effort to modify their behavior and obedience to norms (Goffman 1962). The fact that these "resocialization" efforts commonly take place in hierarchical institutions and that inmates are usually poor and disadvantaged persons who have not "properly" followed society's hierarchically-designed norms, indicates the extent to which society will go in order to maintain order.

Socialization helps to train and instruct people to follow hierarchical norms and re-socialization aims to adjust those for whom earlier socialization efforts seemingly failed. But, anarchists seek the re-socialization of people to "better" norms that will help them live their lives in anarchist fashions. Unlike the bountiful resources at the disposal of society's many total institutions, there are formidable and pronounced impediments to anarchist re-socialization efforts.[7] Even though norms do change in revolutionary situations, re-socialization efforts tend not to last. Consider the widespread changes in norms that took place in Barcelona, Spain in 1936 during the Spanish Revolution, as described by Orwell (1980):

> Waiters and shop-walkers looked you in the face and treated you as an equal. Servile and even ceremonial forms of speech had temporarily disappeared. Nobody said 'Señor' or 'Don' or even 'Usted'; everyone called

---

[6] Other common examples of total institutions include prisons, military training camps, and boarding schools.

[7] It should be noted that although re-socialization, rehabilitation, reform, etc. are the *stated* goals of total institutions, research has tended to indicate that their successes are mixed and questionable. One could explore other explanations for total institutions and perhaps suggest that inmates are sent to them out of convenience, spite, revenge, ignorance, malevolent design, or neglect.

everyone else 'Comrade' or 'Thou', and said 'Salud!' instead of 'Buenos días'. Tipping had been forbidden by law since the time of Primo de Rivera; almost my first experience was receiving a lecture from a hotel manager for trying to tip a lift-boy. (5)

But, the revolution did not last, in part because re-socialization did not take place or did not embed itself long enough in Spanish society for the population to permanently change norms. External forces, including Communists and fascists, ended the opportunities for additional re-socialization efforts. In the present, many other barriers exist, far less time sensitive in nature. It is worth considering these barriers and pondering how they could be overcome.

First, there is much confusion about alternatives. People are rarely aware that alternative norms exist. Even when people understand problems and would like change, there is a familiar response: "But what choice do we have?" or "What else can we do?" Media and formal schooling tends to ignore non-hierarchical organizations and practices, such as cooperatives, collectives, popular assemblies, and syndicalist unions. Of course, most media is itself hierarchical and media-makers are not socialized to consider alternatives. Open discussion of alternatives would also ultimately be detrimental to the corporate and state interests that support most media. Consequently, most people have to seek out information on alternatives. The Internet helps, but one must know what to look for in order to find other models. Information may be in inaccessible formats or shrouded in weird jargon making adoption a bewildering prospect. Familiarity is one problem, but is accompanied by an equally problematic lack of alternative examples to emulate. Very few alternatives exist in most societies. For example, worker cooperatives are now numerically small in most places and have shrunk since the slow death of the 1970s cooperative movement.[8] Re-invigorating the cooperative movement seems like a lot of work, especially without the driving passions of the 1960s. Alternatives also tend to be emphasized for economic value, not their "dual power" capacity to create egalitarian institutions in place of hierarchical ones. Consequently, alternatives do not seem like "alternatives," but rather just "another option" and thus are not as attractive as they could be. Credit unions are seen as "cheaper than banks," rather than

---

[8] Lindenfeld and Wynn (1997) attribute cooperative failures and successes to variations in 1) the technological, economic, legal-political, and socio-cultural environments in which cooperatives operate; 2) interactions with other cooperatives and other organizational actors; and 3) the organizational structure and culture of the cooperative itself.

as revolutionary anti-capitalist organizations. Labor unions are seen to distribute benefits, rather than for their ability to grow working class power and create self-management. And community gardens are viewed as cheaper ways to get food, rather than a means to replace corporate agribusiness and supermarkets, and to gain local food independence.

Second, there is a strong tendency to confuse legitimate concerns with liberal-ish "solutions" that do not address underlying problems of hierarchy. Lots of people are "concerned," but how to solve problems that people face? Without widespread acceptance of radical norms, there is an inappropriate pairing of means with ends. Thus, concern with poverty is treated by charity. Concern with environmental devastation is treated by "green consumerism." Concern over political corruption is treated by periodic voting ("If only we could elect principled, moral politicians!"). Concern with "social inactivity" and apathy is treated by volunteering at a large, mainstream non-profit organization. And concern with crime is treated by supporting get-tough-on-crime and extra policing approaches. These ready-made, yet illusory, responses to people's sincere concerns with problems deflect substantive remedies. It is important to appreciate that applying Band-Aids to gunshot wounds will not work in the long term. But, the system seeks to channel people into controllable, reformist directions, in the hopes that this approach will maintain the system's stability over time. Liberal-ish solutions will not change the fundamental arrangements of power, nor will they provide people with empowerment, self-efficacy, or liberation. Witness how the welfare state absorbs strain through rhetoric and bureaucracies. For example, Piven and Cloward (1993) argued that formal, liberal-ish organizations are often established to quell larger disruption. People get directed into the mainstream or get "cared for" instead of radicalized or encouraged to self-manage their lives. With various aspects of their lives being (briefly) cared for, people never fully understand their problems and appropriate potential solutions. The state tends to withdraw liberal benefits once societal tension dissipates. Thus, welfare state policies merely serve as capitalism's shock-troops and public-relations agent.

Third, a casual evaluation of prized norms may lead to superficial, weak, or even contradictory adherence to anarchist practice. For example, norms based upon values (like a "freedom norm") are often Rorschach inkblots that may mean nearly anything to different people. "Freedom" does not have one, solitary meaning, but many divergent even conflicting meanings. To George W. Bush, "freedom" meant the freedom to acquire unfettered access to foreign reserves of oil, to enforce regime change upon other countries, or the freedom to invest in the stock market without concern for "unintended consequences." To an anarchist, "freedom" has a different meaning: freedom from unwarranted authority, freedom to choose how to live one's life, freedom to seek a better future with others, and so forth. Anarchist freedom implies a rejection of domination and unilateralism that is the very basis of Bush's freedom (recall Chapter 1's discussion of freedom). To many observers, Western countries are already bastions of freedom, equality, justice, etc. Consequently, many people may accept anarchist norms on the basis of face value or non-agreed upon meaning, yet not have any sympathies for practiced anarchist norms. The subjective interpretation of norms is different than the off-hand, abstract reference to norms; these terms must be defined and differentiated in order to be meaningful.

Fourth, for the few "deviant" examples that do exist and are practiced openly, positive reinforcement is not given. Few people transmit positive feedback to those who practice alternatives, consequently re-socialization is apt to be unsuccessful. Instead, rebels are shunned, criticized, and scorned for their differences with mainstream society and their contempt for its norms. Media are not likely to complement those who walk a different path, since media must play to popular opinions as well as vested interests—thus, the anti-mainstream will always lose. Politicians are also not likely to work with (let alone cede power to) those who want to disrupt their power. Given these restrictions and anarchism's deviant image, who will want to find alternative ways of living, without approval or support from others?

Fifth, structural restraints prevent anarchist practices even for those who appreciate anarchist norms. An anarchist professor, for example, may like egalitarianism and anti-authoritarianism, but is still required to submit letter grades for student performances at the end of a semester. The positive appreciation of norms does not necessarily mean that one is able to follow that norm given constraints placed upon them in hierarchically organized institutions. A government worker may honestly wish for a society filled with mutual aid, but is likely unable to empower citizens with collective decision-making means since power is monopolized by the state and its policy-makers, and because rules stand in the way of allowing citizens to create binding rules in their communities. Kropotkin famously pointed to this problem, noting the ways in which the state—although we could extend his logic to all hierarchical institutions—gets in the way of "natural" human tendencies for mutual aid and social solidarity, and stunts people's skills and desire to help each other (Kropotkin 2006).

Sixth, the status quo is simply comfortable and easy. The roles, privileges, and positions we are socialized into seem more attractive than the costs associated with shedding such things (see Laurer 1991). Consider how it is easier to be macho, than to be a pro-feminist male (or pro-feminist female for that matter!). It is easier to pay taxes, than go to jail for tax evasion. Workers find it much easier to be obedient than to form a labor union. Many people find it easier to be quiet about the plight of disadvantaged persons, than experience ostracization, shame, and attack from others who share one's privilege for speaking up in support for the disadvantaged. With these rewards for status quo behavior, it is very challenging to attempt counter-normative behavior that is likely to entail strong societal sanctioning.

Lastly, there is regularly roll-back after the occasional revolt. When rebellions and insurrections occur, new norms do not easily establish strong roots. Even if new norms are egalitarian, there are powerful centripetal forces pulling people back to latent, hierarchical norms. For example, Orwell (1980) noted (not long after his above quotation) that Barcelona ceased to be run by the working classes, that open displays of opulence returned to the city streets, and people expressed being "tired" of the revolution and war. Re-socialization efforts face the prospects of eternal vigilance. Thus, there is always a risk that all the prior years of socialization and sanctioning in obedience to hierarchical norms will be too imprinted in the popular consciousness to easily discard after revolutionary fervor subsides.[9] Below, Figure 2 presents the problems associated with roll-back on re-socialization efforts. While re-socialization prior to revolts and revolutions may help to hasten such episodes, they may only create alternative spaces in society, easily crushed by the weight of long-standing convention and training. If more egalitarian norms are not strongly rooted, the old hierarchical order can re-establish itself after anti-establishment sentiment settles down.

Anarchist Re-Socialization

If most people tend to be socialized within hierarchical societies to obey authority figures, then counter-socialization strategies are mandatory to create even a limited degree of autonomy from those hierarchical

---

[9] The aftermath of the Russian Revolution of 1917 and the May/June 1968 events of Paris provide other examples of how roll-back can occur.

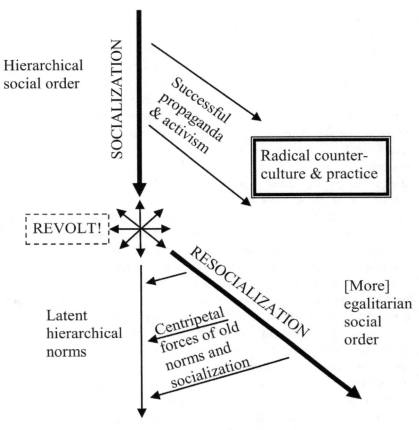

Figure 2. Revolt: resocialization or roll-back?

institutions. Fostering this autonomy within "the system" is a central anarchist goal. Murray Bookchin wrote in *Post-Scarcity Anarchism* (2004) that

> [anarchists] try to prevent bureaucracy, hierarchy and elites from emerging in their midst. No less important, they attempt to *remake themselves*; to root out from their own personalities those authoritarian traits and elitist propensities that are assimilated in hierarchical society almost from birth." (141, emphasis in the original)

And according to Graeber (2002), "ultimately [anarchism] aspires to reinvent daily life as whole" (70). These prescriptions are no easy task. The goal of "taking-in" hierarchically-socialized people, broadening their world-views, and perhaps make them anarchistic requires long-term, rigorous, wide-spread, and thoughtful efforts on the part of anarchists.

As indicated above, political or economic revolution without a parallel revolution in social norms is unlikely to remain a permanent revolutionary current and will be apt to roll-back into hierarchical practices.

James C. Scott (2009), a southeast Asia scholar, has discussed the differences between state-repelling and state-preventing characteristics (pp. 278–279). Communities outside the immediate reach of the state often attempt to repel its influence, while at the same time attempting to prevent state-like forms from emerging within. To consider this dualism in relation to anarchism, the movement tries to repel the state from taking over more of civil society (and encroaching upon the movement itself, e.g. spying, subversion, arrest), but also has tried to prevent state-like forms from growing organically within the movement (e.g. strong leaders, bureaucracy, standing armies, etc.). Thus, some norms ought to be aimed at inhibiting internal hierarchies from emerging in countercultures and movements. Other norms ought to be established to transform non-anarchists/non-radicals/institutions (that exist outside of anarchist circles).

However, according to early "collective behavior" scholar Neil Smelser, social movements themselves are of two varieties: norm-based movements and value-based movements. One could interpret the norm-based movements as more reform-oriented, as they are trying to change the more superficial patterns of individual behavior. Value-based movements are, perhaps, more revolutionary as they are attempting to transform the moral basis upon which society rests. Anarchism has implicitly this value-based analysis, but it operates on a norm-basis (most of the time) by trying to change practices, thereby combining together both of Smelser's forms concurrently. As with the rest of society, anarchism's norms flow directly from its values—the difference is that anarchists have a more hostile orientation towards status quo values/norms.

Anarchists have a long and rich history of attempting conduct the re-socialization they believe necessary for long-term transformation. For example, in the decades leading up to the Spanish Revolution, anarchists organized across Spain. By the 1930s a particularly Spanish form of anarcho-syndicalism had deeply embedded itself into Spanish working class culture. The influence of anarchism grew—most noticeably with the success of the CNT-FAI—through the slow, organic formation of affinity groups. Once the Republic was declared and Franco's uprising occurred—creating both space and motivation—it was only "natural" for sizable portions of the Spanish working class to act upon their anarchist socialization and behave in-line with anarchist norms.

The counter-cultural movements of the 1960s and 1970s—which contained a strong anarchist aesthetic—also attempted to established different norms that were at odds with the dominant society. For example, housing communes, intentional communities, food cooperatives, and squats, as well as more temporary configurations like "be ins" or Rainbow Gatherings (Amster 2003) were designed to foster alternative norms, socialize people in the ways of positive deviance, and create social spaces autonomous of dominant norms. Many of these examples still persist and are places of refuge for individuals with values at odds with hierarchical society.

Contemporary, yet usually unidentified, examples of anarchistic norms exist, too. In most small groups of friends there is often a sense of egalitarianism and comradery. Neighbors regularly cooperate with and aid each other. Sizable minorities (and sometimes majorities) in most societies harbor a strident distrust of authority figures, especially politicians. Many profess solidarity with the disadvantaged (however inappropriately manifested). The people of most societies have strong support for various "commons" and collective property, ranging from social security to libraries to public parks. Regardless of how ill-formed or superficial some of these patterns are, they do exist, and it is important to highlight them and consider their persistence in society, despite relentless efforts by state capitalism to atomize people into obedient workers and consumers. But, how to expand the desirable norms and weaken the undesirable norms? Anarchist opinion on this question differs from state socialists and communists in that it is unethical to force others to adopt new anarchist norms, or to merely preach the merits of revolution. Instead, anarchists show by example the merits of more desirable norms, in the hopes of non-coercively convincing wider anarchist norm adoption.

Anarchists, along with many other politically-active groupings, attempt to re-socialize others. These efforts to "anarchize" sympathetic and interested persons take a variety of approaches. First and foremost, anarchists are actively involved in re-socialization through propaganda. Propaganda raises anarchist concerns, critiques, and alternatives that can be applied to everyday life by their intended recipients. Most of the central anarchist theorists that historians identify were also authors and publishers of anarchist propaganda that attempted to sway the masses of Europe and North America towards revolution. In fact, Jun (2009) considers the populist medium of the pamphlet to be a central factor that helped to position anarchism within the militant working class labor movement. Today, propaganda takes a variety of forms, in addition to the traditional pamphlet and newspaper: books, websites, radio programs, magazines and zines, graffiti and stencils, and guerilla art and culture jamming (see Atkinson 2006, Atton 1999, Downing 2003, Hertog and McLeod 1995). These mediums are designed to reach wide and diverse audiences, challenge their assumptions, rationally convince, and provoke and inspire emotions.

Re-socialization also takes place through the regular interactions that anarchists have with other non-anarchists. By "practicing what they preach," anarchists demonstrate what their beliefs are in both conversation and action. This is likely the most common way in which "new anarchists" are created—through basic, perhaps mundane, conversations and relationships. Once this connection has been made and the character of anarchism is clear to the new adherent (even if not identified as "anarchist ideology"), re-socialization can begin. Anarchists re-socialize non-anarchists in the practice of anarchist norms using anarchist-friendly rewards and sanctions. Relationships between anarchists and non-anarchists are advanced by utilizing supportive rewards for non-anarchists' more anarchistic behaviors; for example, the expression or practice of collectivism or anti-authoritarianism is verbally affirmed and endorsed. "Soft" sanctions are also used for un-anarchistic behaviors, such as classism, racism, or sexism; anarchists tend to express general disagreement with these ideologies, provide evidence for their inaccuracies or inappropriateness, and indicate better orientations to others.

Various anarchist-sponsored events help to re-socialize people. Protests provide the opportunity for many to experience collective and (hopefully) liberatory participation with others. Anarchist tactical approaches differ from conventional protest and are premised upon anarchist values like autonomy, self-determination, and anti-authoritarianism. Protest tactics including blockades, lock-downs, sit-ins, black blocs, snake marches, disobedients, flying squads, and others teach people about the merits of these anarchist values and provide practical experience of anarchy in action (see Atkinson 2001, Starr 2006). But, it is not just the mere experience *during* an event that matters, but also the skills, values, and aesthetics absorbed during the planning of events with other anarchists. One can learn the importance of incorporating as many people as possible in an event, designing the protest to be radical in orientation, and working to defend the event against those who would take it hostage for their own purposes (whether liberals, fascists, or police). Less physically-intense events like teach-ins or workshops serve a similar function for anarchists.

Here, energy is focused in a more explicitly intellectual way and efforts are made to raise consciousness, and offer an anarchist critique and resolution to some social problem.

Anarchists also re-socialize others within their organizations and informal groupings. For example, formal collectives often intensely discuss not only their goals, but the means by which they are attempting to achieve them. Collectives usually discuss their internal power dynamics and attempt to refine their working relationships, decision making processes, and socio-political vision (c.f. Rothschild-Whitt 1979, Fitzgerald and Rodgers 2000). More broadly, anarchist circles (or scenes) allow for social networking and the creation of an independent counter-culture. Anarchist infoshops are an example of geographically-rooted projects that practice anarchist values, while actively spreading such ideas (Atton 2003). It is within these loose communities that anarchists learn from each other and develop new ways of living. The eventual norms that emerge from this complex process serve as the ground rules and framework that guide the local anarchist movement's operation and direction.

Finally, the act of creating dual power institutions also accomplishes re-socialization. Dual power is the establishment of counter-institutions that serve useful functions for society, accomplishing goals and fulfilling needs, but in a way in-line with anarchist values (Mumm 1998). For example, instead of trying to change corporations to be kinder and gentler, dual power means the creation of producer and consumer cooperatives accomplish necessary economic functions. In doing so, the power, necessity, and attractiveness of the corporate capitalist model would diminish and eventually disappear. Or, as opposed to mandatory schooling, the legitimate goal of learning could be alternatively achieved during the life-long process of learning via homeschooling, alternative schools, free skools, popular education, teach-ins, skill-shares, and the like. In the practice of these alternative institutions, people will learn better ways of acting that are founded on values like cooperation, anti-authoritarianism, horizontalism, and self-determination (c.f. "revolutionary transfer culture," Ehrlich 1996). Dual power requires people to adapt oneself and one's community to the calculus of values and practicality, often in a free-flowing and emergent environment. Learning to solve problems in the absence of hierarchy is challenging, as well as an amazing re-socializing experience. Re-socialization could help to guarantee the thorough overthrow of hierarchical institutions, through the permanent establishment of anarchist norms.

Present Concerns for the Future

But, how well do these re-socialization efforts work? In particular, is there "roll-back" for participants? It is unknown—and no conclusive efforts have been made to understand—for whom re-socialization fails, why it fails, and how. Not only do some "anarchists" unsuccessfully adopt anarchist norms, but would-be anarchists regularly "drop-out" of anarchist scenes, perhaps through burn-out, disillusionment, frustration, value-change, or some combination of these. These questions are not only concerned with the short- and long-term sustainability of local anarchist scenes, but the eventual success of anarchistic social revolution. If nurturing a justice-oriented society is a goal, how best can anarchists and like-minded people guarantee progress and critical mass?

Past anarchist movements socialized youth into anarchist norms and values less painfully. During anarchism's "golden age" (late-1800s, early-1900s), working class culture and labor movements kept anarchist norms alive from generation to generation. Various phenomena have wiped out this anarchist culture, thereby reducing the capacity of the anarchist movement to reproduce itself through conventional socialization agents (such as families and peers). Many popular commentators have remarked (usually disdainfully) upon the seemingly youthfulness of the anarchist movement and how it lacks "elders" and older, experienced cohorts. Supporting anarchist aging in an affirming and supportive culture not only assists "institutional memory," but also establishes wizened socialization agents who can assist in the re-socialization of younger would-be anarchists. Thus, anarchist re-socialization strategies must appreciate the long-term vision and effort needed to expand, diffuse, and strengthen anarchism within most societies.

Ultimately, "revolution" cannot be a singular event, disconnected from the past, with no uncomfortable growing pains before or after the fact. Deliberate efforts to change society are hard work, as are efforts to retain the revolutionary nature after rebellions occur. Revolution will likely involve fits and starts, and years (or even decades) of re-socialization to change practices, values, and attitudes. Anarchist norms must be fostered prior to revolution, remade during the process of revolution, and then spread and defended afterwards. Crucially, anarchists and others interested in a just social order need to appreciate the quiet strength that social norms have and seriously consider how to transform these as much as they consider the transformation of the polity and economy.

According to Geertz (1980), performances occur to illustrate relationships of power. These performances are composed of meaningful symbols that need to be understood in order to understand—and dismantle— hierarchical power. Following this logic, it is crucial to subvert the performance of everyday actions and common symbols in order to transform social order. For example, orienting chairs in a circle during a meeting not only makes the meeting more direct and functional for all involved, but also symbolically de-centers "leaders" from the meeting. Or, eliminating formal, privileging titles (e.g. "sir," "professor," "your honor") not only makes conversations shorter and more multi-directional, but also imbues the conversation with an air of egalitarianism. Of course, it is not enough to just change the symbols—the *form* of relations must also change. But, Geertz argues that symbology is an important part of power relations. Thus, one avenue towards social transformation is through changing the many performances people do that project and reify inequality and domination.

Thus, the key objective for those concerned with seeking greater social justice is to present to others hierarchy as a human creation and something under our control. This means nurturing an anarchist imagination *and* fostering self-efficacy. As German anarchist Gustav Landauer (2010) famously wrote:

> The state is a social relationship; a certain way of people relating to one another. It can be destroyed by creating new social relationships; i.e. by people relating to one another differently. (214)

This destruction/creation requires individual and collective action. The ways that each person decides to engage with this project will vary (especially due to one's skills, interests, values, and social positions). But, the important factor in any anarchist re-socialization will be a principled, value-driven practice (Milstein 2010, Gordon 2007). For example, academics and students within universities could move towards anarchist norms and re-socialization via experimentation with alternative learning environments and pedagogical styles. These approaches could emphasize student-driven learning objectives, student-control over syllabus and course design, and participatory action research and community-service learning embedded within social movement organizations. Efforts could also be made to de-center the site of learning to *outside* of the university itself, through the creation of popular learning institutions, skill-sharing, and community-based networking. Scholars who conduct research could break-down the barriers between the Ivory Tower and "the masses" by embedding themselves within movements (as partially suggested by Burawoy (2005) in his so-called "organic public sociology") and providing their expertise in struggles for emancipation. For example, Howard Ehrlich and other ex-social scientists helped social movement organizations survey their memberships, strategically design campaigns, and pursue other research endeavors beneficial to justice struggles (see Ehrlich 1991). Regrettably, most social science scholarship tends to either be isolated within universities and their inaccessible journals that few non-academics have access to or can understand, or exist for the partisan purposes of social policy makers.

More generally, the promotion of collective organizations that are not based upon profit, self-interest, or consumerism is crucial. If there were more visible groupings within societies (especially in North America) that overtly, unabashedly advocated progressive social change in a democratic, cooperative, and horizontal context, then norms would not merely be affected for those immediate participants, but also those who indirectly encounter such groupings and their values. For example, *anyone* could join together with a number of other colleagues, friends, neighbors, or classmates under the auspice of a collectively-run project that had a deliberate name, agenda, and principles of unity. Such organizations could shamelessly promote the key anarchist values of self-management, horizontalism, solidarity, and direct action, through their words, but also their behavior. The possible objectives are endless, but some possibilities include: a print or web-based collective that provides a critical (anarchist) analysis of local conditions and issues; a study group that would read about and apply ideas about cop-watching, restorative justice, prison abolition, worker cooperatives, community self-defense, direct democracy, or anarchism; or an organizing campaign to help facilitate community empowerment through direct action and dual power creation.

These ideas are not meant to delineate a limit upon strategies for anarchist re-socialization, but to serve as food for thought. As is true with any anarchistic endeavor, strong-armed proscriptions are not only unhelpful for generating anti-authoritarian norms, but also limit the collective, creative imagination of peoples in struggle. Anarchist re-socialization will succeed if and only if people are reflexively active in trying to change themselves, others, and social expectations. Linguist and anarchist social critic Noam Chomsky put it thus in the film *Manufacturing Consent*:

> The way things change is because lots of people are working all the time...
> they're working in their communities, or their workplace, or wherever they
> happen to be, and they're building up the basis for popular movements

which are going to make changes. That's the way everything has ever happened in history... whether it was the end of slavery, or whether it was the
democratic revolutions, ... you name it, that's the way it worked. (cited in
Achbar 1994, 192)

Even though there are many pathways for anarchist action—which undo
hierarchical norms, thus potentially leading towards a less dominated
future—there are still formidable barriers to anarchist movement analysis, a topic to which we turn next.

CHAPTER EIGHT

PROBLEMS OF RESEARCH ON RADICALS (OR ANARCHIST MOVEMENT EPISTEMOLOGY)

Introduction

A dynamic area within the discipline of Sociology is the study of social movements. This field of research is far more dynamic than in the past— now various theories compete with each other, scholars advance new ideas and twists to old ideas, and scholarship has broken out of the stodgy ghetto of "collective behavior" to grow into its own vital area. The questions of "what is a movement?," "where do movements come from?," and "how do movements behave and succeed?" are vital questions that have been addressed for decades now, with many fascinating (although sometimes conflicting) answers (della Porta and Diani 2006). Yet almost none of this scholarly work has focused on the anarchist movement, surely one of the more dynamic and fascinating movements active today.

Anarchism is not, of course, merely a socio-political philosophy, as it has been mainly referenced in earlier chapters. Its proponents constitute a "movement," a large collection of people who share similar attitudes, identities, and goals, and who are working towards (however awkwardly) some form of radical social change. This is how sociologist Mario Diani (1992) defines movements: networks of individuals and organizations who are linked by their common identification with that movement, who act in deliberate, extra-institutional ways to modify the structure of a society. Thus, even though "anarchism" refers to a set of immaterial culture (beliefs, theories, and traditions), it also refers to a constituency of real people who take that culture seriously enough to act upon it in the present. It is this present-day activity, this *movement* (as in "motion," "trajectory"), which makes anarchism a subject worthy of study by sociologists.

Although movements are now routine research subjects for sociologists, some movements offer particularly complicated, contradictory, or counter-intuitive characteristics that befuddle scholars and impede scholarship. The objective of this chapter is to explore these problems of epistemology—the means by which we know something—in order to further the quest to better understand the anarchist movement. In doing so, we will tackle sticky issues of definition, the hurdles that stand in the way of studying anarchists, and the factors which make the aforementioned epistemological problems more formidable for anarchism than for most other movements.

The issues discussed in this chapter may be focused in order to serve a number of practical ends. For example, conventional scholars—say, sociologists—may wish to study anarchists or an anarchist movement. The matters to be discussed herein could help such scholars to focus their research questions, properly operationalize their variables, define appropriate sampling frames, design and administer surveys, or even locate and navigate an anarchist scene ethnographically. Equally important, is this chapter's value to journalists, whether mainstream news reporters, college newspaper editors, web-bloggers, or zine writers. Knowing more about these epistemological questions helps to provide the important nuance necessary to understand anarchism in a way that facilitates useful and meaningful communication to desired audiences. Or, anarchists themselves may benefit from this chapter, as it raises issues—and in some instances, controversies—about that movement. Presumably, to grapple with a wide range of epistemological questions serves not to just intellectually challenge anarchists, but to provide them with appropriate analytical ideas that could grow and strengthen their movement.

More Questions Than Answers: Problems of Conceptual Definition

It is very likely that the first question asked by journalists covering protest demonstrations that include the participation of anarchists is: "Who in the hell is an anarchist?" Likewise, most well-intentioned observers would like to know what anarchism is. Thus, the issue of definition is paramount. So, what is "anarchism" and how do we know it "when we see it"? We could approach the identification of "anarchism" from countless vantage points using a variety of methodological approaches. First, we could identify anarchism by its core values: anti-authoritarianism, solidarity, autonomy, mutual aid, liberty, cooperation, decentralization, egalitarianism, direct action, voluntary association, and so forth. If people espouse such values, they are more likely to be anarchists. But, do not many other movements share some of these values? Could non-anarchists not easily adhere to and practice these values without ever realizing they are "anarchist" values? Must we guarantee that *all* such values are present in order to label something "anarchist"?[1] Does this imply that everything anarchist includes all these traits at all times? And how do we identify these values? If we wait for anarchists to identify these values aloud, we may never notice they are anarchists. We may instead [somewhat] incorrectly categorize many others who use these phrases, but in un-anarchistic ways— for example, many patriotic Americans likely believe in "liberty" as do fanatical consumers who love being able to purchase products created under abominable social and environmental conditions. Yet such "liberty" is very different from that defined by anarchism, who intend it to refer to freedom to live as one chooses, unrestrained by hierarchical power.

Second, we could rely upon people to use the word "anarchist" to describe themselves. We could assume that these self-identified "anarchists" possess anarchist characteristics. Then, by inference we could know what anarchism refers to. But could not anyone simply call themselves an "anarchist" and "make it so"? In fact, this happens semi-regularly, especially in the modern-era. Can capitalists *really* be anarchists? Sizable collections of ultra-individualists—who seem to have very little real world presence and tend to lurk on the internet together (appropriately so!)— identify as anarcho-capitalists. Murray Rothbard and others may theoretically claim the label of anarchism, but they do not oppose all authority, as other anarchists do—they are highly enamored with markets, class inequality, and authority in the workplace. Thus, most "movement anarchists"—those active in community-based protest movements—argue against the inclusion of these folks in the anarchist camp.[2] Can people who advocate violence against civilians be anarchists? How about people who vote? There are even groupings of people who call themselves "national anarchists," who subscribe to a thinly-veiled "third position" fascist ideology who identify as anarchists (Macklin 2005)! Spanish anarchist militants who fought Franco in the 1930s would surely roll in their graves knowing the linguistic gymnastics the label "anarchist" is being put through.

The problem plaguing these approaches is that there is no way of "properly" establishing one set of values or social actors as "legitimate"

---

[1] One probably needs to consider how these anarchist values persist or perish within all areas of society—not just in the government and economy—including within the family, peer groups, cultural organizations, schools, etc.

[2] For example, the popular *Anarchy FAQ* (McKay 2007) includes a thorough critique of so-called "anarcho-capitalism" and gives extensive attention to why such a position is at odds with the anarchist tradition.

anarchists. The movement lacks an "approval agency" or central commit-tee that could verify memberships or one's adherence to strict party-lines. Perhaps it is the general failure of anarchist politics throughout history that has ironically created its flexibility as well as its promiscuity.[3] Had anarchist been forcefully entrenched somewhere—like Marxist-Leninism was under Stalin's multi-decade rule in the Soviet Union—maybe it would be easier to explicate commonly accepted criteria for anarchism. Instead, all varieties of people with no experience with anarchist history, practice, philosophy, relationships, or understanding, can call themselves anar-chists. Consequently, this looseness allows for easy adoption of an anar-chist identity, while simultaneously watering down the central factors that make it a distinct movement. This ambiguity not only exists with new recruits and the founders of new "spin-off anarchisms," but also within the consciously, self-affiliated anarchist movement.[4] The anarchist press debates this question all the time (in newspapers and now on Internet message-boards/listserves): who is or is not an anarchist? To out-siders, this holier-than-thou posturing comes off as sectarian. Such behav-ior is likely the by-product of a small movement, incidentally populated by a number of paranoid and self-righteous people. The phenomenon is divisive of unity and solidarity. For social scientists, ideological loose-ness poses a terrible problem of reference and validation. One grouping or ideological subvariant of anarchists thinks the other is not anarchist (and vice-versa); just witness debates between "organizationalists" and "anti-organizationalists," reds and greens,[5] or anarcho-syndicalists and post-leftists. Who is to be believed? Who is *right*?

Third, it is confusing enough that adherents disagree about what anar-chism is, but the supposedly objective, rational, and learned intellectuals seem to have an equally poor—if not worse—understanding of anar-chism. Select nearly any social science or humanities discipline, and one

---

[3] This perception that anarchism lacked an agreed-upon core set of values and strate-gies led some Russian anarchists to create a "platform" that anarchists could subscribe to, thereby uniting anarchists upon some common ground. See Skirda (2002) for more on the Platform.

[4] New recruits—almost by definition—join movements knowing less about them than long-experienced participants. Is it methodologically-appropriate to generalize about a movement if only analyzing the newest participants? Also, new ideological subvariants—new anarchists such as post-leftism, post-structuralist anarchism, primitivism, etc.—regularly define themselves in opposition to other, more-established strands. This requires a selective adoption and rejection.

[5] See Williams (2009a) for a study on red and green anarchist ideological subvariants and their geographic dispersion in the United States.

is unlikely to receive a definition of anarchism that is borne of an analysis of current anarchist movements. For example, the political science litera-ture is rife with theorizing of "anarchy," referring to the international rela-tions between states where no centralized system controls these relations (see Kaplan 2000). Curiously, no one seems terribly bothered by the sim-ple fact that the major actors in this conception of politics are all states! How un-anarchist can such a theory be?[6] In economics the situation is little better: anarchism is apparently best used as a synonym for laissez-faire capitalism, a dog-eat-dog economic system in which each individual must fend for themselves in a Wild West marketplace. Absent again is the easily verifiable history of modern anarchism as an *anti*-capitalist move-ment, solidly in opposition to private wealth, greed, and parasitic wage slavery. Philosophy and history are both fond of abstracting the ideas of classical age anarchists or developing new applications to old anar-chist ideas; the problem is that these ideas tend to be generated in isola-tion from actual anarchist movements. For example, philosophers debate anarchist epistemology for science generally, while historians dig deeper into the archives of late 19th century labor unions. Far less emphasis and effort is focused on the here and now. The field of sociol-ogy gives scant attention to anarchist characteristics of social order, baffling us and legions of anarchists who seem acute and appropriate students of society. These shortcomings and missed opportunities pro-vide insight into why activists tend to not take intellectuals more seriously.

Issues that Complicate Operationalization

Assuming we can grapple with these questions and realize their full-gravity, we are still left with countless practical conundrums that inhibit the study of anarchism. Even if the theoretical conceptualization of "anar-chism" were easily accomplished, the crucial issues of operationalization remain. In other words, we must find a way to locate, observe, measure, and evaluate our concepts if they are to be useful in enhancing under-standing. How to define terms so as to observe the correct real-world phenomenon that we seek to observe?

---

[6] Thankfully, some recent work in international relations has been done, such as that by Alex Prichard and others, that takes anarchism and its traditions seriously—such as the ideas of P.J. Proudhon—instead of treating "anarchy" as if it were merely a word pulled from a dictionary.

One immediate problem is the casual distinction between "anarchism" and "anarchy." Both are used interchangeably by activists and the broader public. But, are they truly the same? Anarchism is an ideology, idea, and ideal. It refers to aspirations, values, and identity. Anarchists get together in their collectives to discuss anarchism, to create anarchist projects, to fulfill anarchism. Anarchy is a social condition, the real-existing anarchist practices that fulfill the anarchist ideal. Consequently, it could be viewed as the end-goal, the utopian result of anarchist struggle. These distinctions may be minor, but how can researchers study the meaning and intent of actual anarchists without appreciating this? Content analysis or interviews could easily overlook one term and its meaning, or inappropriately associate one with the other. In sum, when studying the anarchist movement, are we interested in anarchism or anarchy?[7]

Does anarchism need to be identified as such in order to be anarchism? Undoubtedly people and groups may behave in an anarchist fashion, but have little or no affiliation to anarchist ideas. For example, researchers could study something (e.g. a group, a protest event, a project) that is explicitly "anarchist" and uses the word openly. Or, researchers could direct their attention to things that are anarchistic: that which acts in accordance to anarchist values and practice, but does not use the word. In this latter case, participants could be unaware that their behaviors involve anarchist tendencies or, they could be—at least on the surface—strong, vocal opponents of what they perceive to be "anarchism" (perhaps relying on the media-fueled stereotypes of chaos). Thus, despite the anarchistic ideas of founder Dorothy Day, the Catholic Worker rarely openly identifies with anarchism. Still, anarchism has had—and continues to have—an undeniable influence upon the Catholic Worker, in terms of societal critique, expressed values, and organizing practices (Boehrer 2000, 2003).

Related to this, are we interested in anarchists who identify openly as such? To publicly apply the word "anarchist" to oneself or one's actions is bound to distinguish one from those who may do identify as or act the same exact way, but do not use the same language. Consequently, overt or covert anarchists are likely to have many different characteristics. We ought to consider the reasons why people choose overt or covert

---

[7] But, the term "anarchy" is popularly maligned, often used derogatorily. Mass media uses both terms (but especially the latter) as synonyms for ideas, behaviors, and conditions far-removed from the anarchist tradition. For example, Hurricane Katrina in 2005 spurred such non-theoretically-rooted correlations with "anarchy" in the news, such as "violence," "chaos," and "looting" (Stock 2007). The associations with states in disorder—such as Somalia—are also endlessly propagated in the news.

anarchism. Those who choose to publicly identify with anarchism may be interested in attracting others based on principles they see in practice (e.g. mutual aid, anti-authoritarianism, self-management), to put a real-world face to abstract ideas, to reclaim the word "anarchist" in a positive way, or to distinguish one's ideas from other forms of radicalism. Others, relying on equally rational thinking, may choose to *not* identify publicly with anarchism to avoid the predictable stereotyping and preconceptions that accompany the label, to prevent attack by authorities, or simply not wanting to be pigeon-holed as "only an anarchist" (when one could also adopt other labels, such as "feminist," "revolutionary," "socialist," etcetera). This legitimate issue of visibility creates practical epistemological problems. How to find both groups? How to count them? How to contrast them? Can covert anarchists be part of a "movement"? Can overt anarchists be considered part of other movements?

If we seek out anarchists only within anarchist organizations, settings, or social spheres we are likely to overlook anarchists and anarchist activity outside the realms of the anarchist movement. Many anarchists, of course, do their anarchist activism within explicitly anarchist organizations, functioning within "scenes" composed only of other anarchists. For example, organizations like the Northeast Federation of Anarcho-Communists, the Anarchist Black Cross, or the International Workers Association are explicitly and wholly anarchist. They practice anarchism directly, by name, and place anarchism at the center of all activities. Many other anarchists (and it is obviously unclear how many) practice their anarchist activism within non-anarchist organizations (but still *as* anarchists). Witness the anarchists who regularly participate in organizations like the American Friends Service Committee, Greenpeace, United for Peace and Justice, or the AFL-CIO—and even more often in countless community organizations. Being an anarchist within a non-anarchist setting is unlikely to completely diminish one's anarchistic qualities, although one's anarchism will undoubtedly be muted. So, what are the motivations for anarchists acting outside the anarchist movement? Hypothetically, these anarchists may be "missionaries" of a sort, acting to encourage these organizations to be more anarchist. Or, less ambitiously, anarchists may simply desire engagement with non-anarchists, or because they agree with the short-term goals sought by reformist organizations (however much these anarchists may wish to eventually surpass such reformism).

As anarchist identity is liquid and easily adopted by people, there is also no strong reason for people to have immediate contact with the "formal" anarchist movement. In fact, during modern times when access to information is readily available through mail-order books or the Internet, people can learn about movements and ideologies easily. Non-movement anarchists are people with no formal attachment to anarchist organizations or movements at large, but still identify with anarchist ideologies and politics. Consequently, anarchists may appear and exist in geographical areas where there is no anarchist scene, organization, or other individuals. It is far more difficult to locate these individuals since there are no visible markers (like an anarchist newspaper, anarcho-punk bands, an Industrial Workers of the World chapter, etc.) that would indicate the presence of anarchists. It is also possible that unaffiliated individuals have independently discovered anarchism, even when there *is* an organized anarchist presence in their area. Whether such individuals are simply unaware or uninfluenced, they may still be worthy research subjects.

Unlike many other movements, anarchism is not a "single-issue" movement. Comparatively, the environmental movement is focused upon matters related to the natural ecosystem, the feminist movement upon things that affect women and gender relations, and the labor movement upon the conditions of paid labor amongst workers. Anarchism sympathizes with and participates in *all* of these movements to some extent, but does not focus on one to the neglect of others. The anarchist movement overlaps with many social movements, participating in their most radical wings. Thus, instead of an emphasis upon a particular issue of localized struggle, anarchism is more an aesthetic or general approach to such issues. The few identifiable, core "issues" that link anarchist action together are matters related to hierarchy and authority. Consequently, anarchist activism could—theoretically, at least—be located in nearly all areas of society, as well as within many social movements. For example, Earth First!ers and community gardeners may be part of the anarchist movement *and* the environmental movement. Anarcha-feminist collectives, reading groups, and individuals are just as much part of the feminist movement as the anarchist movement. While the Workers Solidarity Alliance is an anarchist organization and the *Anarcho-Syndicalist Review* an anarchist magazine, both also represent the radical, anarchist-wing of the labor movement.

Finally, it is worth making a bell hooks'-like distinction (2000) regarding anarchism. To speak of "the anarchist movement" is highly naïve. There is no hegemonic character to anarchism throughout the world. Anarchist activity in different geographic locations is undoubtedly different and unique. For example, witness the strains of *especifismo* in South America, Platformism in the United States, or autonomism in Central and

Southern Europe. Perhaps a way to address this overgeneralization would be to note *multiple anarchist movements* (plural) as opposed to one uniform anarchist movement (singular). Thus, we could consider slight regional flavors or those differences amongst anarchists of varying ideological orientations. hooks, writing about feminism, recommends using "movement" as a verb. Movements move; they are in a constant state of evolution, changing to meet new conditions and challenges. It may be useful to refer to "anarchist movement" as the effect of countless anarchists acting within an abstract "movement," engaging in struggles against very different forces of domination. Seen this way, movements are not static, nor are they strictly space-specific, but are liquid configurations of people struggling to reach their goals.

The Subjects and Scale of Anarchist Movement Research

All movements exist at multiple social scales. This means that there are different-sized configurations of anarchists and their groups. For example, movements consist of individuals, groups of individuals, formal organizations, and large networks or federations of individuals and groups. Consequently, any given movement is best viewed as a network of these various collections of people and their created structures (whether loose or firm).

Thus, when speaking about anarchism and anarchists, it is crucial to distinguish between the type and scale of one's research frame. When the FBI describes "anarchists" as a threat to the internal security of the US or propertied interests of corporate America (FBI 1999), to what and whom is it referring? Is the FBI referring to random anarchist individuals (probably), anarchist scenes (implicated, undoubtedly), formal organizations (yes, such as the Anarchist Black Cross, or less formal with the Earth Liberation Front), or broader networks (perhaps)? Or, when the mass media warns (read: rants hysterically) a community that anarchists are about to descend upon them during a large demonstration, does it mean to implicate all anarchists (perhaps living throughout the city), specific anarchist groups or organizations (maybe a "counter-summit" coordinating organization), or large anarchist networks (a regional anarchist federation)? Of course, it is unclear whether the FBI and mass media are *really* interested in these important issues of scale and specificity, or if they are more interested in fear-generation, retaliation, and suppression. Yet, if the anarchist movement is to be genuinely and accurately understood, these questions are of prime importance!

Individual anarchists could be any person (young or old, employed or unemployed, short or tall) who has a conscious identification with some sort of anarchist-specific ideology. Although there are problems (as noted above) with accepting any self-identified ideology into the anarchist movement, all *could* theoretically be counted. Ideologies may range from syndicalist, ecological, or feminist to communist, primivitist, punk, post-left, and so on. These individuals exist at what sociologists call the "micro-level." Individual interaction and relationships occur between people, first and foremost. The micro-level is where encounters take place, friend-ships occur, and community begins. Symbolic interactionists are apt to note the importance of the micro-level in constructing reality from the ground-up, interaction-by-interaction, relationship after relationship. Most anarchists likely know more individuals than they know groups or organizations, and probably interact more frequently with individuals on a one-to-one basis than within the context of a larger structure.

Still, society is not merely composed of random individuals casually bumping into each other and living their lives without deliberate order. Groups are some of the most routine configurations created by anarchist individuals yet are one of the most difficult to locate and observe. For example, anarchist "scenes," collections of anarchist friends, or crowds of anarchists are all casual, informal, but deliberately-created groups in the anarchist movement. Groups represent a great epistemological challenge and raise crucial questions. How does one delineate the boundaries of a city's anarchist scene? How do you locate pockets of anarchist friends or comrades, who might live in the same house together, but probably not? Or is it even possible to predict when and where crowds of anarchist indi-viduals will form (and for how long), and then for a researcher to swoop in quickly to study that crowd?

Anarchist organizations are intentionally-created, formally-designed, and usually named. Organizations exist on the meso-scale (or "between level"); they are not composed of mere individuals, nor are they large superstructures, institutions, or bureaucracies. The possible structures of such organizations are incredibly varied. For example, small affinity groups are made of trusting individuals who intermittently re-form for specific purposes. Collectives aim to accomplish explicit goals like publish an anarchist magazine, run a Food Not Bombs food distribution project, or drive fascists out of their local political scenes. Cooperatives are member-based economic organizations that have strong anarchist characteristics, and may be organized to produce some sort of item or pro-vide a service (a book publisher or bicycle manufacturer), or to consume something (a food cooperative or punk rock record store). Such formal organizations create systems for dealing with decision-making, structures for who can participate and how, and work towards some type of collectively-determined goals. These organizations often, but not always (the best exception being many affinity groups), are visible to the wider anarchist scene and mainstream society. To the extent that they are visible, they are more easily studied from the outside; the less visible (and the more covert), the more it may be necessary for direct participants to analyze them.

It is difficult to conceive of the anarchist movement in "macro-level" terms. There are no real large-scale structures to speak of, since a core anarchist principle is decentralization (Ehrlich 1996). But, anarchists have constructed international federations and networks—such as the International Workers' Association, Independent Media Center network, the Anarchist Federation, and others—but none qualify as hegemonic institutions like states, bureaucracies, religious institutions, or capitalist marketplaces.

Consideration of the appropriate geographic scale may not be enough to account for the temporal condition of anarchist groups and organizations. The relative permanence of a grouping will indicate the ease or extent to which it may be studied. An important anarchist group may be difficult to study if it is short-lived, while an organization that has little meaningful impact over decades may have a greater chance of impacting movement history since there is more opportunity to study it. Thus, the variation in organizational longevity will affect those attempting to understand how organizations persist within the movement environment. Often, if movement participants to do not personally document their roles and activities in these groupings, such episodes may be lost from history, as will the decisions and rationale that generated that history.

Challenges to the Active Study of the Anarchist Movement

Once the problems of defining anarchism and anarchist movements are solved (or at least addressed) and the question of research frame is dealt with, still more challenges await. These challenges are practical matters that can restrict scholar access to anarchist movements, such as sampling, trust, and confidentiality.

In order to study anarchists or anarchism, one needs to find anarchists. Because overt anarchists are relatively small in number today, it is tough to locate anarchist populations to sample. Covert anarchists obviously do not wish to be found and almost surely seek to avoid being studied. Where there are important ethical concerns to consider when studying covert anarchists, such research is still meaningful, valuable, and worth the effort to protect privacy. The behind closed-doors decision-making of covert anarchists can help to inform the future efforts of anarchists, who act under the gaze of watchful states and other authority figures. For example, what strategies are used for affinity group formation? How do covert anarchists participate overtly in the mainstream? How do people decide to engage in illegal activities instead of legal activities?

The fact that covert anarchists wish to avoid study is relevant within representative democracies, where information on membership in affinity groups, Animal Liberation Front cells, or squat residences is completely unavailable. But, this reluctance is particularly true in authoritarian countries. For example, the Nigerian anarchist organization called the Awareness League requests that anarchist comrades not include the "Awareness League" name on mailed letters (or any mention of political matters) out of fear of government censorship. Likewise, anarchists in Zimbabwe fear government repression (again, with good cause!), and consequently conceal their politics behind "arts and culture" community groups. More generally, locating anarchists requires some sort of personal contact information that most people do not regularly have. Consequently, having access to broad social networks is especially important for those interested in studying anarchist movements.

Even when located, anarchists are often hesitant to help scholars pursue their research. Why? Anarchist movements have long been spied upon and then persecuted by governments, corporations and wealthy land-owners, religious institutions, and others. Anarchists are usually aware of this history, and when combined with present-day repression, activists may develop a keen sense of paranoia.[8] Thus, access to movement participants may be thwarted by distrust of outsiders, including (and maybe especially) academics. North American anarchists sometimes call this healthy paranoia "security culture," which results in a refusal to speak about tactical matters (and sometimes political matters) to anyone they do not know personally and well. Inter-organizational matters of dissension and controversy may be particularly off-topic to outsiders. As many scholars are employed at publicly-funded universities, scholars may be distrusted as either interlopers with little sympathy for anarchist goals

---

[8] Not coincidentally, paranoia is one of the very mental states that governments seek to foster amongst radical movements.

or as spies for governments. The former are viewed as parasites who make careers off the struggles of others, the latter as enemy agents intent upon disruption.

Anarchist activists have other reasons to be skeptical of participating in academic research. Even for studies conducted by activist-scholars with the best of intentions, the research process is fraught with risks. Confidentiality may be threatened by authority figures, especially if research seems to isolate and identify individuals. What is to stop a powerful elite from trying to track down original contacts, interviewees, or survey-takers, in order to spy on them, arrest them, or worse? Or more mundanely, employers could harass or fire, landlords refuse to rent to, and family and friends could shun if anarchists' identities became public in the wrong way. Even when confidentiality has been actively protected, the very existence of published research may be a valuable tool to attack a movement. Research that helps scholars and activists to better understand how movements work and how to improve strategies, can also be used by the state to identify movement weaknesses and target those movements for disruption, especially if source data become "public data," which anyone could then access and analyze independently. Anarchists are rightfully suspicious and hesitant to help authority figures undermine their own movements.

Anarchist-sociologists will likely have to go out and collect such data, participate in the aforementioned types of conversations, and live and observe these experiences. For those with no immediate access to research subjects, scholars might wish to seek out other forms of data to analyze. Unfortunately, there are no real good sources of data on anarchists for obvious and previously discussed reasons. There have been some secondary sources we have found useful, albeit imperfect. Very few surveys have been done of anarchists, although some data exists on attitudes about anarchists. One of us has published research using online surveys (e.g. user survey from Infoshop.org), which while not too generalizable, can answer some questions about individual anarchists (see Williams 2009a, 2009b). Organizational directories, such as the International Blacklist (from the 1980s) or the more recent Anarchist Yellow Pages, catalog the existence, location, and character of anarchist organizations (see Williams and Lee 2008). Recent anarchist history has been and is being compiled by various projects, like the A-Infos News Service (see Williams and Lee 2012 as a use of this "data") and the Independent Media Center network. These projects— and many others—describe and record anarchist events, political news, organizational and movement histories, and other documents of note.

Mainstream and alternative press could be used as data for content analysis that indicates the popularity, controversy, or successes and victories of the anarchist movement. For example, long-running newspapers like the *New York Times* has recorded decades of anarchist history—albeit through an unfavorable, elite lens and in superficial contours. Library collections—such as the Labadie at the University of Michigan—have many complete series of anarchist newspapers and magazines from the near and distant past (Herrada 2007). One underused—and perhaps less accessible—source of data is that collected by various law enforcement authorities, who often have a near-pathological institutional mandate to collect information on enemies of the state (see Borum and Tilby 2005 for analysis premised upon police data and perspectives). The data law enforcement collects will generally reflect the perceived, relative threat posed by anarchists and anarchist movements.[9] Still, this kind of data could be a fascinating treasure trove.

The preceding sources of data are not only suggestive of possibility, but also deserving of caution. We end this chapter with a brief discussion of methodological strategies and their weaknesses as they pertain to the study of anarchist movements. The major concerns that deserve attention include incompleteness, inaccuracy, non-generalizability, and challenges to access.

Standard sociological methods, such as survey questionnaires, provide some nice benefits, but are rife with problems when studying anarchists. For example, it is impossible to properly sample anarchists, since no sample frame for anarchists exists. Compared to other groups of people—such as Sierra Club members who are recorded on master lists by the national organization—it is impossible to know who all the potential anarchists in a given area are. Therefore, any anarchists that *are* included in a study will not accurately represent the entire population, since the constitution of the entire population is unknown. Additionally, an unavoidable selection bias results since not everyone given a survey will actually complete it—consequently, any conclusions drawn from these surveys will only reflect the patterns of those who choose to do the surveys, not those who refuse them. Thus, surveys are bound to be

---

[9] Ironically, anarchists have been unintentionally instrumental in the founding of the FBI and Secret Service in the US (via FBI founder J. Edgar Hoover's pathological obsession with "reds" and his participation in the deportation of anarchists Emma Goldman and Alexander Berkman to Russia in 1919, and the backlash following Leon Czolgosz's assassination of President William McKinley in 1901), and the European-based Interpol policing agencies (Jensen 1981).

non-generalizable to the larger population of anarchists. Even efforts to ascertain opinions about anarchists, collected by generalizable surveys, will still be problematic, as secondary data can rarely answers questions that they were not designed to answer originally. Researchers will be grappling with operationalization issues and trying to apply old data to new research questions.

All manner of field methods—ranging from ethnographies to simple face-to-face, open-ended interviews—have other, unique challenge. One formidable problems, previously discussed, has to do with the establishment of trust between anarchists and those wanting to know about anarchism. As a result of distrust of outsiders, committed anarchists are probably the best people to interview other anarchists. As with all qualitative research, questions of generalizability abound: are the people who get observed or interviewed at all alike other anarchists? It is likely that those willing to be observed or interviewed have certain commonalities—e.g. an outward focus, overt status, etc.—that set them apart from other groups of anarchists, such as those who participate in black blocs, do targeted property destruction, advocate armed struggle, are racial or ethnic minorities (or of immigrant status), have been previously arrested, and so forth. There is also always the question of time and expense when doing in-depth observation and interviews: such research tends to span long periods of time and require substantial financial resources for travel and living expenses.

Passive methodologies that do not require direct contact with research subjects, like content analysis, introduce still different issues. Depending on the medium under study, content analysis could be biased (in one direction or another), incomplete, or simply unhelpful. In each case, it is important to honesty consider the source of the data under analysis and reflect on just how helpful it can be. For example, movement documents—statements from anarchist organizations, the movement's magazines, or claims made in anarchist histories—may reflect desires and critiques of anarchists, as opposed to reality and fact. Thus, all movements (anarchism included) put forth propaganda to convince allies to join them, enemies to give up, and for themselves to keep fighting. It is likely quite regular for movements to brag and exaggerate about the success of actions or the attendance at an event in order to make it seem better than it actually was. Movements (and obviously the groupings and organizations within them) are not always good at keeping records about themselves; their decisions, the logic that led to those decisions, and the result of decisions are regularly omitted in meeting minutes or public pronouncements. Thus, for researchers trying to understand how and why something was done, movement documents might make it seem as if nothing actually happened, although the opposite is more likely true. Consequently, many researchers have to read between the lines, a troubling endeavor as it requires projecting one's own conclusions about other's actions.

The mainstream media is an equally complex source of data for content analysis, but for different reasons. Media often present anarchists in a negative light—when they are presented at all. Thus, an "anti-halo effect" likely surrounds anarchist activities. Selective coverage will focus on the most dramatic (and probably most unflattering) behaviors, such as property destruction, while mundane, heroic, or positive acts like sharing food with the homeless, watching police patrol poor neighborhoods, or making long, consensus-decisions at meetings will be overlooked. The media includes a range of anarchist behaviors that is non-representative of the true spectrum of activities. Last, media regularly misquotes people or places their words and actions out of context—whether through reporter misunderstanding, deadline pressures, or deliberate, ideological editorialization. While, this problem affects many movements, it is bound to be of particular significance for radical movements like anarchism who have ideas beyond the typical realm of discourse and otherwise unintelligible to mainstream media.

Finally, going further into protectors of the status quo, one could analyze records kept by law enforcement. While, there are likely extreme issues of limited access (as mentioned earlier), there are also problems related to police mischaracterization. Thus, something that has a clear meaning to anarchists, may be highly misunderstood, mis-categorized, and presented in a fashion that misconstrues anarchist intentions. Also, given police reliance upon informants (paid or unpaid), researchers would have to consider the motivations of those relaying information. Do informants seek to validate their own importance to police by playing up perceived anarchist threats—or even to insure that they continue to get paid for their spying? Or, are informants telling police what they think police want to hear? And if so, what exactly is that "truth"? Regardless, content analysis of law enforcement records would have to sharply filter data based on these rampant biases. Such problems should not deter the use of this kind of data—in fact, it may reveal a good deal about how police perceive and frame threats posed by anarchists—but it should caution the conclusions arrived at.

ANARCHISTS IN THE ACADEMY

Anarchist academic and anthropologist David Graeber devotes the first section of his book *Fragments of an Anarchist Anthropology* to his attempt to answer the question, "Why are there so few anarchists in the academy?" For Graeber this is a pressing question given the veritable explosion of anarchist theory and lively debates over anarchism outside of the academy, especially within the numerous social movements which have emerged recently. Despite the blossoming of anarchist thought and practice, David Graeber is perplexed that this flowering of anarchism has found little reflection in the academy. Graeber seems to long for the type of success that Marxists have enjoyed in their move into the academy following the rise of Marxist theory among the students of the New Left. As he notes in his disappointed comparison of anarchist successes with those of the Marxists: "In the United States there are thousands of academic Marxists of one sort or another, but hardly a dozen scholars willing openly to call themselves anarchists" (2004: 2). In his view this is something that should be a cause of concern for anarchists.

Yet it would seem that Graeber's fears are quite unfounded. A glance across the academic landscape shows that in less than a decade, since the anti-World Trade Organization protests in Seattle in 1999, there has been substantial growth in the numbers of people in academic positions who identify as anarchists. Indeed, it is probably safe to say that unlike any other time in history, the last ten years have seen anarchists carve out spaces in the halls of academia—and (although we lack the hard data to prove it) likely at a quicker rate than any other politically-radical ideology. This is especially true in terms of people pursuing graduate studies and those who have become members of faculty (the authors of this book included). Several anarchists have taken up positions in prominent, even so-called elite, universities, including Richard Day at Queen's University in Canada, Ruth Kinna at Loughsborough University in England and, for a time, David Graeber at Yale. Indeed, the Politics Department at Loughsborough has actively recruited graduate students for a program of study that focuses specifically on anarchism. The flourishing of anarchism in the academy is also reflected in other key markers of professional academic activity. These include: academic articles focusing on varying aspects of anarchist theory and practice; the publication of numerous books on anarchism by most of the major academic presses; and growing numbers of courses dealing in some way with anarchism or including anarchism within the course content. There have also emerged, perhaps ironically enough, professionally recognized associations and networks of anarchist researchers and teachers, such as the Anarchist Studies Network of the Political Science Association in Britain. And another variant across the Atlantic Ocean called the North American Anarchist Studies Network (NAASN) has held four successive years' worth of conferences in Hartford (Connecticut), Toronto (Ontario), San Juan (Puerto Rico), and New Orleans (Louisiana). The NAASN boasts dozens of "members" in numerous disciplines and has had hundreds, possibly thousands, of conference attendees. Suddenly it's almost hip to be an anarchist academic.

At one time, not so long ago in fact, this would have been a curious situation for anarchists to find themselves in. Anarchists once held (and many still do) a rather healthy suspicion of the academy as an elitist institution fully bound up with the reproduction and extension of power structures within capitalist societies. As Graeber (2004: 96) suggests, most modern academic disciplines, and we would certainly add sociology to the list, were made possible by programs of conquest, colonization, and mass murder. Yet the growing enthusiasm among some anarchists over their newfound acceptance within the academy, and the encouragement this gives growing numbers of anarchists to consider academic programs, has not been matched by critical reflection on the limitations of a turn to the academy by anarchists. This postscript offers the beginnings of such a reflection and raises certain cautions.

We should also be clear that we are in no way criticizing individual anarchists for choosing to pursue academic work. We are certainly not suggesting that anarchists stay out of school or leave the academy in the manner of earlier generations of socialists who abandoned universities to take up industrial work. For sure the more places in which anarchist thought might develop and flourish the better. The advances made by neo-conservative academics in shifting economic and social policies, providing the intellectual capital for neo-liberal capitalism and imperialism, while making post-secondary education even less accessible for working class students, shows what can happen when we abandon or are defeated in any field of struggle.

At the same time it is important to contextualize anarchist academic activity in relationship to other types of anarchist activities. If anarchists are to be effective in waging struggles in the academy, and even more importantly, if academic anarchism is to contribute anything to struggles outside the academy, then we need a clear discussion of the matter, one which does not tilt towards uncritical celebration or an envious longing for something we could as well do without. We write this as people from less economically-privileged backgrounds (although we are privileged by our race, gender, sexualities, etc.), who have also spent perhaps way too much time in school, so we have witnessed this issue from multiple perspectives.

Academic Anarchy?

David Graeber describes his recent work *Fragments of an Anarchist Anthropology* as "a series of thoughts, sketches of potential theories, and tiny manifestos—all meant to offer a glimpse at the outline of a body of radical theory that does not actually exist, though it might possibly exist at some point in the future" (2004: 1). The theory, the non-existence of which is of such concern to Graeber, is, primarily, an anarchist current within academic anthropology. We say "primarily" because Graeber also asks similarly why there is no anarchist sociology, anarchist economics, anarchist literary theory or anarchist political science. In posing these questions, and in failing to acknowledge that on some level anarchist versions of each of these "sub-disciplines" do in fact exist, Graeber betrays what is really at the root of his concern. That is the existence of academic or professional versions of anarchist thought in these areas and the acceptance of anarchist theories within established academic disciplines and institutions. Certainly this is understandable for someone who has put a great deal of effort, both personal and collective, into establishing his own academic credentials and who has waged his own high profile battles against the intellectual gatekeepers at the elite institution, Yale University, where he worked for several years.

Indeed in asking the question, "why is there no anarchist sociology?", Graeber entirely overlooks the significant sociological works of people like Colin Ward, Paul Goodman, and John Griffin to name only a few. One could make the same point in identifying significant contributors to an anarchist economics, people such as Tom Wetzel and Larry Gambone. Notably these writers, while extremely important in the development of contemporary anarchist thought and influential within anarchist circles occupy only marginal places, if any in professional, academic sociology or

economics circles. So the problem is not so much the existence of anarchist sociology, but its recognition, acceptance, and legitimation among
academics or professional sociologists. Curiously, Graeber even overlooks
the contributions of anarchist sociologists who have succeeded in bringing anarchist theory into the academy such as Lawrence Tifft and Jeff
Ferrell, again, to name only a few.

The case is the same when one returns to anthropology. Graeber
(2004: 38) claims that "an anarchist anthropology doesn't really exist" and
them sets it as his task to lay the groundwork for just such a body of theory
and practice. Yet to make this claim, and even more to set himself up as
the person to correct the situation, Graeber does a disservice to people
like Harold Barclay who have been working tirelessly for decades to establish an anarchist anthropology within accepted academic circles. Barclay
is a name that appears nowhere in Graeber's writings. And the obsession
with "big names" (that we are, in part, replicating here) also belies the far
more numerous anthropologists who have studied and appreciated the
anarchistic characteristics of countless "traditional" cultures, for a great
many decades of scholarship.

At this point, however, we would point out, in light of Graeber's desire
to see anarchism recognized within the academy, that many anarchists
have been quite good at developing analyses that go beyond mainstream
social science. Indeed such has been the invaluable work contributed by
what can be called constructive anarchist *theorists* from Gustav Landauer
to Paul Goodman to Colin Ward. Again, the problem has not been the
absence of anarchist theory or theorists, low or high, but rather the acceptance of those theories and theorists within the academy. This is what
concerns Graeber deeply in *Fragments,* but we have to ask whether such a
concern might be overemphasized, if not misplaced. At the same time,
there are aspects of anarchism that have made an uneasy fit with some
academic disciplinary approaches.

Academonization

To unproblematically advocate the move of anarchist theory into the
academy is to present an uncritical rendering of the perils and processes involved in academic knowledge production. Beth Hartung, in a
much earlier, and less optimistic account of the engagement of anarchy
with the academy, sounded this cautious note: "Once a theory is taken
from the streets or factories and into the academy, there is the risk that

revolutionary potential will be subverted to scholarship...in other words, knowledge becomes technology" (Hartung 1983: 88). Howard Ehrlich has also repeated this critique in noting that a lecturer's podium is the wrong "barricade" to stand behind during a revolution (Ehrlich 1971) As Murray Bookchin (1978: 16) has similarly argued, academic works often subject social movement perspectives and practices, as in anarchism, to a reformulation in "highly formalized and abstract terms". Almost thirty years after Bookchin's observation, it seems that the recent academic works on anarchism, produced by self-identified anarchists such as Newman and Day it might be added, have indeed continued this practice of making anarchist thought conform to the style and substance of the academic discourse of the day.

Even with graduate training in social theory and familiarity with the language used in such texts, one can find these works to be rather inaccessible. They are texts directed primarily at other academics, addressing issues almost exclusively of concern to academics in a specialized language that is most familiar to academics. Such approaches contradict the anti-vanguardist commitment shared by most anarchists.

Some try to excuse this use of language by arguing that the complexity of ideas being addressed requires a complex language, beyond the grammar of more down to earth expressions. While this might be a fine position for mainstream academics, we might argue that anarchists have to work harder to break the exclusivity of academic discourses.

Anarchists, from the earliest exponents who first identified their perspectives as anarchist to contemporary activists, have generally not viewed anarchist theory as anything unique or new, an approach that clashes somewhat with the pursuit of "original knowledge" that tends to preoccupy certain quarters of the academy. Indeed, anarchist ideas are often considered intuitive, common-sensical, and even "natural" for people. Anarchists, more modestly than most academics, have tended to focus their work on emphasizing types of behavior, such as mutual aid, voluntary association and collaboration, that are regular features of human social life (see Graeber 2004).

Unlike Marxism and its various offspring, Leninism, Stalinism, Trotskyinsm, Maoism, and so on, anarchism is not based on the work of a specific thinker and is not closely associated with the work of a specific theorist or grouping of theorists. While, of course, there are figures who have been recognized as important contributors to the development of anarchist theory (e.g. Proudhon or Kropotkin), they are usually situated as interlocutors within a broader conversation about anarchy than as theoretical fountainheads or "masters". As Graeber (2004) notes, anarchists do not treat ideas, even the ideas of prominent figures, whether Bakunin, Kropotkin, Foucault, or Marx, as the results of some individual's unique genius. Rather, anarchists treat ideas as primarily or most importantly as the products of specific intellectual and material engagements, within specific contexts. From an anarchist perspective, theoretical ideas are the products ongoing conversations and arguments among often quite large numbers of people (Graeber 2004).

> None of it was presented as some startling new doctrine. And in fact it was not: one can find records of people making similar arguments throughout history, despite the fact that there is every reason to believe that in most times and places, such opinions were the ones least likely to be written down. We are talking less about a body of theory, then, than about an attitude, or perhaps one might even say a faith: the rejection of certain types of social relations, the confidence that certain others would be much better ones on which to build a livable society, the belief that such a society could actually exist. (Graeber 2004: 4)

Graeber (2004: 5) notes that of the many and diverse schools of anarchism—from anarcho-syndicalists to anarcho-communists, to platformists to individualists to insurrectionists—none name themselves after some "great thinker". Note that there is no Goldmanism or Bakuninism or Malatestaism in the history of anarchism.

Approaching the Academy

For anarchists, as Graeber (2004) points out, the role of intellectuals is in no way to form an elite that attempts correct political lines or analyses by which to lead the masses. Graeber (2004) suggests that academia might benefit from an engagement with anarchist approaches to knowledge production and sharing. Such an engagement would, in his view, allow social theory to be refashioned along the lines of direct democratic practice. Such an approach, drawing on the actual practice of the newest social movements, would encourage a move beyond the medieval practices of the university, which sees "radical" thinkers "doing intellectual battle at conferences in expensive hotels, and trying to pretend all this somehow furthers revolution" (Graeber 2004: 7). An approach taken from social movements, beyond its rejection of "winner take all" attempts at conversion, might also allow for a move beyond a "great thinkers" approach to knowledge.

Yet we're not convinced that anarchists' energies are best spent in trying to reform the academy in this way. The real problem is the existence of a hierarchical and in-egalitarian social structure that separates and ele-vates knowledge production in such a way as to reproduce the existence of universities as exclusive and privileged institutions (see Martin 1998a). Over the last two decades, largely through the hard work of feminist and anti-racist researchers, there has been a move to more participatory and community-based research. This has certainly been an improvement over the days of grand theory, (fancifully conjured in armchairs), or the positivism-on-steroids infecting much social science of surveys, statistics, and social subjects. Nevertheless, all of this new research, no matter how "community-based" still takes place within and is conditioned by its exis-tence within an authoritarian and unequal political economy of knowl-edge production. The presence of a hundred or a thousand more anarchist professors within the hallowed halls is unlikely to change this much more than the presence of a few thousands Marxist academics has over several decades—unless, of course, they start acting more like anarchists, and less like academics.

A serious concern remains: rather than tearing down the walls between "town and gown", "head and hand", "academic and amateur", the move of anarchists into the academy may simply reproduce, reinforce and even legitimize, the political and economic structures of the academy. It cer-tainly lends a certain shine to the claims of those conservative academics who like to boast about academic freedom and the openness of the neo-liberal university: "Look, we don't exclude anyone. We even allow anar-chists a place at the table".

Then, what happens when anarchists, through the "publish or perish" pressures of promotion and the pursuit of tenure, begin to mold anar-chism to fit the language and expectations of academic knowledge pro-duction rather than the other way around? This has been one of the fatal flaws of academic Marxism. There is much to oppose in the practice of taking a language of the people, born of their struggles and aspirations, and turning it into something distant, abstract, and inaccessible to the people, who have now been turned into little more than passive subjects of study or "social indicators" where they appear at all. Much of academic Marxism has become yet another variant of grand theory, something of a parlor game, exciting for its ideas perhaps, but of little social concern. Could the same not happen to anarchism? Some critics of the academi-cally inspired "post-anarchism", which has tried to meld anarchist theory with the esoteric philosophies of post-structuralism, might suggest it is already happening.

Graeber (2004) notes that most social science approaches to social movements and questions about the real, immediate issue that emerge from transformative projects adopt an emphasis on "policy issues", or demands, negotiations, or concessions (on either side) at the level of the state.

> The notion of "policy" presumes a state or governing apparatus which imposes its will on others. "Policy" is the negation of politics; policy is by definition something concocted by some form of elite, which presumes it knows better than others how their affairs are to be conducted. By participating in policy debates the very best one can achieve is to limit the damage, since the very premise is inimical to the idea of people managing their own affairs. Even more than High Theory, what anarchism needs is what might be called Low Theory: a way of grappling with those real, immediate quesions that emerge from a transformative project. Mainstream social science actually isn't much help here, because normally in mainstream social science this sort of thing is generally classified as "policy issues", and no self-respecting anarchist would have anything to do with these. (Graeber 2004: 9)

The question of whether or not anarchists might, at particular moments within particular struggles, have anything to do with "policy issues" can for now be set aside. We have concluded from years of political activity and involvement that in fact there are times when anarchists, at least those engaged in everyday social struggles beyond the comfort of an anarchist milieu do in fact need to engage with policy issues, even if simply to make a small gain that might allow one to go on and fight another day in pursuit of bigger goals.

There is certainly something of value in drawing upon the works of social science, for example, to inform anarchist thought. Even mainstream social science can provide important information and analysis that might aid anarchists in examining, understanding, critiquing and changing society. The works of anarchists from Peter Kropotkin and Emma Goldman to Élisée Reclus to Paul Goodman and Colin Ward have shown the beneficial aspects for anarchist theoretical development of an informed engagement with academic research. Similarly, there have been a number of amazing works provided by historians providing insights on anarchist movements that might otherwise have been lost to time. Certainly the works of historians have made the greatest and longest term contributions to anarchist movements recently.

Mutual Aid Against Precarity in Academia

One thing that academic anarchists can insist upon is that their practice within the academy reflects and draws upon their practices outside the academy. Anarchists, in particular, have focused on the value of mutual aid within human social organization. As we wrote in Chapter 1 in respect to the forms that anarchist sociology could take, academic anarchists can work to ensure that mutual aid becomes a regular feature of organizing, working, and interacting within academic spaces. This is especially important given the precarious position many anarchist, and other critical faculty, find themselves in within the neo-liberal campus of the twenty-first century.

A central plank in the corporatization agenda in post-secondary education has been movement away from secure, tenure-track positions towards increased reliance on precarious adjunct or contract faculty who lack security, funding and benefits. Efforts by university administrations to keep contract faculty working without even minimal job security provisions or provisions for adequate working conditions is a key part of the push to "flexibilize" labor as campuses are made to fit the lean production models of other sectors. Many new scholars will face years of work as adjuncts before, if ever, gaining full-time, permanent employment (see Berry 2005 for a longer discussion of issues facing adjunct faculty in the North America).

Reliance upon adjunct faculty has been a major part of attempts by university administrators to contain costs by paying adjunct faculty on a per-course basis, rather than as part of a salaried professorship, to teach courses that have often been passed over by full-time faculty. Typically, adjunct faculty must apply for their jobs every four to eight months regardless of seniority. Even those who have taught a course for 20 or so years have to re-apply to teach it, with no guarantee that they will be employed. To protect against this eventuality, contract faculty have tried to fight for an increase in the number of conversions of adjunct faculty to tenure stream positions. Adjunct faculty are often assigned courses that are outside their research areas and enjoy little advanced notice. For example, the first year Shantz worked as an adjunct, he was assigned his third of three courses less than a week before the semester started. In some ways, this situation is reinforced by the individualism of academic career paths, from graduate school through tenure and promotion practices that emphasize individual creativity, research, and publication records.

On campuses throughout North America, contract faculty, those who are hired to teach on a temporary, per-course basis without any prospect of tenure, and the intellectual protection it affords, are particularly vulnerable to threats of discipline by university and college administrators. Some schools even claim ownership over the material and contents of lecturer's office computers. For some schools, this control extends to the right to confiscate the office computer and claim possession of everything on it. That can include confiscation of e-mails, coursework materials, and research notes or data. The issues facing adjunct instructors are familiar of the corporatization drive in other public service sectors: privatization, reduced job security, the absence of collective representation, and reductions in wages and benefits.

Compounding the already numerous problems facing adjunct faculty is the fact that many adjuncts have no collective representation, whether through existing faculty associations or combined adjunct and teaching assistant locals or through separate adjunct unions. In Canada, as in the US, the vast number of adjuncts remain non-unionized. This has made it easier for universities to maintain the inequitable adjunct system, and it has also meant that few adjuncts have had experiences in a union setting and the important lessons, as well as real material gains, that can be gained from such conditions. Adjuncts' organizing combines broader concerns with accessibility and quality with specific concerns for job security and promotion.

Higher learning, and the conditions and contexts in which it is pursued, have been characterized recently by economic and political precarity, or conditions of insecurity affecting material and emotional well-being. Collaboration in research, writing, teaching, and professional development can potentially play a crucial role in developing active and collective input on matters affecting critical aspects of academic decision-making. Such collective and participatory work can provide a possible counter to conditions of insecurity faced by precarious academic workers.

Mutual Aid and Collaboration

A key contemporary issue—one that is socially and politically charged—involves the question of whether collaborative practices in diverse areas, and the growth of opportunities for mutual aid, could pose a serious hallenge to the hegemony of international regimes of neo-liberalism and the corporatization of post-secondary education. Collaborative work extends throughout human communities historically and finds vibrant contemporary expressions in a variety of places, including academic research and teaching, open source software, and community service networks. At the same time, collaborative efforts and mutual aid are perhaps more than ever before confronted by powerful institutions and organizations, with the full weight of multinational corporations and national states behind them, seeking to extend private control and management, driven by a lean "cost-benefit" approach, of both the processes and products of creative activities.

As Rishab Ghosh (2005a) suggests, intellectual property rights and policy decisions that treat knowledge and art as physical forms of property, far from enhancing creativity, actually limit public access to creativity, and discourage collaborative creative efforts while threatening to decrease creativity overall. For Ghosh, a clear indicator of how dramatic the conversion from knowledge and art to "intellectual property" is the widespread assumption that creative production is necessarily individual and private, with collaboration occurring only under specific commercial conditions. Collaboration, as in open source software development where thousands of people might organize informally without ever meeting, to produce high quality works, is often viewed as being an exception. Even more this exceptionality is often explained as having a predominantly ideological basis (among those already committed to communalism or socialism of various sorts). As Ghosh suggests, it is a somewhat romanticized notion that collaborative production and ownership on a large scale are driven by ideology and require the commitment of idealists in order to occur (2005b: 1).

Lost in hegemonic neo-liberal discourses of proprietary rights and market competitiveness is the recognition of human sociality—that the greatest human achievements have been collaborative efforts, as anarchist have long stressed. In the current context collaboratively creating knowledge has come to be viewed as a novelty (Ghosh 2005b: 3). As Ghosh suggests: "Newton should have had to pay a license fee before being allowed even to see how tall the 'shoulders of giants' were, let alone to stand upon them" (2005b: 3).[1] At the same time, open source and free software movements have played important parts in renewing public interest in collaborative creation more broadly.

Yet a strong and compelling case can be made that collaborative approaches to creativity are desirable and viable alternatives to frameworks based on the isolation, individualization and, indeed, privatization that characterizes much academic work in the context of neo-liberal transformations of post-secondary education. This collaboration can

---

[1] Additionally, see Conner (2005) for an interesting argument about the role of "ordinary" people in the creation of knowledge.

extend to include innovative approaches to research, teaching, professional development, and administration. Such collaborative practices can help to overcome the divisions between teaching and research and between ideas and implementation in academic planning.

A useful approach is to adopt collaborative administrative practices that involve adjunct faculty as equals. One, often overlooked, contribution to addressing issues of isolation can be the inclusion of adjuncts and students in departmental decision-making meetings and committees. This is a very basic form of collaboration in day-to-day aspects of departmental life, but one from which precarious academic workers are often excluded. Too often the voices of precarious workers find little opportunity for expression within established and official venues.

This can be extended to refuse the top-down imposition of administrative positions, beyond departmental levels, that are not essential to learning. Mutual aid among faculty can provide a means to avoid or reduce or stop the growth of bureaucratic administrative positions or tasks. Collaborative labor could stem the creation of growing layers of management (assistant deans, vice presidents and so on) while ensuring that those who provide a substantial portion of the work carried out in departments have an actual say in the vision and future planning of the institution. Savings gained from the reduced administrative costs could be used to create more permanent full-time positions, course offerings, books and/or student grants. Post-secondary institutions can be run by faculty and staff but winning back aspects of decision-making will require collective organizing. Early steps might include the collective attendance of administrative meetings but could develop autonomous institutions organized on a collective, non-hierarchical basis.

Mutual aid can also be useful in the development of course materials or in working with new faculty, who are generally overworked, to prepare course materials. This can help to lessen the workload of adjunct and new faculty as well as serving as a useful form of skill-sharing among instructors. This can include collaboration in the development as well as the delivery of courses. Collaboratively prepared and taught courses can provide important means of skill sharing among faculty. It can also allow contract faculty to achieve some seniority accumulation and pay during periods when they might otherwise not. It also allows for recognition of teaching for adjunct faculty.

Another proposal is the development of collaborative research projects, jointly formed by full-time faculty and precarious faculty. This may include, perhaps more controversially, making research funds available to precarious faculty as a means of subsidizing or "equalizing" their different salaries and resource bases.

Mutual aid can provide an alternative to the academic "star" system in which "big names" sell themselves to the highest bidding institutions or to endowed chairs. This system reproduces notions of knowledge production as an individual rather than collective process, reinforcing existing hierarchies. Ideally, an anarchist approach to social networks could turn them functionally against themselves: instead of the top-ranking graduate programs reproducing the upper-class faculty of the future (c.f. Burris 2004), networks could be used to subvert the privileging effects of the most elite within the Ivory Tower.

Collaborative approaches can also contribute to professional development, beyond the benefits of collaborative teaching. Mutual aid and collaboration in research, teaching and administration are ongoing practices and should allow adjunct faculty access to office space, library resources, computer accounts travel grants, and professional development funds. By including adjuncts within ongoing collaborative processes they can be viewed as making regular contributions to scholarship and departmental life, rather than as merely the providers of specific limited courses.

Economic precarity in institutions of higher learning is also reflected in the material reality of student and adjunct poverty. Rapidly increasing tuition along with the elimination of financial grants and insufficient loan amounts means there is little left over for food or rent. Thus students, as well as temporary faculty, have to turn to food banks which are springing up on campuses. Here, too, collaboration can play an important part.

One successful example of campus-based collaboration against precarity initiated by anarchists is the Anti-Poverty Working Group (APWG) of adjunct and teaching assistant union local 3903 of the Canadian Union of Public Employees (CUPE) at York University in Toronto, Canada. The Working Group acts beyond the expectations of traditional unionism to assist people (members and non-members) experiencing problems with collection agencies, landlords, bosses and police and to help anyone having difficulties with welfare or other government bureaucracies. The APWG is available to assist students and non-students studying or living in the low-income neighborhoods near campus.

Precarity is part of broader processes of privatization, isolation and individualization in diverse spheres of social life. This includes and is facilitated through the breakdown of collective activities, decision-making, solidarity and collaboration, as in cases of de-unionization or the stratification, and exclusion, characterizing contemporary academic workplaces. Responding to precarity requires new forms of collaboration, the development of solidarity, to overcome isolation experienced by many academic workers and to contest corporatization more broadly.

Collaboration in areas of teaching, research, administration, and professional development might work to resist the neo-liberal transformation of the curriculum and the breakdown of solidarities that neo-liberalism both fosters and relies on. It might help to restore a system in which intellectual inquiry takes precedence over market "relevance" and corporate productivity. Mutual aid could also extend beyond the normal reach of the academy to place academics within various communities. Lots of models—some borrowing heavily from "participatory action research"—envision intellectuals actively helping non-academics (e.g. "public sociology"). More radical efforts at mutual aid see academics less as missionaries, than as providing training (where needed) or simply warm bodies in the effort to better understand the problems communities face and the alternatives they could utilize in their struggles (Ehrlich 1991, Martin 1998b).

Conclusion

Overall, the emphasis should remain on using the academic work to inform and enrich anarchist analysis rather than using anarchist analysis to bolster academic disciplines or theoretical positions that have little connection with people's lives. In terms of social theory, we would suggest that the work done by theorists such as Paul Goodman, Colin Ward, Murray Bookchin, and Howard Ehrlich—people who may have been trained in universities but who have consistently offered complex analyses in engaging and accessible terms—offer more for anarchist movements "on the ground". This is the case both in terms of the applicability of their analyses and in terms of the issues and concerns that they devote their attention to.

The primary orientation of anarchist academics must remain the anarchist movements actively involved in struggles against capitalism, the state, and all other forms of domination. In some senses anarchist academics are subsidized by the movement activists who are doing the day-to-day work of building movements while the academics are pursuing their own, often very personal, interests. Anarchist academics need to recognize that while they do academic work (much of which is involved in "departmental work" or "professional development" which contributes little to social struggles), someone else is taking care of the organizing work (that the academic may only be theorizing about). This is not to say that anarchist academics are not able to contribute to organizing at the same time as getting their work done; it is instead more a call to remember the appropriate division of labor.

It is important to point out again that this is not to criticize those anarchists who have taken work as professors for their choice of employment. Arguments that claim academic work represents some sort of sell-out or compromise are ridiculous. There are worse jobs under capitalism—trust us we have had some of them—and there is no shame in taking a job that offers good pay, benefits, and generally decent working conditions (as long as one does not become an administrator or an academic boss with exploited teaching and research assistants working for them, of course). The greater concern is the extent that creating a space within the academy is prioritized as "anarchist organizing" or such activity comes to take up time that active and thoughtful anarchists might put toward less exclusive contexts. Ultimately, the choices of prioritization are up to the individual anarchist academic to make, while the larger anarchist movement ought to hold such academics (us included) accountable for the application of those choices.

BIBLIOGRAPHY

Achbar, Mark. 1994. {ed.} *Manufacturing Consent: Noam Chomsky and the Media: the Companion Book to the Award-winning Film*. Montreal: Black Rose Books.

Alinsky, Saul. 1972. "Empowering People, Not Elites". *Playboy*. Available: http://www .progress.org/2003/alinsky5.htm.

Alvi, Shahid. 2000. *Youth and the Canadian Criminal Justice System*. Cincinnati: Anderson Press.

Amster, Randall. 2003. "Restoring (Dis)order: Sanctions, Resolutions, and 'Social Control' in Anarchist Communities". *Contemporary Justice Review*, 6, 9–24.

Amster, Randall, Abraham DeLeon, Luis A. Fernandez, Anthony J. Nocella, Deric Shannon. 2009. *Contemporary Anarchist Studies: An Introductory Anthology of Anarchy in the Academy*. London: Routledge.

Arrigo, Bruce and Yoshiko Takahashi. 2006. "Recommunalization of the Disenfranchised: A Theoretical and Critical Criminological Inquiry". *Theoretical Criminology*, 10, 307–336.

Atkinson, Ian. 2001. "May Day 2001 in the UK, the News Media and Public Order". *Environmental Politics*, 10, 145–150.

Atkinson, Joshua. 2006. "Analyzing Resistance Narratives at the North American Anarchist Gathering: A Method for Analyzing Social Justice Alternative Media". *Journal of Communication Inquiry*, 30, 251–272.

Atton, Chris. 1999. "Green Anarchist: A Case Study of Collective Action in the Racial Media". *Anarchist Studies*, 7, 25–49.

Atton, Chris. 2003. "Infoshops in the Shadow of the State". In J. Curran and N. Couldry, *Contesting Media Power: Alternative Media in a Networked World* (57–69) Lanham, MD: Rowman and Littlefield.

Avrich, Paul. 2005. *Anarchist Voices: An Oral History of Anarchism in America*. Edinburgh: AK Press.

Baldwin, Roger N. {ed.} 1968. *Kropotkin's Revolutionary Pamphlets: A Collection of Writings by Peter Kropotkin*. New York: Benjamin Blom.

Beck, Colin J. 2007. "On the Radical Cusp: Ecoterrorism in the United States, 1998–2005". *Mobilization: An International Quarterly Review*, 12, 161–176.

Berry, Joe. 2005. *Reclaiming the Ivory Tower: Organizing Adjuncts to Change Higher Education*. New York: Monthly Review Press.

Boehrer, Fred. 2000. "The Principle of Subsidiarity as the Basis for a Just Community". *Contemporary Justice Review*, 3 (2), 213–224.

—— 2003. "Anarchism and Downward Mobility: Is Finishing Last the Least We Can Do?". *Contemporary Justice Review*, 6 (1), 37–45.

Bookchin, Murray. 2004 {1971}. *Post-Scarcity Anarchism*. Edinburgh: AK Press.

—— 2005. *The Ecology of Freedom: The Emergence and Dissolution of Hierarchy*. Oakland, CA: AK Press.

Borum, Randy and Chuck Tilby. 2005. "Anarchist Direct Actions: A Challenge for Law Enforcement". *Studies in Conflict and Terrorism*, 28 (3), 201–223.

Bourdieu, Pierre. 1990. *In Other Words: Essays Toward a Reflexive Sociology*. Stanford, CA: Stanford University Press.

Bracewell, Michael C. 1990. "Peacemaking: A Missing Link in Criminology". *Criminologist*, 15, 3–5.

Brennan, Luann. 2003. *Restoring the Justice in Criminal Justice*. Detroit: Wayne State University, Department of Interdisciplinary Studies.

Brooks, Carolyn and Bernard Schissel (eds). 2008. *Marginality and Condemnation: An Introduction to Critical Criminology*. Halifax: Fernwood Books.

Burawoy, Michael. 2005. "For Public Sociology". *American Sociological Review, 70*, 4–28.

Burning River Revolutionary Anarchist Collective. 2002. *Constitution/Structure and Strategy Document*. Cleveland, OH: Burning River.

Burris, Val. 2004. "The Academic Caste System: Prestige Hierarchies in Ph.D. Exchange Networks" *American Sociological Review, 69* (2), 239–264.

Butler, Judith. 1990. *Gender Trouble: Feminism and the Subversion of Identity*. New York: Routledge.

Chomsky, Noam 2005. *Chomsky on Anarchism*. Oakland, AK Press.

Clawson, Dan, Robert Zussman, Joya Misra, Naomi Gerstel, Randall Stokes, Douglas L. Anderton, and Michael Burawoy. 2007. *Public Sociology: Fifteen Eminent Sociologists Debate Politics and the Profession in the Twenty-First Century*. Berkeley, CA: University of California Press.

Cleaver, Harry 1992a. "The Inversion of Class Perspective in Marxian Theory: From Valorization to Self-Valorization". In *Essays on Open Marxism*, (eds.) W. Bonefeld, R. Gunn, and K. Psychopedis. London: Pluto, 106–144.

—— 1992b. "Kropotking, Self-valorization and the Crisis of Marxism". Paper presented at the Conference on Pyotr Alexeevich Kropotkin, Russian Academy of Science, Moscow, St. Petersburg, and Dimitrov, December 8–14.

Cohen, Albert. 1955. *Delinquent Boys: The Culture of the Gang*. New York: Free Press.

Collins, Patricia Hill. 1991. *Black Feminist Thought: Knowledge, Consciousness, and the Politics of Empowerment*. New York: Routledge.

Collins, Randall. 1992. *Sociological Insight: An Introduction to Non-Obvious Sociology, 2nd Edition*. Oxford: Oxford University Press.

—— 1994. *Four Sociological Traditions*. New York: Oxford University Press.

Conner, Clifford D. 2005. *A People's History of Science: Miners, Midwives, and "Low Mechanicks"*. New York: Nation Books.

Cordery, Simon. 2003. *British Friendly Societies, 1750–1914*. New York: Palgrave Macmillan.

Cornell, Andrew. 2011. "A New Anarchism Emerges, 1940–1954". *Journal for the Study of Radicalism, 5 (1)*, 105–132.

Dahrendorf, Ralf. 1959. *Class and Class Conflict in Industrial Societies*. Stanford, CA: Stanford University Press.

Day, Helen Caldwell. 1954. *Not Without Tears*. New York: Sheed and Ward.

Day, Richard J.F. 2005. *Gramsci is Dead: Anarchist Currents in the Newest Movements*. London: Pluto.

de Cleyre, Voltairine. 2004. *The Voltairine de Cleyre Reader*. Oakland, CA: AK Press.

DeKeseredy, Walter. 2000. *Women, Crime and the Canadian Criminal Justice System*. Cincinnati: Anderson.

DeKeseredy, Walter and Barbara Perry. 2006. *Advancing Critical Criminology: Theory and Application*. Lanham, Md.: Lexington Books.

della Porta, Donatella and Mario Diani. 2006. *Social Movements: An Introduction*. Malden, MA: Blackwell.

Diani, Mario. 1992. "The Concept of Social Movement". *The Sociological Review, 40 (1)*, 1–24.

Dolgoff, Sam. 1972. *Bakunin on Anarchy: Selected Works by the Activist-Founder of World Anarchism*. New York: Alfred A. Knopf.

Douglas, Dorothy. 1929. "P-J Proudhon: A Prophet of 1848. Part 1: Life and Work". *American Journal of Sociology, 34(5)*, 781–803.

Downing, John D.H. 2003. "The Independent Media Center Movement and the Anarchist Socialist Tradition". In J. Curran and N. Couldry (eds.), *Contesting Media Power: Alternative Media in a Networked World* (243–257) Lanham, MD: Rowman and Littlefield.

Durkheim, Emile. 1964. *The Division of Labor in Society*. Glencoe, Illinois: Free Press.

—— 1956. *Education and Sociology*. London: Glencoe.

Drinnon, Richard. 1961. *Rebel in Paradise*. Chicago: University of Chicago Press.

Ehrlich, Howard J. 1971. "Notes from a Radical Social Scientist: February 1970". pp. 194–211 in *Radical Sociology*, edited by J.D. Colfax and J.L. Roach. New York: Basic Books.

—— 1991. "Notes From an Anarchist Sociologist: May 1989". pp. 233–248 in *Radical Sociologists and the Movement: Experiences, Lessons, and Legacies*, edited by M. Oppenheimer, M.J. Martin, and R.F. Levine. Philadelphia: Temple University Press.

Ehrlich, Howard. 1996. *Reinventing Anarchy, Again*. Oakland: AK Press.

Ehrlich, Howard J. 1996. "How to Get From Here to There: Building Revolutionary Transfer Culture". pp. 331–349 in *Reinventing Anarchy, Again*, edited by H.J. Ehrlich. Edinburgh: AK Press.

—— 1996. "Anarchism and Formal Organization". pp. 56–68 in *Reinventing Anarchy, Again*, edited by H.J. Ehrlich. Edinburgh: AK Press.

Ehrlich, Howard, Carol Ehrlich, David DeLeon, and Glenda Morris. 1996. "Questions and Answers about Anarchism". In *Reinventing Anarchy, Again*, ed. Howard Ehrlich. Oakland: AK Press.

Epstein, Barbara. 2001. "Anarchism and the Anti-Globalization Movement". *Monthly Review, 53* (*4*), 1–14.

Falk, Candace. 1984. *Love, Anarchy, and Emma Goldman*. New York: Holt, Rinehart, and Winston.

Feagin, Joe R. and Hernán Vera. 2008. *Liberation Sociology*. Boulder, CO: Paradigm Publishers.

Federal Bureau of Investigation. 1999. *Terrorism in the United States*. Washington, DC: Department of Justice.

Ferrell, Jeff, Keith Hayward and Jock Young. 2008. *Cultural Criminology*. Los Angeles: Sage.

Ferrell, J., and C.R. Sanders (eds.). 1995. *Cultural Criminology*. Boston: Northeastern University Press.

Fitzgerald, Kathleen J. and Diane M. Rodgers. 2000. "Radical Social Movement Organizations: A Theoretical Model". *The Sociological Quarterly, 41*, 573–592.

Foucault, Michel. (1978). *The History of Sexuality: Volume 1: An Introduction*. New York: Pantheon.

Freeman, Jo. 2002. "The Tyranny of Structurelessness". pp. 54–61 in *Quiet Rumours: An Anarcha-Feminist Reader*, edited by Dark Star Collective. Edinburgh, UK: AK Press.

French, Marilyn. 1986. *On Power: Beyond Women, Men and Morals*. London: Abacus.

Fuller, John. 2003. "Peacemaking Criminology". In *Controversies in Critical Criminology*, edited by Martin D. Schwartz and Suzanne E. Hatty. Cincinnati: Anderson, 85–95.

Geertz, Clifford. 1980. *Negara: The Theatre State in Nineteenth-Century Bali*. Princeton, NJ: Princeton University Press.

Ghosh, Rishab Aiyer. 2005a. "Introduction". In *CODE: Collaborative Ownership and the Digital Economy*, edited by Rishab Aiyer Ghosh. Cambridge, MA: The MIT Press.

Ghosh, Rishab Aiyer. 2005b."Why Collaboration is Important (Again)". In *CODE: Collaborative Ownership and the Digital Economy*, edited by Rishab Aiyer Ghosh. Cambridge, MA: The MIT Press, 1–6.

Gibbs, J.P. 1965. "Norms: The problem of Definition and Classification". *American Journal of Sociology, 60*, 586–594.

Goffman, Erving. 1962. *Asylums: Essays on the Social Situation of Mental Patients and Other Inmates*. Chicago: Aldine.

Gordon, Uri. 2007. *Anarchy Alive! Anti-Authoritarian Politics from Practice to Theory*. London: Pluto.

Goldman, Emma. 1969. *Anarchism and Other Essays*. New York: Dover.

—— 1970. *Living My Life*. New York: Dover.

—— 1972. *Red Emma Speaks: Selected Writings and Speeches by Emma Goldman*. New York: Random House.

—— 2003. *My Disillusionment in Russia*. Mineola, NY: Dover.

Goldman, Emma and Max Baginsky. 1907. "The Relation of Anarchism to Organization". *Mother Earth* II: 310.

Gordon, Linda. 1976. *Woman's Body, Woman's Right: A Social History of Birth Control in America*. New York: Penguin.

Graeber, David. 2002. "The New Anarchists". *New Left Review, 13,* 61–73.

—— 2004. *Fragments of an Anarchist Anthropology.* Chicago: Prickly Paragdigm.

—— 2007. *Possibilities: Essays on Hierarchy, Rebellion, and Desire.* Oakland, CA: AK Press.

Griffin, John. 1991. *A Structured Anarchism: An Overview of Libertarian Theory and Practice.* London: Freedom Press.

Grusky, David B. and Szonja Szelényi. 2007. "The Rise and Fall of Benign Narratives About Inequality. pp. 1–13 in *The Inequality Reader: Contemporary and Foundational Readings in Race, Class, and Gender,* edited by D.B. Grusky and S. Szelényi. Boulder, CO: Westview.

Haaland, Bonnie. 1993. *Emma Goldman: Sexuality and the Impurity of the State.* Montréal: Black Rose Books.

Habermas, Jürgen. 1985. *Lifeworld and System: A Critique of Functionalist Reason.* Boston: Beacon Press.

Hall, C. Margaret. 1971. *The Sociology of Pierre Joseph Proudhon, 1809–1865.* New York: Philosophical Library.

Harbold, William. 1976. "On Alan Ritter's 'The Anarchist Justification of Punishment.'"*Political Theory, 4*(2), 237–238.

Hardy, Dennis. 1991. *Campaigning for Town and Country Planning 1899–1990: From Garden Cities to New Towns: Campaigning for Town and Country Planning 1899–1946.* London: Routledge.

Harney, Stefano. 2002. "Fragment on Kropotkin and Giuliani". *Social Text, 20 (3),* 9–20.

Harris, Angela P. 1990. "Race and Essentialism in Feminist Legal Theory". *Stanford Law Review, 42,* 581–616.

Hartung, Beth. 1983. "Anarchism and the Problem of Order". *Mid-American Review of Sociology, 8 (1),* 83–101.

Heckert, Druann Maria. 1998. "Positive Deviance: A Classificatory Model". *Free Inquiry in Creative Sociology, 26,* 23–30.

Herman, Edward S. and Noam Chomsky. 1988. *Manufacturing Consent: The Political Economy of Mass Media.* New York: Pantheon.

Herrada, Julie. 2007. "Collecting Anarchy: Continuing the Legacy of the Joseph A. Labadie Collection". *RBM: A Journal of Rare Books, Manuscripts, and Cultural Heritage, 8 (2),* 133–140.

Hertog, James K. and Douglas M. McLeod. 1995. "Anarchists Wreak Havoc in Downtown Minneapolis: A Multi-level Study of Media Coverage of Radical Protest". *Journalism and Mass Communication Monographs, 151,* 1–47.

Hirschi, Travis. 1969. *Causes of Delinquency.* Los Angeles: University of California Press.

Hong, Nathaniel. 1992. "Constructing the Anarchist Beast in American Periodical Literature, 1880–1903. *Critical Studies in Mass Communication, 9,* 110–130.

hooks, bell. 1981. *Ain't I A Woman? Black Women and Feminism.* Boston: South End Press.

—— 1989. *Talking Back: Thinking Feminist, Thinking Black.* Boston: South End Press.

—— 2000. *Feminism is for Everybody: Passionate Politics.* Cambridge, MA: South End Press.

Hurd, Heidi M. 2005. "Why You Should Be A Law-Abiding Anarchist (Except When You Shouldn't)". *San Diego Law Review, 42,* 75–84.

Jasso, Guillermina and Karl-Dieter Opp. 1997. "Probing the Character of Norms: A Factorial Survey Analysis of the Norms of Political Action". *American Sociological Review, 62,* 947–964.

Jensen, Richard Bach. 1981. "The International Anti-Anarchist Conference of 1898 and the Origins of Interpol". *Journal of Contemporary History, 16 (2),* 323–347.

Jun, Nathan J. 2009. "Anarchist Philosophy and Working Class Struggle: A Brief History and Commentary". *Working USA: The Journal of Labor and Society, 12,* 505–519.

Kaplan, Robert D. 2000. *The Coming Anarchy: Shattering the Dreams of the Post Cold War.* New York: Random House.

Kelling, George L. and Catherine Coles. 1996. *Fixing Broken Windows: Restoring Order and Reducing Crime in Our Societies.* Glencoe: Free Press.

Kingston-Mann, Esther. 2006. "The return of Pierre Proudhon: Property Rights, Crime, and the Rules of Law", *Focaal, 48*, 118–127.

Kinna, Ruth. 1995. "Kropotkin's Theory of Mutual Aid in Historic Context". *International Review of Social History, 40* (2), 259–283.

Kissack, Terence. 2008. *Free Comrades: Anarchism and Homosexuality in the United States, 1895–1917*. Oakland, CA: AK Press.

Kohlberg, Lawrence. 1969. "Stage and Sequence: The Cognitive-Developmental Approach". In *Handbook of Socialization Theory and Research*, edited by David A. Goslin. Chicago: Rand McNally.

Kollontai, Alexandra. 1971. *The Social Basis of the Woman Question*. New York: W.W. Norton.

Kropotkin, Peter. 1902. *Mutual Aid: A Factor in Evolution*. London: Heinemann.

—— 2006. *Mutual Aid: A Factor in Evolution*. Mineola, NY: Dover.

Landauer, Gustav. 2010. *Revolution and Other Writings: A Political Reader*. Oakland, CA: PM Press.

Lanier, Mark M. and Stuart Henry. 2004. *Essential Criminology*. Boulder: Westview Press.

Laurer, Robert H. 1991. *Perspectives on Social Change, Fourth Edition*. Boston: Allyn and Bacon.

Lea, John. 2002. *Crime and Modernity: Continuities in Left Realist Criminology*. London: Sage.

Lea, John and Jock Young. 1984. *What is to be Done About: Law and Order?* Harmondsworth: Penguin.

Lenz, Elinor and Barbara Myerhoff. 1985. *The Feminization of America*. Los Angeles: Jeremy P. Tarcher.

Lilley, P.J. and Jeff Shantz. 2004. "The World's Largest Workplace: Social Reproduction and Wages for Housework". *Northeastern Anarchist, 9,* http://jeffshantz.ca/reproductiverights.

Linden, Rick. 2008. *Criminology: A Canadian Perspective*. Toronto: Nelson.

Lindenfeld, Frank and Pamela Wynn. 1997. "Success and Failure of Worker Coops: The Role of Internal and External Environmental Factors". *Humanity and Society, 21*, 148–161.

Lombroso, Cesare. 1911. *Crime: Its Causes and Remedies*. Boston: Little Brown.

Loomis, Mildred J. 2005. *Decentralization: Where It Came From, Where Is It Going?* Montreal: Black Rose Books.

López, Ian Haney. 1996. *White By Law: The Legal Construction of Race*. New York: New York University Press.

Macklin, Graham D. 2005. "Co-opting the Counter Culture: Troy Southgate and the National Revolutionary Faction". *Patterns of Prejudice, 39* (3), 301–326.

Mansbridge, Jane. 1979. "The Agony of Inequality". Pp. 194–214 in *Co-ops, Communes and Collectives: Experiments in Social Change in the 1960s and 1970s*, edited by J. Case and R.C.R. Taylor. New York: Pantheon.

Marshall, Peter. 1993. *Demanding the Impossible: A History of Anarchism*. London: HarperCollins.

Martin, Brian. 1998a. *Tied Knowledge: Power in Higher Education*. http://www.bmartin.cc/pubs/98tk/ Date accessed: July 28, 2006.

—— 1998b. *Information Liberation*. London: Freedom Press.

—— 2007. "Anarchist Theory: What Should Be Done?" *Anarchist Studies, 15* (2), 106–108.

May, Todd. 2009. "Anarchism From Foucault to Rancière". pp. 11–17 in *Contemporary Anarchist Studies: An Introductory Anthology of Anarchy in the Academy*, edited by R. Amster, A. DeLeon, L.A. Fernandez, A.J. Nocella, and D. Shannon. London: Routledge.

McKay, Iain. 2007. *An Anarchy FAQ: AFAQ Volume One*. Edinburgh: AK Press.

McLeod, Douglas M. and James K. Hertog. 1992. "The Manufacture of 'Public Opinion' by Reporters: Informal Cues for Public Perceptions of Protest Groups". *Discourse and Society, 3*, 259–275.

Merton, Robert K. 1968. *Social Theory and Social Structure*. New York: Free Press.

Michels, Robert. 1958. *Political Parties: A Sociological Study of the Oligarchical Tendencies of Modern Democracy*. Glencoe, IL: Free Press.

—— 1962. *Political Parties: A Sociological Study of the Oligarchical Tendencies of Modern Democracy*. New York: Collier.

Miller, J. Mitchell, Christopher J. Schreck and Richard Tewksbury. 2008. *Criminological Theory*. Boston: Pearson, Allyn and Bacon.

Mills, C. Wright. 1959. *The Sociological Imagination*. Oxford: Oxford University Press.

Milstein, Cindy. 2010. *Anarchism and Its Aspirations*. Oakland, CA: AK Press.

Mumm, James. 1998. *Active Revolution*. http://www.infoshop.org/texts/active_revolution.html. Date accessed: July 1, 2003.

Nisbet, Robert A. 1966. *The Sociological Tradition*. New York: Basic Books.

Noland, Aaron. 1970. "Proudhon's Sociology of War". *American Journal of Economics and Sociology*. 29(3), 289–304.

O'Grady, William. 2007. *Crime in Canadian Context: Debates and Controversies*. Don Mills: Oxford University Press.

Olson, Mancur. 1965. *The Logic of Collective Action: Public Goods and the Theory of Groups*. Cambridge, MA: Harvard University Press.

Orwell, George. 1980 [1952]. *Homage to Catalonia*. San Diego: Harcourt Brace Jovanovich.

Osgood, Herbert L. 1889. "Scientific Anarchism". *Political Science Quarterly*. 4(1), 1–36

Parsons, Talcott. 1968. *The Structure of Social Action: A Study in Social Theory With Special Reference to a Group of Recent European Writers, Volume 1*. New York: Free Press.

Pepinsky, H.E. 1978. "Communist Anarchism as an Alternative to the Rule of Criminal Law". *Contemporary Crises*, 2, 315–327.

Piven, Frances Fox and Richard A. Cloward. 1993. *Regulating the Poor: The Functions of Public Welfare, 2nd Edition*. New York: Vintage.

Proudhon, Pierre-Joseph. 1840. *What is Property?*. New York: Humboldt.

—— 1858. *De la justice dans la révolution et dans l'église: nouveaux principes de philosophie pratique adressés à son éminence Monseigneur Mathieu, cardinal-archevêque de Besançon*. Paris: Garnier frères.

—— 1888. *System of Economic Contradictions: or the Philosophy of Poverty*. Princeton: B.R. Tucker.

—— 1923. *General Idea of the Revolution in the Nineteenth Century*. London: Freedom Press.

—— 1924. *De la Capacite politique des classes ouvrieres*. Paris.

—— 1927. *Proudhon's Solution to the Social Problem*. New York: Vanguard Press.

—— 1969. *General Idea of the Revolution in the Nineteenth Century*. New York: Haskell House.

—— 1969a. *General Idea of the Revolution in the Nineteenth Century*. New York: Haskell House Publishers.

—— 1969b. *Selected Writings of Pierre-Joseph Proudhon*. Garden City: Anchor Books.

—— 1979. *The Principle of Federation*. Toronto: University of Toronto Press.

Purchase, Graham. 1994. *Anarchism and Environmental Survival*. Tucson, AZ: See Sharp Press.

Purkis, Jonathan. 2004. "Towards an Anarchist Sociology". pp. 39–54 in *Changing Anarchism: Anarchist Theory and Practice in a Global Age*, edited by J. Purkis and J. Bowen. Manchester: Manchester University Press.

Quinney, Richard. 1974. *Critique of Legal Order: Crime Control in Capitalist Society*. Boston: Little Brown.

—— 1980. *Class, State and Crime*. New York: Longman.

Reichert, William O. 1967. "Toward a New Understanding of Anarchism". *The Western Political Quarterly*, 20(4), 856–865.

Rieman, Jeffrey. 2006. *The Rich Get Richer and the Poor Get Prison*. Boston: Allyn and Bacon.

Ritter, Alan. 1967. "Proudhon and the Problem of Community". *The Review of Politics*, 29(4), 457–477.

Ritter, Alan. 1975. "Godwin, Proudhon and the Anarchist Justification of Punishment". *Political Theory*, 3(1), 69–87.

Rocker, Rudolf. 1998. *Nationalism and Culture*. Montréal: Black Rose Books.

Rothschild-Whitt, Joyce. 1979. "The Collectivist Organization: An Alternative to Rational-Bureaucratic Models". *American Sociological Review, 44*, 509–527.

Sandefur, Melissa and Vicky M. MacLean. 2007. "Emma Goldman". pp. 2004–2007 in *The Blackwell Encyclopedia of Sociology*, edited by G. Ritzer. Malden, MA: Blackwell.

Sarre, Rick. 2003. "Restorative Justice: A Paradigm of Possibility". In *Controversies in Critical Criminology*, edited by Martin D. Schwartz and Suzanne E. Hatty. Cincinnati: Anderson, 97–108.

Schmalleger, F. 2003. *Criminology Today: An Introduction*. Upper Saddle River, N.J.: Prentice-Hall.

Schmidt, Michael and Lucien van der Walt. 2009. *Black Flame: The Revolutionary Class Politics of Anarchism and Syndicalism*. Edinburgh: AK Press.

Scott, James C. 2009. *The Art of Not Being Governed: An Anarchist History of Upland Southeast Asia*. Hartford, CT: Yale University Press.

Shantz, Jeff. 1997. "Listen Anarchist: Murray Bookchin's Defence of Orthodoxy". *Alternate Routes: A Journal of Critical Social Research, 14*, 69–75.

Shantz, Jeffrey. 2012. *Crime/Punishment/Power: Sociological Explanations*. Dubuque, IA: Kendall Hunt.

Simon, David R. 2007. *Elite Deviance*. Boston: Allyn and Bacon.

Skirda, Alexandre. 2002. *Facing the Enemy: A History of Anarchist Organization from Proudhon to May 1968*. Edinburgh: AK Press.

Smelser, Neil. 1963. *Theory of Collective Behavior*. New York: Free Press.

Spangler, Brad. 2007. "Proudhon and Market Anarchism".

Spreitzer, Gretchen M. and Scott Sonenshein. 2004. "Toward the Construct Definition of Positive Deviance". *American Behavioral Scientist, 47*, 828–847.

Spring, Joel. 1998. *A Primer of Libertarian Education*. Montréal: Black Rose Press.

Starr, Amory. 2006. "'Excepting Barricades Erected to Prevent Us From Peacefully Assembling': So-Called 'Violence' in the Global North Alterglobalization Movement". *Social Movement Studies, 5*, 61–81.

Stock, Paul. 2007. "Katrina and Anarchy: A Content Analysis of a New Disaster Myth". *Sociological Spectrum, 27*, 705–726.

Stoehr, Taylor [ed]. 1994. *Decentralizing Power: Paul Goodman's Social Criticism*. Montréal: Black Rose Books.

Sullivan, Dennis, Larry Tifft, Georgia Gray, John Laub, and Michael Buckman. 1980. "Let the Water Be Wet, Let the Rocks Be Hard: Anarchism as a Sociology of Quality of Life". *Humanity and Society, 4 (4)*, 344–362.

Sydie, R.A. 1987. "The Value of Reproduction: A Partial Re-examination of Tönnies' Gemeinschaft and Gesselschaft". *Atlantis, 13*, 137–147.

Tepperman, Lorne. 2006. *Deviance, Crime and Control: Beyond the Straight and Narrow*. Don Mills: Oxford University Press.

Tifft, L. and D. Sullivan. 1980. *The Struggle to be Human: Crime, Criminology, and Anarchism*. Orkney, U.K.: Cienfuegos Press.

Turner, Scott. 1998. "Global Civil Society, Anarchy and Governance: Assessing an Emergent Paradigm". *Peace Research, 35(1)*, 25–42.

Umbreit, Mark S., Robert B. Coates, Betty Vos and Kathy Brown. 2002. *Victim Offender Dialogue in Crimes of Severe Violence: A Multi-Site Study of Programs in Texas and Ohio*. Minneapolis: Center for Restorative Justice, University of Minnesota.

Ward, Colin. 1973. *Anarchy in Action*. New York: Harper Torchbooks.

—— 1996. *Anarchy in Action*. London: Freedom Press.

—— 2004. *Anarchism: A Very Short Introduction*. Oxford: Oxford University Press.

Ward, Colin and David Goodway. 2003. *Talking Anarchy*. Nottingham: Five Leaves.

Weber, Max. 1958. "The Three Types of Legitimate Rule". *Berkeley Publications in Society and Institutions, 4(1)*, 1–11.

—— 1978. *Economy and Society: An Outline of Interpretive Sociology*. Berkeley, CA: University of California Press.

Welsh, Ian. 1997. "Anarchism, Social Movements, and Sociology". *Anarchist Studies, 5* (2), 162–168.

West, Candace and Don H. Zimmerman. 1987. "Doing Gender". *Gender and Society, 1,* 121–151.

Wexler, Alice. 1984. *Emma Goldman: An Intimate Life.* New York: Pantheon Books.

White, Rob, Fiona Haines and Lauren Eisler. 2009. *Crime and Criminology.* Don Mills: Oxford University Press.

Wilbert, Chris and Damian F. White. 2011. *Autonomy, Solidarity, Possibility: The Colin Ward Reader.* Edinburgh: AK Press.

Williams, Dana M. 2009a. "Red vs. Green: Regional Variation of Anarchist Ideology in the United States". *Journal of Political Ideologies, 14* (2), 189–210.

—— 2009b. "Anarchists and Labor Unions: An Analysis Using New Social Movement Theories". *WorkingUSA: The Journal of Labor and Society, 12* (3), 337–354.

Williams, Dana M. and Matthew T. Lee. 2008. "'We Are Everywhere': An Ecological Analysis of Organizations in the Anarchist Yellow Pages". *Humanity and Society, 32,* 45–70.

—— 2012. "Overthrowing the State Without Using It: Political Opportunities for the Anarchist Movement". *Comparative Sociology, 11,* 558–593.

Williams, Frank P. and Marilyn McShane. 2004. *Criminological Theory.* New Jersey: Pearson Education.

Wilson, James Q. 1975. *Thinking About Crime.* New York: Vintage Books.

Winslow, Robert and Sheldon Zhang. 2006. *Criminology: A Global Perspective.* Toronto: Pearson.

Woodcock, George. 1962. *Anarchism: A History of Libertarian Ideas and Movements.* New York: World Publishing Company.

—— 1972. *Pierre-Joseph Proudhon: His Life and Work.* New York: Schocken.

—— 1983. "Emma Goldman: A Life of Anarchy". CBC Radio transcripts.

Yarros, Victor. 1936. "Philosophical Anarchism: Its Rise, Decline and Eclipse". *American Journal of Sociology, 41*(4), 470–483.

Young, Jock. (ed.). 1994. *The Exclusive Society: Social Exclusion, Crime and Difference in Late Modernity.* London; Thousand Oaks: Sage Publications.

—— 1997. "Left Realist Criminology: Radical in its Analysis, Realist in its Policy". In *The Oxford Handbook of* Criminology edited by M. Maguire, R. Morgan and R. Rainer. Oxford: Oxford UP, 473–498.

INDEX